Feminists are aware of the diversity of thinking within their own tradition, and of the different approaches to moral questions in which that is manifest. This book seeks to describe and analyse that diversity by distinguishing three distinct paradigms of moral reasoning to be found within feminism. Using the writings of feminists themselves, the major strengths and weaknesses of each theory are considered, so that creative dialogue between them can be encouraged. Three common themes are drawn out of these paradigms, and are discussed in depth in the second part of the book. These themes are also on the agenda of new developments in philosophical and Christian ethics: namely the search for an appropriate universalism, the possibility of a redemptive community, and the development of a new humanism. Feminists may be encouraged, through this account of their considerable scholarship in ethical thinking, to contribute to these new developments with their special concern for the lives and the fulfilment of women.

FEMINISM
AND CHRISTIAN
ETHICS

NEW STUDIES IN CHRISTIAN ETHICS

General editor: Robin Gill

Editorial board: R. L. Clark, Antony O. Dyson,
Stanley Hauerwas and Robin W. Lovin

In recent years the study of Christian ethics has become an integral part of mainstream theological studies. The reasons for this are not hard to detect. It has become a more widely held view that Christian ethics is actually central to Christian theology as a whole. Theologians increasingly have had to ask what contemporary relevance their discipline has in a context where religious belief is on the wane, and whether Christian ethics (that is, an ethics based on the Gospel of Jesus Christ) has anything to say in a multi-faceted and complex secular society. There is now no shortage of books on most substantive moral issues, written from a wide variety of theological positions. However, what is lacking are books within Christian ethics which are taken at all seriously by those engaged in the wider secular debate. Too few are methodologically substantial; too few have an informed knowledge of parallel discussions in philosophy or the social sciences. This series attempts to remedy the situation. The aims of New Studies in Christian Ethics will therefore be twofold. First, to engage centrally with the secular moral debate at the highest possible intellectual level; second, to demonstrate that Christian ethics can make a distinctive contribution to this debate – either in moral substance, or in terms of underlying moral justifications. It is hoped that the series as a whole will make a substantial contribution to the discipline.

A list of titles in the series is provided at the end of the book.

FEMINISM AND CHRISTIAN ETHICS

SUSAN FRANK PARSONS

Principal, East Midlands Ministry Training Course,
Nottingham

CAMBRIDGE
UNIVERSITY PRESS

Published by the Press Syndicate of the University of Cambridge
The Pitt Building, Trumpington Street, Cambridge CB2 1RP
40 West 20th Street, New York, NY, 10011-4211, USA
10 Stamford Road, Oakleigh, Melbourne 3166, Australia

© Cambridge University Press 1996

First published 1996

A catalogue record for this book is available from the British Library

Library of Congress cataloguing in publication data

Parsons, Susan Frank.
Feminism and Christian Ethics/Susan Frank Parsons.
p.   cm. – (New Studies in Christian Ethics)
Includes bibliographical references and index.
ISBN 0 521 46281 9 (hardback). – ISBN 0 521 46820 5 (paperback)
1. Christian ethics. 2. Feminist ethics. 3. Feminist theology.
I. Title.   II. Series.
BJ1278.F45P37   1996
241'.082–dc20   95–13211 CIP

ISBN 0 521 46281 9 hardback
ISBN 0 521 46820 5 paperback

Transferred to digital printing 2004

CE

To
MOTHER

Contents

General editor's preface

This is the eighth book in the series *New Studies in Christian Ethics*. It seeks to analyse in detail the increasingly complex relationship of feminism to Christian ethics. There can be little doubt that such an analysis is much needed.

The complexity is caused in large measure by the development of different, and sometimes opposing, approaches within feminism. A decade ago it might have been possible to ignore differences amongst feminists – although even then this would probably have been a mistake. Today such differences will be obvious to many. They are differences that divide both secular and religious feminists. If those on the fringe of feminist debates within theology once tended to regard them monolithically, today and especially after the publication of Ann Loades' very helpful *Feminist Theology: A Reader* (SPCK, 1990), they have less excuse. Simplifications in this area are manifestly inappropriate.

The great merit of Susan Parsons' work is that it brings real philosophical clarity to this complex subject without oversimplifying it. Her main focus is upon women writers who identify themselves as feminist – some of them secular or humanist and others explicitly Christian. She argues that they can be analysed in terms of three broad paradigms. The first of these paradigms, which she terms 'liberalism', is the one most obviously derived from the Enlightenment. On its basis many of the early feminists argued for equality of rights and respect. Rational individualism and a stress upon personal autonomy could be applied as much to women as they could to men. The second paradigm, which she terms 'social constructionism', derives from the rise of the social sciences, and especially Marxism, in the nineteenth century. Within this paradigm feminists are more concerned with patriarchal social structures than with individual autonomous rationality. The third paradigm, termed simply 'naturalism', focuses instead upon differences between men and women arising from their different biologies or natures.

Parsons argues that Christian feminists, like their secular colleagues, can be located in any of these paradigms. Indeed some, like Rosemary Radcliffe Ruether, have shifted over the years from one paradigm to another. This is an important insight which helps to explain some of the differences and tensions within Christian feminism. The tensions between individualism, structuralism, and biology cut across disciplines, including Christian feminism, and cannot easily be resolved.

These three paradigms provide the overall shape for this book. Each paradigm is outlined and then criticised in detail. The liberal paradigm has come under increasing attack from the ascendant postmodernists. The social constructionist paradigm has introduced a degree of relativism which sometimes seems to endanger the whole feminist project. The naturalist paradigm has found little agreement amongst feminists about what really constitutes 'female nature'. Yet together they do suggest that the feminist project itself points in certain (albeit still unresolved) directions. In the final part of her book Parsons seeks to unpack these. Three she finds particularly important – the quest for an appropriate universalism, the search for redemptive communities which are not blemished by patriarchy, and the hope for a new vision of humanity. In all three she argues that Christian theology has something distinctive and crucial to contribute.

There are many points of contact between this book and others in the series. Parsons makes direct use of both Lisa Cahill and Jean Porter. Their books for the series – *Sex, Gender and Christian Ethics* and *Moral Action and Christian Ethics* respectively – make many complementary points. Kieran Cronin's *Rights and Christian Ethics* and Ian McDonald's *Biblical Interpretation and Christian Ethics* also offer overall analyses of their subjects which bring similar clarity to otherwise complex issues. Finally many of her conclusions about communities and the misuse of power compare usefully with James Mackey's *Power and Christian Ethics*.

This is an important critical analysis of a subject of major importance.

ROBIN GILL

Preface

This book traces a journey through feminism and Christian ethics which has been very much my own. I remember so clearly thinking, in my early feminist awareness, that really, if we would all simply obey Kant's categorical imperative and treat women as ends-in-themselves, the matter, as far as ethical inquiry was concerned, could be closed. Making this claim, however, far from settling things, seemed to open a gate into entire areas of inquiry that had not yet been touched. To undertake a closer exploration of the territory that then lay before me has been to enter places of great turmoil, in which whatever one says is offensive, of great confusion, in which it is difficult to get one's bearings, and yet of great potential, in which we might be able to discover something better to say. I have thus lived through each of the ways of feminist thinking sketched here, and have found, within each movement and writer, insights to value and criticisms to bear. What I offer here is both a description of that journey so far, with significant markers along the way, and an anticipation of what now seem to me to be the threads that will guide our steps into the future, even as we weave them in our continuing debates. This journey has been for me a theological investigation of great importance, and I share with so many feminists a conviction that the matter of the divine is intimately bound up with the understanding of our humanness. That feminism and Christian ethics might engage in this work together seems the obvious, but nevertheless essential, conclusion.

I would like to thank those who have especially stirred my theological thinking in times past, whose critical minds and generous spirits have in so many ways nourished my self. I am grateful to my teachers in the Department of Philosophy and Religion at Depauw University, particularly Russell Compton, who first awoke my interest in ethics, Robert Newton, and John Eigenbrodt. Their teaching will always be exemplary to me, and the community of scholars which they sought to build up was the most creative context in which to learn critical reasoning. My tutor at Durham University, John Heywood Thomas, was a patient guide to my doctoral research, and continues to challenge my thinking as a good friend. I am also grateful both to my colleagues in the Department of Religion at Trinity College, Hartford, with whom I shared such a very happy four years from 1971 to 1975, and to my women colleagues there, with whom early feminist ideas and frameworks of thinking began to be formed.

There are special thanks to be given to those who have helped in the reading of this book, to Tim Jenkins, Ann Morley, and John Heywood Thomas, who read and commented upon some of the early parts of the text, and to Eric Forshaw, Rosi Jarvis, Pauline Mulligan, and Barbara and Michael Taylor, who have so kindly read it all, and offered me their advice. Discussions of women's writing with Barbara have been especially thought-provoking, while Michael has been a much-valued colleague and a keen partner in theological debate. Pauline held my hand throughout the whole project, feeding me with provocative bits of theological sense and nonsense, without which the outcome of my work would have been so much poorer. My thanks to Gillian Maude for her helpful work as copy editor, and to Rosi for her great care in proof reading. All of them have contributed in special ways to this book, for which I thank them most sincerely. I alone must now be responsible for the result.

To be honest, I have not found the task of writing an easy one. Speaking to a word processor is not my natural form of communication, and I have at times found the enforced solitude uncomfortable. I have been hugely supported by the students and staff of the East Midlands Ministry Training Course, by Ted O'Neil and Vanessa Johnson, who kept the office running so smoothly, and by the Council of the Course, who kindly granted me a study leave during which so much of the reading and preparation could be done. My neighbours and friends have been patient with my extended absence from their good company. My husband, Mark, has been my true companion throughout this work, and our son, Andrew, says he expects no more bad moods or moaning, now that this is finished.

Lastly, I thank my parents, within whose home I first cut my theological teeth, in a context of Christian faithfulness to tradition and inspiration for what might yet be true. Most especially, this book is dedicated to my mother, Wilma Alice Sedoris Frank. She would not like to be called a feminist of any kind whatsoever. Yet, she has lived much of her life on an edge that has been too narrow for others to accompany her, and it is only in my own growing up that I have begun to grasp something of her inner struggles. My sensitivities to the quality of women's lives, and my awareness of the spiritual potential which they hold, has been nurtured, even across the miles, in her embrace. I now believe that, 'It is impossible to ask a woman to be holy . . . as long as she is unable to recognize the potential holiness of her own mother.'[1] This book is an expression of a mother's love, returned to her with great affection.

---

[1] The reference is to Luce Irigiray: 'Equal to Whom?' in *differences*, a Journal of Feminist Cultural Studies, 1:2, p. 72.

CHAPTER I

On Diversity

To enter the area in which feminism and Christian ethics interact is to enter a territory characterised by broad and deep diversity, a diversity which is challenging and creative to those who may take hold of the opportunity it presents. Careful observers of contemporary culture will have become aware of the very great number of belief systems and moral frameworks which are used by different groups and by individuals in making moral decisions and in settling major political and social issues. The contemporary world has been described as pluralistic, suggesting that there are a variety of frameworks available for justifiable and reasonable commitment, to which people are intensely attached, and which provide for them the essential foundation and rationale for the practice of their personal and social lives. The presence of these alternatives has been discussed and analysed by numerous moral philosophers and Christian ethicists, who have attempted in various ways both to understand the nature of the differences and to recommend a reasonable way through the alternatives for moral agents. This book shares in that task by engaging in an analysis of the interactions of feminism and Christian ethics, interactions which are themselves indicative of the complexity of current moral thinking.

Diversity of belief makes itself known in a number of ways, in academic teaching and writing, in political debate, and in dilemmas of daily life. The nature of this diversity is such that, while people are clear and certain about the decisions made within one of these frameworks, being able to be decisive in judgements about matters which come to their attention, there is confusion as people from within different frameworks talk to each other and try to work together. As people enter into moral and political debates, they come to the discussion with certain basic moral reference points which they take to be fundamental, with a set of definitions, with some understanding of matters on which there is uncertainty or which may be open to alternative interpretation and even compromise. They come with stories of lives which illustrate the effectiveness of their own moral framework in bringing fulfilment and, by contrast, the distressing or debasing impact of an alternative framework on human life. The presence of these different moral frameworks makes debate on any particular issue perplexing for participants and interpreters alike.

Several examples of this situation could be given to illustrate the nature of the complexity. Consider the debates being conducted throughout the western world over the matter of abortion.[1] There are some participants who believe that human rights are at stake in the debate. The kind of moral reasoning which is appropriate to a dilemma like this is reasoning which measures itself with reference to the universal and objective principles by which such rights are affirmed and enforced. The conflict within this framework of moral reasoning develops as a conflict between such rights, each of which is supported by principles that admit no exceptions in order that consistency in the moral life be maintained. Some support the 'right to life', expressed in a principle which requires protection of all human life however dependent and unformed, and in a set of definitions which asserts that the fœtus, at a certain stage in its development in the womb, is actually 'human life' and that anything which deliberately stops the growth and flourishing of that life to full-term birth is killing. Together this principle and these definitions are supported by illustrative stories from parents and from professional health carers and social workers, with photographs, which are intended to be persuasive and to draw people into this way of understanding the dilemma and its consequences.

On the other hand, some support the 'right to choose', and enter the debate with a fundamental principle of freedom

which calls for treating persons as ends-in-themselves, together
with a set of definitions regarding what constitutes 'consent' in
sexual intercourse and the importance of being 'wanted' or
'chosen' in the flourishing of human life. This is accompanied
with stories from raped or abused women, with illustrations of
the unhappy lives, the increased poverty, and the continuing
vulnerability of those who are deprived of freedom. In both
cases are participants who understand the debate to be about
principles and the human rights which such principles embody
and justify, and who can disagree with one another from a
common ground, for they share a conception of the nature of
moral reasoning. The abortion debate is thus usually represented as a conflict within this framework, a conflict between
those who are basically 'pro-life' and those who are generally
speaking 'pro-choice'. To engage in the debate has required
the acceptance of moral reasoning as a consideration of human
rights. There is, however, considerable dissatisfaction with the
terms of reference which this framework adopts. It may be
argued that this view of moral reasoning generates exactly this
kind of unresolvable conflict, for its presuppositions are inadequate to a full appreciation of the complexity of human life. It
is clear that today the 'conflict of rights' description is not so
helpful as a guide to the many interacting strands of argument
that are actually involved.

Thus there are those who participate in this debate whose
understanding of morality is not this, and who offer quite a
different view of the project of moral reasoning itself. A second
interpretation of morality emerges here. These participants use
as fundamental reference points, not principles, but sharp
insights into the operation of social structures, the apparatus of
power by which these structures are sustained, and the result-
ing deprivation of genuine human moral agency. Their understanding of morality is set in a framework which considers the
politically necessary striving for domination to be the key
factor in any moral debate, and the history and present forms
of that domination to be the central narrative underlying those
debates. In the matter of abortion there are very powerful
institutional pressures from the churches, from political groups,

and from the medical establishment. These combine with forms of language, in which social ideologies are fixed, to constrain the discussion and to channel its results into enforced social patterns. The moral concern of the participants is to expose the motivations of those institutions which seek to retain their hold on public order through the ideology of the family, and to demonstrate that moral principles are merely the tools of the powerful to uphold oppressive social structures. This demonstration is effected by allowing the voices of the victims of such oppression to be heard, in their speaking to crack open the solidity of such ideological and institutional control of human life, and to discover the language of their own authentic moral agency.[2] The definitions and stories accompanying this moral case are themselves examples of such exposure and reclamation, for new and critical insights are offered as the family is redefined as a bourgeois capitalist necessity, sexual intercourse is redescribed as an assertion of phallic power, and abortion itself is viewed as a sacrament.[3]

Thirdly, there are those in the debate whose understanding of moral reasoning centres neither on human rights, nor on social critique, but rather on a description of the fundamentals of biology. In knowing how it is that life is formed, what contributes to its sustenance, and what physical realities are essential to its continued development, is to discover a law of nature binding upon that life. This law is understood to be the expression of the purposiveness of nature inherent in the make-up of all things, in obedience to which life is lived and fulfilled. What is needed in the moral debate is the description of these natural realities, descriptions which are value-laden with affirmation that life is good and which offer without recourse to other considerations compelling reasons for action. Moral decisions are thus to refer to the natural world in the midst of which what is good can be discovered, and this world is to be given priority over the world of universal principles of the first view or the psycho-socio-political world of the second. The point these participants make in the abortion debate is that, in arriving at a moral decision, we are to affirm the natural and avoid the unnatural, since this natural material is the stuff from which human beings develop in all their fullness of possibility and experience. The stories accompanying this account of moral reasoning are thus illustrations of the deeper meanings of our decisions which do not affect 'mere' matter, but which signify what we believe about the purpose of life, about pain and suffering, and about the potential of love.[4]

As this discussion has proceeded, it has been possible to detect all kinds of overlapping concerns and partial agreements between these frameworks, and to see ways in which temporary compromises have been possible in order to effect decisions. Those who are critical of the advancing power and control of medical technology in the name of free choice join hands with those of strong religious conviction whose loyalty to a divine power prohibits such freedom; and the second two frameworks, while differing significantly from one another, share in criticism of the insufficiency of the first. These have, however, not altered the fact that between these understandings of moral reasoning there are deep differences and incompatibilities. It comes as no surprise, therefore, that at times great rifts have opened up between them, making it difficult for a person within one of them to speak sensibly and coherently to a person from another, for the nature of their disagreement is profound.[5] They operate within different belief systems which are internally coherent, but which cannot engage with each other because their basic moral reference points may not be compatible, and their definitions are so different as to prevent in some cases even basic understanding of what another is saying.

A second and briefer illustration relates to present considerations of the nature and responsibilities of government, in which once again alternative moral frameworks run together head-on in offering different interpretations of the state, and incompatible proposals for present and future politics.[6] One moral framework sees in the modern state a minimalist approach to government, in which non-intervention is the principal consideration. The state is understood in a negative sense as that framework within which the full expression of individual liberty, in ownership, in work, in making choices regarding life style and use of wealth, is to be upheld and protected. Persons who live within such a structure are taken to be autonomous, separate beings who are basically and deeply alike; each has a will and a mind and a body independent of other persons, each owns the things accrued through their own activities, and each confronts other persons as potential competitors or suspicious allies in any social working. The principles for effective functioning of such a state posit the existence of 'human rights', which give expression to the basic requirements for living this kind of life without constant warfare, and which can be referred to in moral dilemmas and legal decisions as 'inalienable'. This approach understands moral discussions about the state to be a matter of conformity to, and application of, the appropriate principles that define and ensure the just distribution of these rights, so that the basic equality of persons may be sustained.

Another moral framework reads into this interpretation of the state a more insidious tale of the emergence of controlling institutions and ideologies. Underneath the rhetoric of *laissez-faire* is the reality of the colonialisation of the eastern world by the west, of the economic enslavement of peoples of colour by white people, and of the physical, spiritual, and emotional containment of women's lives by men. These realities are what the state actually embodies, and in its operations of governance seeks by whatever necessary means to preserve its power. People who live within such a reality may be defined as either oppressors or victims, as those who are dominant or those who are submissive, as part of the problem or part of the solution. What is important, as moral debate proceeds, is for that identity to be clear from the start so that decisions may be judged according to whose interests are served. In this approach, moral discussions about the state are a matter of unmasking ulterior motives, and of allowing the repressed to be expressed in whatever unpopular or disruptive forms that may take.

Yet another framework emphasises, in understanding the nature of government, that there is a true and natural order of things which the state embodies. This view expresses a positive concern for human well-being within that order, and encourages the state to be actively involved in the development of a society within which personal life may flourish. Here the moral reference points are not human rights and individual liberty, nor the awareness of hidden motive and structural power, but rather a description of the place and function of individual human life in an overall scheme of common human good. In this approach, persons are taken to be developing beings, whose lives are constituted by the interactions and relationships which social roles can provide, and who develop fulfilled and happy lives in appreciation of their differences and variety. The state is to provide the matrix within which these networks of relationship thrive, its existence being the embodiment of the purposiveness of human life. Accordingly, the state preserves meaningful social groupings, so that human life is lived in the best possible setting. In this case, moral discussions about the state are understood to relate essentially to an understanding of what is true order.

Once again the ideas that come together within each of these frameworks form clusters of interrelated notions, which are coherent, but between which are unpredictable relationships. Sometimes they exist separately, as when one is clearly taken up by a political party or forms the basis for some measure or other. Sometimes strands from one become tangled with strands from another, which results in a more unsteady state of affairs. Close examination of recent arguments regarding freedom of the press reveals both that these clusters form recognisable positions in relation to the debate, but also that there are frayed edges in which strands from different clusters come together. Thus each framework may have the strangest set of bedfellows, team supporters, and adherents, some of whom one would not have suspected of being sympathetic. We cannot therefore be entirely sure who will be taking which side in which debates, and which kinds of attachments will be made by various groups and individuals to particular causes. In political debate, the identity and the policy platforms of modern political parties have become confused, as people from different traditions and loyalties ally themselves in new ways.

The reason for concentrating upon this present state of

culture and its ramifications in theoretical and practical moral concerns, is that it also describes the interrelation of feminism and Christian ethics. Contemporary feminism has developed out of one reasonable and persuasive belief system, in which certain principles are taken to be crucial to human life and necessary to any debate regarding social and personal justice, certain definitions are taken for granted as the essential cornerstones of moral argument, and narratives of the life recommended by this framework are provided. This belief system, broadly labelled as liberal and identified with the Enlightenment period of philosophical thinking, nurtured the growth of feminism. That would be altogether straightforward, not that everyone would agree with the conclusions pressed by feminists or believe that they were possible or practicable, but at least people would understand and broadly empathise with the framework in which these things were being proposed. Straightforward, that is, were it not for the fact that this paradigm is now deeply and seriously challenged by others which offer alternative explanations of the same events and problems, and which lead to different conclusions regarding the living of life within them.

The present state of feminism is thus far from being a straightforward matter. There are now a variety and diversity of feminists who operate within broad frameworks of belief that are fundamentally different from each other, such that it is now rather more difficult than it might have been at one time to define what a feminist is.[7] One may offer a general definition, that a feminist is one who takes most seriously the practical concerns of women's lives, the analysis and the critique of these conditions of life, and the ways in which women's lives may become more fulfilling. Each of these features is understood and analysed today from quite different theoretical and political stances. This confusion of alternatives suggests the need for some clarity in explicating these paradigms one by one, so that some broad schema may be mapped out by which we might be able to get our bearings in present debates.

Three different forms of feminism will be considered: the liberal, the social constructionist, and the naturalist. Each of these forms will be shown to be basically related to an overall framework of belief, shared with others whose concerns are not primarily feminist, but which gives the structure necessary for reasonable debate about moral matters. The setting of feminist thinking within these frameworks will aid the analysis of the basic moral principles, the significant definitions, and the stories of life upon and around which feminists construct the case regarding women. In addition it will be important to examine ways in which these frameworks have been challenged and criticised, and that will be a second task of this work. Each framework has been, and continues to be, assessed and questioned by feminists working within one of the others, and the material which is available for evaluation of the alternatives is now considerable. What is revealed by the criticisms is both a much sharper picture of the original framework, with its presuppositions and its implications, and an awareness of the underlying questions which are unresolved within that framework which any further development in thinking may need to take on board.

It has been suggested that between differing moral frameworks there is rivalry, that each is a fixed thing competing with the others for belief and commitment, and that there may be no common ground on which to form a unified or unifying set of concerns.[8] This understanding of diversity might imply that the moral agent must therefore choose which stance to cling to, like deciding which political party to vote for, and in that choosing will immediately distinguish between this view and those others. This, I want to suggest, is inappropriate as an understanding of the diversity within feminism. There is the obvious point that there exists already a unifying concern regarding the lives of women. There is the point already made about these frameworks being clusters with frayed edges. There is a personal point that individual feminists have lived through these frameworks, and have discovered in each of them something of significance which illuminates the nature of women's personal/political lives, and may now continue to draw from each of them important resources for understanding and action. This suggests that, through the diversity, there is a serious and critical commitment to understanding the meaning of human life, to gaining insight into the conditions in which life might be most fulfilling from this perspective and that one, and to discovering the creative potential for reordering the conditions of life. In these matters, conversation between moral frameworks is essential, as each is allowed to present the best possible case it can make, and each is encouraged to engage with the others at the most deep level of moral debate. This can only be a constructive effort out of which the future agenda and direction of feminist theory and practice may emerge.

The relationship of Christian thinking to all of this is again another matter of some complexity. For just as feminists work within these three frameworks of belief and practice, so it is the case that these frameworks provide the structure for certain understandings of the nature of the Christian life, and indeed definitions of the theological task itself. Christian thinking has both contributed to, and been influenced by, the Enlightenment, and the emerging liberal paradigm of moral thinking has been expressed in a theistic context in which its commitment to principles and its basic humanism have been enriched. Theologians have worked out the ethical consequences of this framework, and many believe it to be consistent with both the essence of the biblical record and the working of the Spirit in the world today.

There are also Christians who sympathise and work within the social constructionist framework, which presents itself in opposition to Enlightenment morality. The social construction of morality is a challenge to the form of Christian ethics which has adapted to the first framework, and thus it makes very particular demands to reconceive morality as the product of a community's life. Christian ethicists may claim that this paradigm refreshingly clears away the pretensions of a false universalism, and offers a more profound recognition of morality as a human task. Yet feminists and Christian ethicists alike are concerned about the implications which this framework might have for moral and political action, since to claim that moral guidelines are socially produced and manipulated may be to deprive them of the authority necessary for effectiveness in moral decision. This deprivation is directly related to questions about the authority of faith in relation to moral guidance, and, as such, reopens considerations of truth-claims in matters both of morals and of faith.

Likewise there are Christians who work within the naturalist framework, and who would argue that the reinstatement of this kind of morality may be one of the clearest responses to present social and ethical confusion. A fresh consideration of this paradigm is appropriate given some of the weaknesses evident in the other two. This is however the one paradigm in which the most intense arguments and accusations and recriminations lie between feminism and Christian ethics. There are feminists who agree with Christians from within this framework, that the basic source of moral principles must be found within a description of nature, but who disagree that such a description has ever adequately been given which takes account of the concerns of women's lives, or indeed even contemporary biology. They object to the tendency to absolutise particular conceptions of nature, depriving human beings of the freedom necessary to the moral life. There are Christians who share this understanding of the moral project, but who utterly reject the possibility of another description of nature, particularly human nature, since this is too great a challenge both to the tradition and to what is believed to be the once-for-all revelation of God's purposes for creation. Between these two, it is often difficult to see possibilities for genuine dialogue or co-operation.

Through this analysis and critique of three frameworks of belief, the nature of the task which lies before Christian ethicists may also become more clear, and we may appreciate more fully the project of Christian ethics. Precisely the same diversity, the same confusion in moral debate, and the same discussions at cross-purposes occur in Christian ethical debate as elsewhere in our contemporary culture. This leads not infrequently to an impasse in moral debate between Christians, in which the questions raised earlier, regarding how and in what sense the participants may be understood to be inhabiting the same moral universe, are greatly intensified. Diversity amongst Christians thus becomes one of the matters about which Christian ethicists are concerned, and through which they consider what is essential for the continuation of a tradition which is itself a complex and varied tapestry. Out of this consideration is the hope that we may be able to offer some description of reasonable belief which does not rely upon the arbitrariness of blind choice or the sheer strength of commitment to what one hopes is the winning side. Which strands of the fabric of tradition are drawn out and used to weave the next pattern is a matter for serious reflection, for critical and passionate debate, and for attentiveness to the details of our lived humanness.

It is the aim of this work to demonstrate in the midst of this diversity that the concerns of feminism and the concerns of Christian ethics are intrinsically related to one another, such that a consideration of one is tied up with, and has implications for, a consideration of the other, and such that, in the end, the future of the one is tied to the future of the other. This means that the easy dismissal by Christians of feminism as a secular phenomenon, a cultural development which at its most innocuous has nothing to do with Christianity, or at its most harmful is at odds with the truths of Christian faith and morals, or which in particular forms is anti-church and anti-Christ, is too simple a response to the complex history and present faces of feminism and to its deeply theological affirmations and assumptions.[9] Likewise this means that the rejection by feminists of Christianity as a hopelessly exclusive tradition, the model *par excellence* of patriarchal domination through language, institutional order, and cultural collusion, in which women cannot find themselves or their voices, is also too simple a response to the varied understandings of theological method and the deep commitment to truth which lies at the heart of Christian theology.[10]

Feminists share with many Christian ethicists the deep sense of dissatisfaction with the fundamental assumptions in which modern moral inquiry has been conducted. There is a certain collaboration in critique which can be mutually supportive and encouraging. Likewise feminists are challenging the Christian ethical tradition to understand the ways in which, and the reasons why, previous, pre-modern, descriptions of the moral project available in the tradition are not now wholly satisfactory. In this challenge they are joined by Christian ethicists who also understand that to be faithful to a tradition requires its being lived anew in each age. Beyond these mutual concerns of critique and challenge however, is the constructive task which lies ahead for both.

The final part of this work will examine ways in which this creative effort is being expressed and elaborated.[11] Feminist theory offers important insights into a possible reformulation of our understanding of morality, and with it a reconception of what might constitute a good life for human beings, and these may engage directly with the kinds of insights which the Christian tradition might bring to bear. These insights from Christian ethics are not already fully worked out so that they can be applied to feminism as answers to questions or resolutions to dilemmas. The Christian ethical tradition does not provide us with principles which only need to be applied to the 'case' of feminism. Rather the areas we examine are areas of interwoven concern that require dialogue for mutual enhancement. Three areas of interdependent interest will be explored: – the search for an appropriate universalism by which justice may be known; the emphasis on community as the site of redemptive relationships; and the possibility of a gender-sensitive natural law ethic in which the basic features of our humanness may yet be developed and sustained. Feminists are working in just these areas of interdependence, in which some of the most creative developments within Christian ethics may be taking place.

CHAPTER 2

The liberal paradigm

In September 1791 in Paris, 'The Declaration of the Rights of Women Citizens' was issued by Olympe de Gouges. Caught up in the fervour of the French Revolution, she spoke of the 'natural, unchangeable and sacred rights of women' which it was the duty of government to protect and affirm.[1] Conversely, the corruption of government, she argued, was due to 'ignorance, neglect or contempt of the rights of women'. De Gouges believed that the same kinds of natural rights which men were proposing for themselves also applied to women. There was in her view no cause for distinction. She believed these natural rights to be established and expressed in the form of principles, and so her moral argument was that our reasoning in making decisions must be based on 'clear and unarguable principles'. It was by reference to these that the logic of the feminist case was to be presented.

These principles were founded in nature itself. De Gouges claimed that limits had been put upon the lives of women through men depriving women of what is naturally theirs, and these limits 'must be reformed by the laws of nature and of reason'. It was the task of rationality to discover the principles that lie at the heart of nature, and no longer to base political or moral judgements upon superficial distinctions or social tradition. Reason was to penetrate nature, to understand the fundamental laws upon which nature is established and by which it operates. These laws would then prohibit unnatural, unjust, or immoral extensions of one set of human rights over against another. Reason could reform society.

The logical outcome of this would be that 'all citizens,

women and men, being equal in the eyes of the law, must have equal access to all honours, positions and public posts, according to their abilities and with no other distinctions than those of their strengths and their talents'. Here is a new view of society emerging, in which de Gouges claimed for women what men were claiming in their liberal vision for society, namely equality – equality of persons regardless of established distinctions, equality of persons according to the true knowledge which rationality has given of our nature, equality which the law must express and a just society embody. The principle of equal responsibilities included responsibilities not only for the benefits, privileges, and rewards of society, but also for its tasks and for its difficult and dirty work. Unpleasant duties and tedious chores, de Gouges claimed, must also be included, along with jobs that bring influence and honours. These should be distributed throughout the society.

Lastly, in this piece de Gouges expressed the common call of the Enlightenment period for liberation from slavery:

the powerful hold of nature is no longer circumscribed with prejudice, fanaticism, superstition and lies. The torch of truth has cleared away all clouds of foolishness and usurpation. Man the slave has increased his strength and needed to use yours too to break his chains . . . Oh women, women, when will you open your eyes?

Men have escaped the tyranny of nature by the mastery of the light of reason, in which they have discovered fundamental principles of natural human rights. It was now clearly time for women to claim their same rights, logically, according to the same principles of reasoning which men used for their own freedom. Slavery, if not justified for the one, was clearly also not justified for the other. De Gouges believed that women would be able to march forward for this freedom 'under the banners of philosophy'. This new understanding of rationality would provide both the light by which to illuminate their previous situation of oppression and slavery, and the new insight into nature and human rights upon which a positive vision for society in the future could be established. De Gouges was guillotined for her trouble.

Our exploration of the relationship between feminism and

Christian ethics begins with the feminism which emerged with
the Enlightenment, which historically has been most significant in the development of contemporary feminism. Contemporary feminism was born out of the new humanism of the
Enlightenment, and thus is a child of the liberal paradigm of
moral reasoning. The liberal way of understanding the nature
of morality has now become part of the overall cultural milieu
in which contemporary debates about moral issues are conducted, and current thinking in a whole range of matters is
carried out within its context. The terms of this paradigm are
now commonplace, and are so taken for granted as basic
elements of our moral discourse that it is often difficult for us to
see them with any critical distance, or to know that they may
present any special problems. So we are accustomed to speaking about human rights and to arguing that people ought to
have equal access to these rights; and we have come to believe
that to assert the basic equality of persons is a moral trump
card which is hard to beat in any argument. Such language has
become the common currency that we need to exchange for
much serious progress to be made in moral considerations and
in political debates. Within the language of rights and respect
for human dignity lie the main features of this liberal humanist
paradigm of moral thinking which give it shape and structure.

   The growth of liberalism occurred at a particular time and
place in western history, and the cultural conditions out of
which it developed not only motivated the changes which
liberal thinkers proposed, but shaped those proposals themselves in important ways. The 'Enlightenment' is so called
because many took it to be literally a time of the bringing of
light to a world and a society which was in darkness. Therefore
there is a sense, in the liberal description of human life, of
trying to offer something radically new that would affect our
understanding of all aspects of that life. One of the accomplishments of this Enlightenment was to be the discovery of the
key to this illumination, to be found in a description of rationality, engagement with which allows new insights into the
social and the natural world. This new kind of rational thinking brought with it an alternative version of truth which

challenged the epistemological presuppositions and framework of previous eras. The growth of early modern science is the product of this rationality and embodies its new approach to the world, while the growth of liberal politics and morality is an expression of a new rational approach to the world of human affairs. Having once captured the key to unlock this darkness, there is a kind of philosophical and political and theological purging which makes its own contribution to changes in western societies. One of the characteristics of the Enlightenment is thus an enthusiasm for liberation, liberating the mind from superstition, liberating people from fixed social and economic patterns based on natural law, liberating the natural world from the illusions of an earlier science, and liberating society from tradition.

Preceding these developments had been changes in theological thinking, from which were derived liberation themes. The Protestant emphasis on a direct approach to God by each individual frees all persons from what had come to be understood as the tyranny of institutional authority. Each person knowing God in the quiet reason of his or her own heart and mind is a way of liberating individuals from tradition, from mediation between themselves and God, and from hierarchical structures. In such turning to God, the believer has come to realise the futility of human action *per se*, the pretentiousness of any attempts to be good, and is therefore able to accept in complete humility and emptiness the grace of God. Theological writings share with philosophical and scientific ones the same optimism in human possibilities for true knowledge, available to the Christian through faith. Such knowledge from God transcends the partial and limited viewpoints of this world, and offers to the believer an opportunity to affirm what is ultimate. In this affirmation are found the roots of Protestant humanism, with its emphasis on individual responsibility before God. In the conscience of each person are known the demands of God, which address themselves to the deepest level of human awareness within us, and call forth obedience in living an authentic life. From such a cluster of ideas comes prophetic courage to challenge society, and to urge the enhancement of the possibilities of full human life. Protestant ethics, in its diverse forms, shares many of the basic assumptions of the liberal approach to moral reasoning, and is thus entangled with Enlightenment humanism. Early feminist writers and speakers used the central themes of the Enlightenment, both philosophical and theological, in their arguments regarding the position and the responsibilities of women, and found little difficulty in blending the religious with the secular expressions of this approach. Through the late eighteenth and early nineteenth centuries, the ripples of the Enlightenment ideal were beginning to be felt in the lives of women in tentative ways that revealed a developing network of relationships between France, Britain, and the United States. With the developments in evangelical Protestantism during the Second Great Awakening in the United States, women welcomed their acceptance as individuals in the structures, teaching, and mission of the churches. Their involvement in all aspects of church life confirmed their egalitarian understanding of religious commitment, and led to their increased concern for the practical implications of their faith by righting injustices in the wider society. Women were to play important roles in organising anti-slavery and temperance movements, in social action to ease the conditions of increasing urban poverty, in educational work, and in various expressions of concern for the welfare of animals. Their writings contain descriptions of conditions of life which had previously been hidden from view, upon which the new light of reason could now be shed, and in which the work of reforming society could begin.

Perhaps the most important of these was published in 1791 by Mary Wollstonecraft, who directed her attention both to the discernment of 'the pernicious effects which arise from the unnatural distinctions established in society', and to the affirmation of the common human nature of women and men.[2] Both the respect paid to property, from which flow 'as from a poisoned fountain, most of the evils and vices which render this world such a dreary scene to the contemplative mind',[3] and the differential education of women as outlined by Jean Jacques Rousseau, encourage women to sacrifice the most essential elements of their own humanness.[4] Wollstonecraft believed that, through the use of reason, we are able to discover principles for behaviour which apply to all human beings, and which are to be consistently used in moral decisions. These principles are founded beyond the distinctions which society takes so seriously, and present to us a higher court of appeal. Such thinking reveals the separation of values from the world of facts and experiences, and relies upon unique insights which reason is able to provide. Moral principles are thus not based upon judgements about what is the case, in society or in biology, but rather are uniquely derived and established. Moral practice is a matter of obedience to these principles, applying them consistently to cases which the moral agent is considering. Reason presents lofty expectations of moral decision and action, requiring a motive of single-minded adherence and a high degree of consistent obedience in practice. Wollstonecraft argued that even 'if women are by nature inferior to men, their virtues must be the same in quality, if not in degree, or virtue is a relative idea'.[5] Relativity of virtue was inconsistent with the requirements of morality as established by reason, and thus to argue that principles apply to one but not to another was irrational.

This kind of thinking relies upon the assertion of the oneness of truth; 'for man and woman, truth, if I understand the meaning of the word, must be the same'.[6] Discovery of universal truth is here understood as the most important project of human rationality, and is indicative of a particular understanding of the operations of the mind. Underlying Wollstonecraft's argument is a belief that the rational mind is capable of transcendence, being basically independent of the body and of its environment. Some aspect of this mind is able to rise above physical conditions as well as received beliefs, in order to question, to ascertain the deeper truth which lies beyond these realities, and to discover there the salient features of the good human life. Through the use of our rational capacity, human beings are able to detach themselves from present situations and from confinement to physical conditions. Reason is thus characterised by suspicion, doubt, and challenge until that which may not be questioned or doubted appears. The mind has thus the human capacity to transcend, and, through its functioning, human beings are independent and free. Such activity becomes the highest expression of human possibilities and of the real essence of humanness which lies at the heart of each one of us. From this central recognition comes the affirmation of a basic human dignity established by reason.

The expectations which this puts upon the lives of women were serious. For, 'women must only bow to the authority of reason instead of being the *modest* slaves of opinion'.[7] Wollstonecraft presented a challenge to women to adopt this form of reasoning for their own lives, claiming that women need to be educated 'in such a manner as to be able to think and act for themselves'.[8] Rather than training women in their alleged inferiority, women ought to be trained and educated according to the same principles and the same aims as men. Since human beings are all bound by the same rules, 'their conduct should be founded on the same principles and have the same aim'.[9] The task which then lies before women and men alike is great:

To render mankind more virtuous, and happier of course, both sexes must act from the same principle; but how can that be expected when only one is allowed to see the reasonableness of it? To render also the social compact truly equitable, and in order to spread those enlightening principles which alone can meliorate the fate of man, women must be allowed to found their virtue on knowledge, which is scarcely possible unless they be educated by the same pursuits as men.[10]

She urged that women grasp the whole of the truth, which would reveal to them their equality with men, and then set about the great task of spreading those enlightening principles.

Throughout Wollstonecraft's *Vindication* is an emphasis on individuality. While there is a common natural law, giving persons rights which are shared and discovered through the proper functioning of reason, human beings are none the less quite distinctly individuals, who bear responsibility for their own lives, and for their own exercise of reason. As individuals, we each have our own conscience, and moral behaviour is the result of the operation of the individual conscience. She argued therefore that 'private virtue becoming the cement of public happiness, an orderly whole is consolidated by the tendency of all the parts towards a common centre'.[11] Here is an early expression of the democratic liberal society as a collection of individuals, each of whom has exercised their own capacity for reason to understand the truth about themselves, and each of whom has had educational opportunities that allow them to develop to the best of their abilities, without distinction of class or gender. Through education, people would begin to think properly and to exercise their imaginations in the right kind of way towards a consideration of what is our common good, rather than private or personal reward. This, Wollstonecraft believed, would lead to a truly free society. 'Society can only be happy and free in proportion as it is virtuous; but the present distinctions, established in society, corrode all private and blast all public virtue.'[12] Here we have an impressive vision of a new society bound by the common exercise of reason, with the central focus on the good in which all human beings share, a vision which encourages people to set aside all those temporary and insubstantial goals in favour of the one which holds us in our common humanity, men and women together. This vision of society was to exercise a powerful hold on the imaginations of those concerned with liberation of all kinds for centuries to come.

A year earlier, in the United States, another essay had been produced by Judith Sargent Murray, 'On The Equality of the Sexes'. Here, not only are the same themes of liberal moral reasoning present, but Murray sets them in the context of Christian theological affirmations. Like Wollstonecraft and de Gouges, she asserts the equal capabilities of women and men, which require the same education to enhance. Furthermore, as a Christian, Murray argued that there is an equal responsibility for women and for men to approach and to worship the deity, so that woman 'might catch a glimpse of the immensity of the Deity, and thence she would form amazing conceptions of the august and supreme Intelligence'.[13] Through the study of astronomy, and indeed through all the sciences, women would be able to discover in the same way as their brothers the greatness of God through the exploration of the natural world. There is nothing, Murray believed, that would logically prohibit the same kind of exploration which leads to the same worship of God. To prevent such opportunities results in the trivialisation of women's lives. The problem of vanity in women's lives, which was often used to justify their inferior social status and to excuse their separation in educational opportunities, was nothing more than the application of their motivation and their energies to lesser things, because the greater opportunities were not given to them. Their lives become full of resentment and of unhappiness, and they are surrounded by trifles, as a result not of their 'nature', but of social possibilities. Unless they could be encouraged to develop their intelligence in all four of its aspects in the same way as men, women would be consigned to a status that reason did not support and their full humanity could not justify.[14]

Murray asserted that this equality is established in nature by the Creator. 'Yes, ye Lordly, ye haughty sex, our souls are by nature *equal* to yours. The same breath of God animates, enlivens, and invigorates us . . .'[15] For Murray, belief in God as the Creator meant belief that God has made all persons equal, and she argued for that equality of soul, regardless of bodily facts, regardless of differences in physical strength, regardless of what some can do with assistance and others can do independently. Equality of soul was for her something established beyond superficial or bodily differences; it was plainly irrational to attribute 'strength of mind to the transient organization of this earth born tenement'.[16] Like Wollstonecraft, she demanded consistency, and was not convinced that good reasons had been given for taking some bodily distinctions more seriously than others. These alone could not affect the fundamental equality of soul, which God has made and upon which moral worth is based.

In the supplement to her essay, Murray demonstrated just how powerful can be our attachment to unimportant distinctions and to received prejudices, by presenting one of the earliest attempts at biblical interpretation in the light of this new humanism. Recognising that the Judaeo-Christian tradition had based its beliefs about the inferiority of women on a particular interpretation of the biblical story of the Fall, she offered an alternative view. Contrary to the received view of Eve's bodily weakness, through which sin entered human life, Murray claimed that Eve was motivated by the desire to enhance her mind through the knowledge of good and evil, a search which is to be commended, even though she was misled about the method of its attainment. Adam, on the other hand, had little excuse for his eating of the fruit, for he could only have been driven by self-love and by his attachment to her. Thus the tables are turned on the tradition which, Murray believed, had been so caught up with men's absorption in partial admiration of their own abilities, that it was rendered blind to this obviously rational interpretation.[17] The light of the new reason would bring new challenges and new insights in the work of biblical interpretation as well.

In the writings of these early feminists can be found the important assumptions of the liberal paradigm of moral reasoning. The first of these is the belief that the free and transcendent activity of reason is the most essential expression of our uniqueness as human beings. It is through this activity that human dignity is realised and affirmed, and that objective truth is discovered. Reason is able to draw us out of the mundane into the ultimate, out of the particular into the universal, out of the contingent into the free, and out of the bodily into the spiritual. The deeply theological implications of this belief were accepted by those who understood that, in this exercise of reason, God was also approached and known. In the search for ultimate truth, for universal principles of judgement, for real freedom, and for spiritual awareness are expressions of faith that such things are possible and are not illusory. God may be understood as the divine being who supports these realities, in whom the search for them may be most fulfilled. While there were clearly those for whom the Enlightenment meant also the abandonment of religious belief and practice, theologically their arguments may be seen as attempts to clear away the idols which hinder the true apprehension of the divine. Liberal feminist writers have known this, and have accepted that in the most serious criticisms of the Judaeo-Christian tradition are to be found expressions of prophetic insight that can clear away the irrational dross of our social and political lives. The affirmation of transcendent reason is basic to this view.

The second of these presuppositions is that through the exercise of this reason, moral principles for decision and action are discovered. One expression of these principles is the positing of natural rights which are believed to inhere in the fundamental structures of human existence itself. It is claimed that these rights are known by reason, and, by some, that they are written into human nature by the Creator. Once discovered, they provide the framework for moral considerations and the justification for moral behaviour. Since these rights are established within the structures of our humanness, feminists who use this paradigm understand it to be consistent to claim that such rights are equally relevant to women and to men. Another expression of these principles is the Kantian demonstration of the moral law within human life, formulated as a desire to do what one ought to do which can only be fulfilled through obedience to those things that may be willed to be universal law, and that may be enacted without self-contradiction. This moral law places upon the agent an obligation to test the maxim of each action and, only after such testing, to decide upon a course of action. In deciding how to behave with other human beings, the moral law demands that we consider how we would will that all human beings should behave towards one another, and that we test whether this result can be lived without contradicting our moral commitments. For Kant, the categorical imperative to treat other persons as ends only, and never as a means to an end, was the reasonable expression of this moral law. Since its discovery by reason was at the same time a realisation of the divine will of the Creator, this imperative was equally well expressed in the command of Jesus to love our neighbours as ourselves. Again, liberal feminists believe that consistency and universality in moral principles requires the inclusion of women in all moral considerations.

The third assumption within this paradigm is the importance of the individual human being, and the affirmation of each as a person. The development of the language of personhood may be traced to the emphasis on the capacity to reason, from which is believed to stem the essence of personal responsibility. Freedom from established patterns, which the Enlightenment encouraged, brought with it the burden of decision-making for the individual moral agent, for whom the freedom of the will and the freedom of the spirit were essential. Individuals become centres of freedom; how and what they do with this freedom can be traced back to the exercise of their own consciences, which assess alternative possibilities and guide behaviour. This humanistic expression of individualism is one reflection of Protestant ethical emphasis on personal responsibility before God, who holds all persons accountable for their motives and their actions. Theologically, this is expressed through the belief that each person is addressed by the Word of God, in reading the Bible and in hearing sermons, and is thereby challenged to examine the mind and heart, and to respond in obedient assent to God's call. Through the word of God, human personhood is invoked and the essential worth of each individual is confirmed in giving oneself over to God's freedom. The paradox one finds in Luther, namely, that the human person is most free in obedience to God, most powerful in owning human weakness, most dignified in living unto Christ and not unto self, is echoed in the later Enlightenment conviction that personal dignity is discovered through a disciplined following of the dictates of reason. Liberal feminists recognise that in this description of what it means to be a person, whether one is a man or a woman is not relevant, either morally or theologically. Consistency requires the social and political acknowledgement of this belief.

All of these assumptions are carried into twentieth-century developments of feminism, where their implications are explored more fully and their adherence is urged more strongly. In both secular and theological writings, feminists make use of this paradigm of moral reasoning, drawing out the wide-ranging impact which its implementation might have. Several examples of these writers will illustrate the unique emphases which are given to this way of reasoning in contemporary feminism, the theological appropriations of this paradigm by Christian feminists in particular, and the consequences for feminism and Christian ethics of taking seriously this liberal approach to moral concerns.

In contemporary feminism, this paradigm of moral reasoning is extended and elaborated to meet new cultural realities, political events, and an altered philosophical scene. The publication of *The Second Sex*, by Simone de Beauvoir, was an important step in the emergence of contemporary feminism, for, like Wollstonecraft, de Beauvoir accepts the critical function of human reason in sweeping away the irrational aspects of human life. In particular, women have allowed themselves to be made into the 'second' sex, and to be treated as the 'other' by men, who define their lives and describe the limits of their existence. Indeed women have treated men's understanding of them as a form of idolatry, of bad faith in which true freedom is given away, and of enslavement to the imminent and the contingent realities of life which cannot yield full humanness. She writes:

In a sense her whole existence is waiting, since she is confined in the limbo of immanence and contingence, and since her justification is always in the hands of others. She awaits the homage, the approval of men, she awaits love, she awaits the gratitude and praise of her husband or her lover. She awaits her support, which comes from man ... In bed, she awaits the male's desire, she awaits – somewhat anxiously – her own pleasure.[18]

In this description of the present life of woman, de Beauvoir intends to give the impression of a creature who is not fully herself. Her challenge to woman is to rise up and grasp the fundamental freedom and autonomy which it is possible for her to know.

This critique rests upon a description of the life of reason, as the full and free exercise of the human consciousness in controlling the body, not just in its activities, but in giving it meaning and value. The body with its powers and its limitations is an extremely important fact about human beings, and thus for women, it 'is one of the essential elements in her situation in the world'.[19] However, while these facts about ourselves may shape the circumstances and structures in which our lives are lived, they do not determine what meaning these things have for us. This meaning can only be given by the free consciousness in its own choice of patterns for living. Thus de Beauvoir declares that the 'body is not enough to define her as woman; there is no true living reality, except as manifested by the conscious individual through activities and in the bosom of a society'.[20] Women have passively allowed the meaning of their own bodies to be given to them, and de Beauvoir's challenge was for women actively to grasp the power of self-definition.

Woman is the victim of no mysterious fatality; the peculiarities that identify her as specifically a woman get their importance from the significance placed upon them. They can be surmounted, in the future, when they are regarded in new perspectives.[21]

Women may rise out of the conditions of their lives through the exercise of human consciousness, and in so doing will become the authors of their own lives and fates, just as men are. The same struggles characterise the lives of men, 'the same drama of the flesh and the spirit, of finitude and transcendence; both are gnawed away by time and laid in wait for by death'.[22] In the transcendence of reason, there are not morally significant differences between men and women, and true fraternity may be discovered.

This life of reason requires the exercise of total freedom in the creation of our own principles for living, since de Beauvoir shares with Jean Paul Sartre the belief that choice alone creates goodness. Unlike the earlier liberal feminists who grounded their moral arguments in a new understanding of human nature, de Beauvoir takes most seriously the detachment of human consciousness from any such essence. In this separation, values are not discovered as things which already exist, fixed and permanent in a transcendent realm or within nature as illuminated by reason, but rather are created out of the unhindered purposive movement of the human consciousness. This gives to human life its heroic quality, since the primary task of the consciousness of each individual is to detach itself from the 'confused conglomeration of special cases'[23] and to live in the open spaces of independent and lonely choices. There is no God here for consolation, and no divine ground on which to fix moral decisions. De Beauvoir does not require belief in the will of the Creator regarding human beings, since, for her, human nature is not a static thing made by God, but a continuously fluid 'nothingness' which is determined by human decisions and purposes. Thus 'the conflicts in which they are opposed merely mark a transitional moment in human history'.[24] It is this tendency for religious belief to understand humanness as something given by the good will of God which compounds the problem of freedom for women. It is irrelevant whether the believer understands that gift as one of equality or inequality with men. In either case, the woman is deceived regarding her own full human potential, and then avoids through such bad faith the imaginative use of her freedom.[25]

For de Beauvoir, the challenge to women is to take responsibility for their own lives, to make of themselves whatever kinds of persons they choose to be, to become the true authors of their lives. Belief in what is generally true of women or of men is unhelpful in this project, and assumptions about an essence of woman or of man are deceptive and debilitating.[26] This emphasis on individualism requires for its support only the abstract logic of self-consistency and universalisability, principles of the moral law which Sartre derived from Kant; 'I can take freedom as my goal only if I take that of others as a goal as well.'[27] Such individuals become centres of resistance and revolt within society, creating in their own lives the projects by which their full human potential is realised. In so doing, they 'enact the fate of all humanity in their personal existences',[28] and thus recreate the universe. The special opportunities for women to impose their purposes on the world lie ahead of them as they realise the full implications of the belief that 'One is not born, but rather becomes, a woman.'[29]

Another contemporary feminist for whom these issues are important is Janet Radcliffe Richards, a British philosopher whose book, *The Sceptical Feminist*, was both a criticism of certain kinds of feminist thinking and a reassertion of the liberal paradigm for moral reasoning.[30] Radcliffe Richards' roots in the British analytical tradition give her a framework for a certain scepticism regarding nature. While de Beauvoir had found the notion of essential or *a priori* human nature fundamentally deceiving to the freedom of the human will, Radcliffe Richards, following J. S. Mill and H. Taylor, questions such notions on logical grounds.[31] For Radcliffe Richards, any judgements regarding the natural differences between men and women, are purely contingent ones, depending upon circumstance and situation, and there are always counter examples and instances in which such statements do not hold true. While recognising that it is in the vested interests of some women and some men to maintain such natural differences, their commitment to holding on to what is true by nature, she believes, is an instance of irrational stubbornness for which there is no logical case to be made. Following Mill, she argues that 'what is now called the nature of women is an eminently artificial thing', and claims that social conditioning is responsible for our understanding about and experience of the 'natural'.[32] Here she follows quite closely Mill's view that nature is something made or shaped by the will and intentions of human beings, rather than something which appears before us as a matter of objective and uninterpreted fact. Thus, arguments over what is or is not natural, which were a feature of early feminism, are pointless in producing a conclusive moral case one way or another.[33]

Radcliffe Richards constructs her case for liberal feminism upon the concern, which she believes is shared by Hume, Mill, and G. E. Moore, to avoid the naturalistic fallacy in moral reasoning. She uses this argument to assert the rational grounding of moral principles beyond any particular view of the 'natural'.

All three of these writers come to the same two main conclusions. The first is that 'natural' can mean a good many different things. The second is that, according to none of these possible meanings can the natural be taken as any guide at all for distinguishing good from bad.[34]

Avoidance of the naturalistic fallacy requires an alternative source of value and of moral principles, which Radcliffe Richards finds in an uncompromising expression of freedom for individual persons to make and choose their own lives. In a definition of freedom which echoes that of de Beauvoir, she claims that freedom is measured by the extent to which people *'are in control of their own destinies and not controlled by other people or other alien forces'*.[35] This is freedom from any external control, from heteronomy, but it suggests that within that freedom *from*, there is to be a freedom *for* choosing one's own purposes, shaping one's own destinies according to the values that one believes are important. In this sense, she argues that freedom 'is being taken as a fundamental good in its own right, and a thing of which we should therefore all have as much as possible'.[36] In this respect, there are again no morally significant ways in which men and women differ.

From the force of this reasoned argument, Radcliffe Richards believes that the principles which guide feminism may be derived. An understanding of society as a collection of individuals, each of whom has as much as possible of what is good, is presumed here, and it is one in which the case for feminism and the case for liberal morality entirely overlap. This society will be shaped by two fundamental political principles of justice. 'The first of these principles is that *the most important purpose of society is to improve the well-being of sentient things, which should all be as well off as possible.*'[37] The second principle concerns the distribution of these good things, whereby *'everyone's well-being is to be considered equally; when social structures are planned no individual or group is to be given more consideration than any other'*.[38] Radcliffe Richards understands these principles to be 'intuitively acceptable', appealing in the end to what most people, men and women, intuitively want and what most people, men and women, will find acceptable. 'Making people happy and fulfilled' is a matter which 'needs no complicated justification'.[39]

Many feminist theologians have made use of this liberal paradigm as a way of reforming the Christian tradition, and of challenging Christian ethics, and the churches, to take feminism seriously. They understand Christianity not only to be compatible with the requirements of liberal feminism, but to provide an even more helpful foundation for the social critique upon which the concern for liberation ultimately depends. The earlier form of liberalism had been attacked in this century for being too naively optimistic about the positive potential of human social life, and for proving too vulnerable, in its formulation of truth established by reason alone, to the dismissal of the deity. Neo-orthodox theologians set about a restatement of the Reformed tradition in which the utter transcendence of God, the dependence of all moral knowledge and action upon faith, and the necessity for human obedience to the divine will were all reaffirmed.

In the course of this new defence of theology, moral truth is set firmly in a secure foundation beyond the relativities of history and culture. Just at a time when the philosophical description of moral reasoning is left, in the end, to rely upon intuition or the assertions of free choice, neo-orthodox theology offers the prospect of grounding these ultimately in the divine will. Instead of asserting the formulation of abstract rational principles, to which individuals give free assent, and in which they discover a universal perspective beyond their own narrow interests, the neo-orthodox theologian reasserts, in a way consistent with Reformation Protestantism, the discovery of the true moral life in conformity with the commandments of God, rather than the values of culture. Such a possibility offers the adherent an even greater, or more profound, transcendence of this world than the rational consciousness alone can provide. Likewise, instead of denying the givenness of nature, which would open up unlimited choices and possibilities for human development, the neo-orthodox theologian affirms the discovery of true humanness, beyond social distinctions, through obedience to the challenging Word of God. Feminists who write from within this framework are convinced that it provides a continuous resource for social criticism, as well as a challenging vision of the future God intends for creation.

In the early writings of Rosemary Radford Ruether one can find an understanding of the moral project in which Christianity and feminism cohere in the case which is being made

about the lives of women. She argues that it is through theological vision that we are able to discover the transcendent
horizon of human life, and there can find the appropriate
foundations for a serious and radical ethic of liberation. Religion, she claims, is 'man's search to renew his contact with the
ultimate foundations of this being . . . But this transcendence is
not objectifiable as a thing among things'.[40] The insights
derived from this transcendent foundation result in a reassessment of the patterns of behaviour and the institutions in which
one has been caught up, which are judged to be inadequate
and deceptive as guides to the moral life. The problem with
secularism is that it has elevated a particular standpoint into
the position of the transcendent, thereby taking 'an oppressive
status quo as the norm of truth'.[41] The oppressive status quo is
a form of the naturalistic fallacy, in which morality becomes a
matter of doing what *is* the case, rather than seeking for what
ought to be the case. It is precisely this which religious faith
may provide. Following the recognition of sinfulness is the gift
of grace, whereby an individual receives the power and the
motivation to stand against the status quo and rise above its
demands and restrictions. The result of this experience is the
realisation of freedom as an ability to be truly one's own self,
and it is exactly this freedom to be a person in one's own right
that liberation is aiming to achieve.

Such liberation into the fullness of our humanity is not possible, however, to those bound by the requirements of the
secular status quo without a kind of exorcism, an exorcism
which begins within the church, but which then 'touches off a
revolution which must transform all the relations of alienation
and domination'.[42] These theological categories must therefore also be turned upon the Christian tradition itself, which
has absorbed cultural assumptions throughout its history. It
stands accused of allying itself to those things which are temporal and conditional, and which have no ultimate authority.
Relying upon the teaching of Jesus, that there is only one
teacher, only one Father who is in heaven, and only therefore
one Master to whom human beings are to be obedient, she
claims that

If this teaching of Jesus had been maintained, the very root of sexism and clericalist hierarchicalism in biblical religion would have been decisively undercut. The fatherhood of God could not have been understood as establishing male ruling-class power over subjugated groups in the Church or Christian society, but as that equal fatherhood that makes all Christians equal, brothers and sisters.[43]

The theological perspective of neo-orthodoxy provides exactly the Archimedean point on the basis of which the Christian tradition itself may be challenged and its cultural collusion questioned. It is this 'which allows the anti-female passages in Paul and the pastorals to be put aside for more fundamental theological principles',[44] principles which establish the unique role that women have to play in salvation history.

Ruether claims, then, that the affirmation of women as full human beings must become the touchstone of cultural criticism, of biblical interpretation, and of theological truth. Those things which affirm their humanness are true signs of the divine will, and those things which deny, diminish, or distort the full humanity of women are 'therefore to be appraised as not redemptive'.[45] To place women in this position is a recognition of the basic principle which the Bible itself contains with regard to its own internal revisions. Ruether understands the Bible to be a continuous prophetic critique, which is 'in a constant state of revision by situating itself in contemporary issues and contemporary consciousness of good and evil and by becoming a vehicle for the critical consciousness of groups who have been shut out of the social dialogue in the past'.[46] The true witness of the Bible may thus be discerned by reference to its independence from cultural norms, for God's redemptive work in each day is among the despised and rejected. In the contemporary world, that test is provided by the experiences of women, which are instances of exclusion from the cultural status quo. Therefore, she claims a correlation 'between the feminist critical principle and that critical principle by which biblical thought critiques itself and renews its vision as the authentic Word of God over against corrupting and sinful deformations'.[47] When this transcendent vision is apprehended, she believes, then the 'broken fragments begin to swell into a real alternative, not just for women, but for humanity and the earth', for 'the women's movement, properly understood, encompasses all other liberation movements'.[48] This feminist theological appropriation of the liberal paradigm suggests a principle of continuous socio-political criticism, carried out in hope of the future restoration of all creation in the loving presence of God.

The work of Letty Russell reveals a similar neo-orthodox approach to Christian feminist ethics. She understands, like Ruether, that our task is to journey towards freedom, and in such a journey to discover a more humane society for all. The realisation of human potential for women calls into question the rigid sex role into which her life is cast, which has been justified by reference to a so-called 'objective' description of her self. It is through scepticism regarding her biological nature, her capacities for work, and the social expectations of her behaviour, that women may begin to take hold of a critical consciousness. For Russell, this is a prophetic task, under the guidance of the Holy Spirit, and is thus a gift of the new freedom for which Christ has set us free. Against the determination of her life as shaped by others, by which a woman is made into an object, she calls for the

courage to be a *misfit* in society; acting and thinking with those who are groaning for liberation and working to disturb the status quo. The cost of this may mean becoming 'marginal persons', those who don't fit with their peers or into accepted norms in either church or society.[49]

In this work, women are engaging in the most essential work of theology for our day, and are therefore taking their place alongside men as inheritors of the tradition, responsible for its continued proclamation. They are required, in partnership with men, to engage in 'critical reflection – in the light of the Word accepted in faith – on historical praxis and therefore on the presence of Christians in the world'.[50]

Necessary for this process of discernment is the discovery in the tradition of what Russell calls 'usable'. The Christian tradition is a dynamic one in which all people can find for themselves a place in that Tradition by perceiving that God offers to them a *usable future*, a *usable history* and a *usable language*. In this way the reality of God's handing over Jesus Christ into the hands of all generations and nations can be seen as a still living and evolving past with which to shape the future in community with others today.[51]

For Russell, the very reading and interpretation of the Bible is the first and fundamental step on the road to true humanness, for this is the means by which the reality of Jesus as 'a unique revelation of true personhood: One who helped both men and women to understand their own total personhood' is actually apprehended.[52] The reader is touched by the words, which take hold of her life in challenge and in promise, and, through her response to them, she is drawn out of her self and her own horizons. A text, which could otherwise become a dead and static set of words used to legitimate privilege and to exclude those whom God has also called, becomes through this process a living and true witness to humanness, and is thus transformed into a vehicle of human liberation.[53]

To take hold of the possibilities for liberation and transformation in one's own situation is at the same time an affirmation of humanness for all. The Christian tradition contains the foundations for a liberatory ethic for all humanity and all oppressed peoples. Thus Russell argues that 'feminist theology strives to be *human* and not just *feminine*, as other forms of theology should strive to be *human* and not just *masculine*'.[54] Theology is a liberating project, the ultimate goal of which is the increased humanisation of the world:

The particular interpretive key that assists me in continuing to give assent is the witness of scripture to God's promise (for the mending of creation) on its way to fulfilment. That which denies this intention of God for the liberation of groaning creation in all its parts does not compel or evoke by assent (i.e., it is not authoritative).[55]

Her central christological affirmation is that Jesus Christ is the new human being, in whom are opened new possibilities for human life. The achievement of this new humanity through the Incarnation and the Resurrection is available to those who participate with him through faith.

Through these two examples of theological appropriations of the liberal paradigm, it is possible to discern the distinctive features of this approach to Christian ethics, and to assess the importance of the contribution which it makes to the continuing theological tradition. One of the strengths of this position is its discovery of the key to cultural criticism, whereby the political and social and religious status quo might be challenged. To be able to measure the conditions of everyday life against the standard of our common human dignity is a powerful weapon to use in argument for social reform and political change. The language of human rights to which it gives birth is crucial to the understanding of justice with which we negotiate in the modern world. To consider that human worth is given by God in the creation adds weight to the case, but also then requires that attention be given to the institutional church. Such a critique had already begun with the Protestant Reformation. Christian feminists who use this paradigm believe that the charges which are made against a one-sided theological tradition, and against the easy accommodation of the disturbing witness of the Spirit of God to cultural norms and standards, are entirely consistent with the prophetic nature of Christian truth. Belief in the possibility of transcendent perspective and insight is essential to this paradigm, and constitutes one of its important contributions to modern moral thinking.

A second strength of this position is its affirmation of basic critical principles which embody the transcendent perspective. In its secular form, this paradigm asserts a belief in a common humanity, which is shared by all persons regardless of circumstance and condition and physical make-up, and which itself provides the code by which we are to live. This common humanness is established by a reasoned understanding of the essential framework of human nature, a process which excludes all of those things that are not of ultimate significance, and includes only those salient features without which we would not be human. Gender can claim no fundamental hold here, as can neither race nor intelligence. It is in affirmation of this fundamental humanness that the liberal model excels. Such common humanness is also affirmed under God, whose creative power is believed to have formed, and to continue to uphold, the conditions which make and keep human life human. In addition, it is hoped that human life will come to fulfilment in the future which God prepares for humanity. For the Christian, there is thus a basic obligation to participate with the Creator in acknowledging and co-operating with this divine intention to lead humanity into the realisation of its own most true nature. The question whether this or that will enhance human dignity and facilitate its developing potential thus furnishes the standard by which moral decision and action is measured.

A third strength of this understanding of the moral project is its important emphasis on the individual person. Liberation for humanity means the particular liberation of individuals to be, and to be treated as, ends-in-themselves. For this reason, men and women are challenged to take on the realities of free choice in their daily lives, and to see themselves as persons who make themselves. To run from this freedom, in forms of passive obedience to authoritarian leadership, or of unquestioned acceptance of social practices, is to lose something essential to the living of a full life. Not only does this have consequences for the person who tries to do so, but it results in social injustices, and in political blindness to inhumanity on a grand scale. Calling for personal responsibility is thus one way of restoring a moral sense to our social dealings as well. There is something in this attention to individual autonomy which is significant in considerations of moral reasoning, and which is also taken up by Christian ethicists. It is the person who stands before God, it is the person whose faith and whose motives are known to God, and it is the person who is addressed by the word of God, in scripture or through preaching and proclamation, to respond to the newness of life which is possible through the redeeming work of Christ. Unless such personal appropriation of the Gospel is made, the Christian ethical life will be a shallow imitation of itself, and Christ will not actually be known in the here and now. Christian feminists believe that exactly the kind of giving of oneself to God which is required of Christian men, is the responsibility of Christian women too, and that those structures, or ideas, which prevent such receptiveness to the will of God are to be confronted and changed. Persons matter, and become a means by which the Holy Spirit makes its presence known in the world.

To present the liberal paradigm in this way demonstrates the entanglement of secular and religious ethical thinking, and the pointlessness of debating whether feminism is a secular product or is theologically inspired. Enlightenment humanism informs the modern world, and, to the extent that feminism takes a uniquely modern form, its approach to moral reasoning will share in these assumptions. While, to some extent, such humanism results in a serious critique, or even a rejection of Christianity, this is not fundamentally incompatible with the self-revising or prophetic nature of either the biblical witness or the later Christian tradition. What is important in our present process of reassessment, is not to try to disentangle one from the other, or to allow one or other position to claim the moral high ground, but rather to examine more closely and critically the basic assumptions on which such humanism rests. Such a fresh consideration of the tradition is suggested by Beverly Wildung Harrison:

Enlightenment humanism had a symbiotic relationship to patriarchal Christianity, and therefore was not without its own arrogance and presumption ... We Christian feminists then are heirs to the secular enlightenment tradition as well as to the radical Jewish and Christian traditions, yet we have to subject all of these traditions to the same searching analysis.[56]

It is to the critique of this model of moral reasoning that we now turn.

CHAPTER 3

Critique of liberalism

After five years of marriage and the birth of a child, the American writer and lecturer, Charlotte Perkins Gilman, produced a short story. Entitled 'The Yellow Wallpaper', the piece describes the terrifying tale of a woman going mad, driven to animal behaviour by her irrational fixation on the pattern in the wallpaper of her room.[1] The story is brief, written in short clipped sentences, and tells with clarity and detail of one person's progressive mental breakdown. The first potential publisher refused the piece, claiming that no one else should be made as miserable as he was upon reading the story, and indeed when it was finally published in *The New England Magazine* in 1892, it was received with cautious praise.[2] There was little that was morally uplifting about the story, so it could not be used as an educational tool for reinforcing social values, yet it was recognised as a competent and medically accurate account of the details of 'incipient insanity'.[3] Because it had qualities similar to works in the horror-story genre, it was to be included in anthologies of works by Edgar Allen Poe and others, as a chilling description of madness caused by obsession with physical objects.

The author was a woman of true New England grit, who learned independence and a strong sense of responsibility and duty at an early age. She clearly was a determined woman, a perfectionist, and one who pursued her goals to their completion. She read and wrote widely with great curiosity, and with a desire to make sense of her observations of personal and social life. As a self-taught woman, she represents many of the educational ideals of the Enlightenment, standing back from

the circumstances of her life to reflect carefully on the underlying explanations of these, and proposing from that standpoint new ways in which society might move forward. She was
committed to social justice particularly for women, and to
making progress towards a better society through the use of
rational argument, debate, and considered judgement. Her
non-fiction work was well known, especially her work on
Women and Economics, used for 20 years as a college textbook and
translated into seven languages, and she made a career for
herself as a lecturer and writer. She was described as 'the
leading intellectual in the women's movement in the United
States' in her time.[4] Clearly she was a fine example of the
liberal paradigm of moral reasoning appropriated and
embodied in a woman.

And yet there is this short story. A married woman is
unhappy; there seems to be 'really nothing the matter . . . but
temporary nervous depression'.[5] Her husband is naturally
worried about her, and because he is a doctor, is able to give
medical advice as well as express husbandly concern. He
decides that she needs complete rest from her worries and her
writing, and takes her to a country retreat. There he recommends that she be confined to a room at the top of the house
which had been designed as a children's nursery with bars over
the windows to prevent accidents, a room without distractions
where her mind could be empty and she could relax. We are
led to believe that this was the most advanced medical knowledge of the day as it was applied to the unexplained maladies
of women, and that her husband was doing his best with
something which he may otherwise have been ill-equipped to
understand. In his kindly way, he called her his 'blessed little
goose' and absolutely forbade her to 'work', referring to her
writing, until she was well again.[6]

While in her room, the woman does indeed become
fascinated by the wallpaper, the pattern and colour of which
seem to her to represent so much that is true of her own life. She
is facing an immediate question of her own identity, and here is
this wallpaper which has an ill-defined and pointless pattern
on it, made up of 'lame uncertain curves'.[7] She has lost her

independence and the power to make decisions about her life, and here is this wallpaper which has a series of meaningless swirls imposed upon it without 'principle of design' or aesthetic quality.[8] She is raising the most difficult questions about the purpose of her life, and here is this wallpaper whose patterns 'suddenly commit suicide – destroy themselves in unheard-of contradictions'.[9] Increasingly, the wallpaper comes to represent her life, until the point at which she discerns the figure of a woman, and finally lots of women, behind the wallpaper trying to free themselves from its prison. At this point, two realities collide with one another. There is, on the one hand, the certainty and self-assuredness of her husband, who says *to* her, 'Bless her little heart', and 'she shall be just as sick as she pleases', in his magnanimous way, and behind whom is ranked the whole supportive social order.[10] There is, on the other hand, the desperation and anguish of the women in the wallpaper who come creeping out of the walls and through the house and garden on all fours. While the heroine of the story has fought throughout her increasing 'madness' the necessity for creeping, nevertheless at the end she too is on her hands and knees, tearing off great strips of wallpaper in her bare hands and hiding behind the door.

It is true that some of our sensitivity to this story is the result of knowing that Gilman herself had been through a similar incident in the early years of her marriage, and indeed that she used the real name of the nerve specialist who examined her in the telling of the story. Beyond this, some part of our interest is in the allegorical nature of the story, which tells of one woman attempting to come to terms with Enlightenment ideals while living in the real world of social pressures and expectations of marriage and family. The story suggests that these two may be incompatible, and therefore that there may be something about the Enlightenment ideal of rational choice and responsible freedom which women cannot fully embody in this society. At a still deeper level, our interest in the story is in its depiction of aspects of human life and consciousness, which the basic tenets of the liberal paradigm of moral reasoning have failed to capture or to illuminate. So it is not simply the case that liberal principles have not yet been fully applied to the whole of social and political life, not simply that there remains a great deal to be done to fulfil the liberal vision of the just social order. Rather this story reveals an awareness that this vision is only a partial expression of what may be meant by justice, by power, and by love, and further that its partiality renders it blind and ineffective in relation to whole areas of human personal and social experience. That the tenets of equality and respect for the dignity of persons may have embodied tacit support for men's awareness and self-understanding means that the introduction of women into these terms may weaken and throw into question the whole structure.

This short story is one expression of a growing dissatisfaction with the liberal paradigm of moral reasoning. In the early days, feminists were convinced that this paradigm gave grounds for belief in the common humanity of women and men, and that to continue to argue for innate or natural differences between them was not only irrational, but unjust. Belief in a shared human nature was discovered through the exercise of the transcendent consciousness, by which the moral agent abstracted herself from the circumstances of everyday life in order to reflect dispassionately upon what is true and good, a process also given theological expression in Christian ethics. However, feminists become increasingly aware of the danger that the process of such reasoning may turn one's attention exclusively to the heavens at the cost of sensitivity to history, and to the very particular circumstances in which people really do live. What may be excellent as a formal method for arriving at universal principles, and what provides a splendid viewpoint from which to be critical of present life, is less satisfactory in application, and ultimately in expression of the fullness of our humanity. To remedy this may mean revisiting the issue of difference, reintroducing the question of the distinctiveness of men and women.

In the early days of Enlightenment enthusiasm, it was hoped that women would actually be able to realise the new possibilities promised by the liberal understanding of the human

person. The story of this period may be written as the progressive gaining of rights for women, as the right to vote is granted
and with it the recognition that women are citizens alongside
men, or as entry into educational institutions and into professional work is gained, and along with these the involvement
of women in the public sphere of paid employment and in
shared responsibility for social institutions. What surprised and
angered many was the negative attitude encountered as such
seemingly logical and reasonable arguments were pressed
forward. One rather glaring example of such negativity is given
in the nineteenth-century 'scientific' arguments regarding the
relative intelligence of women and men, arguments which were
used specifically to exclude women from education. When one
set of 'facts' was reported by many researchers in the mid 1850s,
namely 'that the male possessed noticeably larger and more
well-developed frontal lobes than females', a fact which
apparently existed even in foetuses, this confirmed rather well
the widespread belief that the seat of the intellect lay in the
frontal lobes. Thus women were naturally less intellectually
capable than men, due to an inferior brain. Such belief was not
in the least disturbed by a 'discovery' 40 years later that these
earlier 'facts' were mistaken.

In the cerebrum itself the frontal region is not, as has been supposed,
smaller in woman, but rather larger relatively ... It is now believed,
however, that a preponderance of the frontal region does not imply
intellectual superiority, as was formerly supposed, but that the par-
ietal region is really the more important.[11]

In one sense, this kind of argumentation and the attitude it
reveals could be understood as the last vestige of pre-
Enlightenment prejudice, and it could be challenged and
ridiculed from the transcendent vantage-point of rational
judgement. This, women persistently sought, and still seek, to
do.

However, in another sense, this kind of rational argument
may not be able sufficiently to give voice to the stunning sense
of helplessness which women who were faced with these supposed facts experienced, both in themselves and in relation to
the common social world. Throughout this time is the growing

recognition amongst women that what is being gained, through wider inclusion in the public world, is participation in society as it exists. So women are torn between conformity and challenge, between the belief that involvement on an equal basis with men is the right of women in the liberal society and in all of its institutions, and the recognition that these have already been established without them and with the place which they may effectively occupy already clearly defined. In education, in medicine, in the church, in politics, in business, in all social institutions, the use of universal principles of judgement discoverable by transcendent reason by which human dignity and personhood are established comes up against immovable structures that are impervious to its logic. As there was no attempt from the beginning to include a whole range of people in social and political reforms, their inclusion at a later stage means that they have had to accept existing institutions as the status quo, and relate to these as already given social realities. This suggests that the story of progressive inclusion is at the same time the story of the ascendancy of political, social, and economic institutions as defined and shaped by men. To see the historical application of the liberal paradigm is to observe both that it has been used to establish new social forms of interaction for propertied men in the first instance, and then, when these have been secured, to consider the inclusion of others into them. The helplessness experienced by women is thus the counterpart to the institutional authority of men, whose interests have been well served by liberal reasoning, and whose place in the rational order, immediately next to the divine, has been confirmed.

Not only in its application, but in its expression of the fullness of our humanity, the liberal paradigm is found wanting. Much of the anguish expressed by Gilman in her short story is the result of a series of divisions characteristic of society, which run through the fabric of political and personal interactions. These divisions are formed by a process of exclusion, whereby one reality is defined and given meaning in relation to another to which it is opposed. Oppositional thinking runs consistently through the liberal tradition. Early on, the activity of the mind was distinguished and rendered meaningful by contrast to the activity of the body, the contrast between the two being so thoroughly established that it was difficult to explain how there was ever any interaction, or how they could effectively be combined in a human being. Following this opposition, another appeared between facts and values, the former being known through empirical and publicly verifiable examination of the physical world, while the latter were more elusively and privately known through feeling or intuition. These developments reflect a third opposition between human beings, who have possibilities and the capacity for transcendence, and the world of nature, which is a given and confined reality. In the application of rational principles to social and political affairs, the opposition between the public and the private worlds appears, as the common world of discourse, debate, contracts, and decision-making is supported and sustained by the hidden one of relationships, family life, sexual desire, and personal experience.

Consistent through these oppositions is the higher value which is given to the first term, the one which represents man's best potential for truth and goodness and fulfilment in life. All of them combine in the husband of Gilman's short story, a practical and thoughtful man, dedicated to the science of medicine, concerned to explain and to control 'silly fancies', and dependent upon a woman to be 'his darling and his comfort'.[12] That the world has been defined to his advantage would not have occurred to him, nor can he grasp the consequences which it is having on those who bear the burden of the excluded reality. Yet he asks of his wife greater self-control over those things he seeks to control, and an application of rational authority over her intuitive awareness that things are not well. That women are defined by the excluded term, and conversely that the half of lesser value is explicitly or implicitly identified with women and women's nature, creates a deep sense of discomfort with the inherited framework of liberal thinking. That women have made use of the insights gained from this exercise of reason to create space for themselves in existing institutions, only to find themselves effectively silenced

by these invisible divisions, is one of the painful and dehu-
manising implications of this framework with which contemporary feminists are struggling.

There are indications that, in spite of her emphasis on the
total rational freedom of women, de Beauvoir also recognised
their unique situation, a uniqueness which remains unexplained, but necessary in the framework of existentialism that
she adopts, and which contains the seeds of awareness that this
paradigm is not quite credible as a model for human moral life.
The presence of women presents two problems to this paradigm, which disturb the smooth course of the transcendent
consciousness seeking formal and universalisable principles to
be applied objectively in differing situations. The first is its
duplicity regarding women, revealed in the explicit way in
which Sartre, whose interpretation de Beauvoir used,
delineated the activity of the *pour-soi* in relation to the *en-soi*, as
a contrast between the nothingness that is true freedom on the
one hand, and the sticky, slimy, feminine stuff of matter on the
other.[13] De Beauvoir herself understood that the conception of
transcendence essential to the existential self was a positing of a
particular freedom over against the inchoate stuff of life itself.
She knew that, as man creates values, he transcends life. She
further recognised that, in so doing, man has sought to transcend woman, for 'this activity has prevailed over the confused
forces of life; it has subdued Nature and Woman'.[14] The
opposition of these two realities is fundamental to the Sartrean
picture of human life as one which is caught in a nearly
impossible situation. For Sartrean man combines a belief in
unrestrained freedom of decision as the fullest expression of
human individuality, with a sense of being utterly hemmed in
by its opposite, which lures freedom away from its authentic
activity and fills it with disgust, an opposite which is conceived
and described as feminine.

How are women to respond to this description of life? On the
one hand, there is absolutely nothing which can logically
exclude the consciousness of women from the same kind of
requirement for the maintenance of unique freedom in the face
of bad faith. Thus de Beauvoir accepts that women are not able

to blame their bodies, their social circumstances, their particular psychological make-up, or history for their present situation in life. They must simply get on, and make choices in the same way as men do and by the same method. The moral demand upon the self must be the same for the two persons. On the other hand, the identification of woman with the very stuff against which freedom struggles suggests that women are required to occupy a place of opposition, upon which this framework is logically dependent, and which defies the equality it purports to enhance. That the very nature of the project of freedom is described as one of opposition to the feminine leaves women in a deeply ambivalent relation to its requirements. It is perhaps for this reason that the tenor of de Beauvoir's work is so different from that of Sartre. He is critical of those who fail to exercise autonomy, providing examples particularly of women who cannot live up to the nearly impossible task of human life, and suggesting that feelings of inferiority are in fact the result of the free choice of individuals.[15] She, on the other hands, writes with a sense of painful familiarity, without the air of superiority reprimanding those who do not fulfil this demand. Her work leaves us, not with a sense of certainty that all is clearly worked out for women, but rather with doubt about the extent to which women can adopt for their lives something which at the same time devalues them.

This brings us to the second problem, which is the failure of this paradigm to attend to structural aspects of human life. It is noticeable that de Beauvoir is reluctant to blame women for their situation, and that her descriptions of their various ways of running away from freedom are written, not with contempt, but with descriptive clarity. Thus we need to understand the consistent refrain in her work: 'Once again it is useless to apportion blame and excuses: justice can never be done in the midst of injustice'.[16] It is true that for de Beauvoir, 'women are, at least potentially, subjects and therefore capable of opposition, and yet they do not contest the practical and moral subjugation that men have imposed on them'.[17] She herself says, 'It must be admitted that the males find in woman more complicity than the oppressor usually finds in the oppressed'.[18]

Yet there immediately follows a long section describing 'the situation' in which both find themselves.

We have seen that all the main features of her training combine to bar her from the roads of revolt and adventure. Society in general – beginning with her respected parents – lies to her by praising the lofty values of love, devotion, the gift of herself, and then concealing from her the fact that neither lover nor husband nor yet her children will be inclined to accept the burdensome charge of all that. She cheerfully believes these lies because they invite her to follow the easy slope; in this others commit their worst crime against her.[19]

This turns attention away from the individual self in its determination to overcome circumstances, and focusses instead on cases 'which are incapable of satisfactory solution, because they are determined by unsatisfactory conditions'.[20]

These statements begin to reveal de Beauvoir's awareness that a framework of moral thinking which interprets structures outside the self, either as capable of being overcome by force of will in good faith, or as excuses for inaction in bad faith, is an inadequate framework for the whole of human experience. The relation between structures and personal subjectivity may not be an extrinsic one in this sense at all. Thus she is concerned that 'concrete means' be found for the realisation of women's subjectivity.

The evil originates not in the perversity of individuals – and bad faith first appears when each blames the other – it originates rather in a situation against which all individual action is powerless. Women are 'clinging', they are a dead weight, and they suffer for it; the point is that their situation is like that of a parasite sucking out the living strength of another organism. Let them be provided with living strength of their own, let them have the means to attack the world and wrest from it their own subsistence, and their dependence will be abolished – that of man also. There is no doubt that both men and women will profit greatly from the new situation.[21]

Such thinking may be thought to be only utopian fantasy, but it does open up the possibility that when de Beauvoir speaks of regarding things in 'new perspectives', she may not be arguing that women take on a new understanding of themselves from a transcendent standpoint as individuals. Rather, she holds that a new understanding from within the situation of human life, and with attention to structures and to relationships, will more closely approximate the fullness of the moral life. This the liberal paradigm of moral reasoning may not give us the means to comprehend.

The voice of one theologian stands out as the first indication that all was not well with this way of understanding moral reasoning in theological terms either. An article by Valerie Saiving, published in 1960 in *The Journal of Religion*, manages to break through the massed male voices of Christian ethics to tell of her uncertainty about the way 'the human situation' was being described, particularly in neo-orthodox theology.[22] Intrinsic to its theological anthropology is also the notion that human beings are caught between transcendence and immanence, that they are delicately balanced on a narrow ledge between God and the natural world, in a position which may easily tip over too far in one or other direction. To avoid falling into sin, the Christian must not use his freedom as an opportunity to usurp the place of God, nor his natural life as an occasion for selfishness. The temptation either to elevate the self beyond its rightful position, or to denigrate the self through abandonment of freedom, is constantly present, and can be met effectively only through the experience and acceptance of unconditional self-giving love from God. Such love is then to be the main characteristic of the Christian life, for only self-giving can counterbalance self-interest.

What intrigues Saiving is that this kind of theological reflection is written 'by men who lived amid the tensions of a hypermasculine culture', and that its basic terms reflect both this general cultural milieu and the particular experiences of men within it. Thus,

this modern era can be called 'the masculine age par excellence', in the sense that it emphasized, encouraged, and set free precisely those aspects of human nature which are particularly significant to men. It placed the highest value on external achievement, on the creation of structures of matter and meaning, on self-differentiation and the separation of man from nature ... by these and many more innovations, the modern era presented a heightened challenge to men; and, by the same token, it increased their natural sense of insecurity and anxiety.[23]

Understanding the social context of this theology both illuminates the particular cultural emphases against which it was speaking, and at the same time expresses one kind of experience of this context, in particular, the experience of those who are most valued and potentially flattered by these developments.

Attention to the experiences of women throws into question the scope of universal relevance and application expected from an ethic that was supposedly derived for all persons from the divine will. Different early life experiences in the formation of personal identity challenge the bland assumption of equality, 'that the characters of men and women are essentially alike in all respects'.[24] While the early stages of personal identity are formed for both boys and girls in relation to the mother, this has different meanings. For the girl, it means an awareness, shared with her mother, of being closely bound to nature and to biological functions, a source of strength and of security for her, 'which make it easier, all other things being equal, for her to enter into loving relationships in which self-concern is at a minimum'.[25] Her experience of freedom on the other hand is more restricted, which means that she has a further distance to travel to reach the transcendence of the spirit, and also that, having chosen the feminine role, 'she has chosen a kind of bondage which is not involved in a man's acceptance of his sexual identity'.[26] For a boy, the formation of personal identity is fraught with anxiety in that he may not share his mother's experience, but must distinguish himself from her.

The man's sense of his own masculinity, then, is throughout characterized by uncertainty, challenge, and the feeling that he must again and again prove himself a man. It also calls for a kind of objective achievement and a greater degree of self-differentiation and self-development than are required of the woman *as* woman.[27]

Saiving suggests that theological writings reflect this pervasive sense of anxiety about the self and about its uniqueness in the face of other tempting possibilities, an anxiety which in a special way belongs to men. For a man, the problem of life will be defined by the need to differentiate himself explicitly from nature (i.e. from woman), and yet not to get so carried away by pride in this achievement that he forgets he is a creature of God. Indeed, identifying himself as God's may be a way of securing his uniqueness as a man, and of holding him on that narrow ledge between heaven and earth from which his selfishness and his pride threaten to tumble him.

Observing these different kinds of experience leads Saiving to argue that the central themes of a Christian ethic formed out of the special experience of men may not speak to that of women, and, more critically than this, may actually devalue the very things women need to be able to do to respond to the divine in their own lives. Women discover, in the experience of mothering, the need for self-giving love which seems to stem naturally from the physical experience of nurturing, and thus to be an expression of ordinary life as a woman. This differs from the experience of many men who find that self-giving love must be imposed upon them, and that it confronts them as an external demand, because their own development has required such assertion of self to establish personal identity. That such love is a key strand of the Christian moral life, intended as a universal and equal requirement, may therefore hide quite different ways in which it is understood, received, and appropriated.

Similarly, the things a woman may experience as barriers to an open and truthful relation with the divine may not be the same as those of her brothers. While his concerns are pride and selfishness, her concerns

are better suggested by such items as triviality, distractibility, and diffuseness; lack of an organizing center or focus; dependence on others for one's own self-definition; tolerance at the expense of standards of excellence; inability to respect the boundaries of privacy; sentimentality, gossipy sociability, and mistrust of reason – in short, underdevelopment or negation of the self.[28]

For her to remove these barriers requires self-assertion, the learning of a measure of pride, development of a sense of self-importance and dignity, all of which mean that she should not give herself up wholly to serving others. That these are the very things of which the central theme of Christian moral life disapproves, in its praise of humility and self-emptying, again places women in the position of the excluded other. Saiving calls for a new approach to 'the human situation' in Christian ethics which can take account of differing experiences, which does not frame its requirements around the exclusion and devaluation of some aspect of human life, and which does not dress the experiences of some human beings in the clothing of universality.

Each of the writers examined here absorbed the model of moral reasoning expressed in Enlightenment ideals as part of the overall cultural milieu in which they lived, and each attempted to work within that framework to understand the moral dimensions of women's situation in the contemporary world. What emerges from their use of this framework is a deep awareness of its inadequacy as a way of illuminating the morally salient features of our human personal and social lives. From these early expressions of dissatisfaction with the liberal paradigm of moral reasoning, we may note three themes of continuing interest, themes which have been taken up by more recent feminist writers. Here we find more full exploration of the limitations of the liberal paradigm, and the implications these might have for moral reasoning generally, and for Christian ethics in particular.

The first theme concerns the understanding of justice in the liberal paradigm. It was the great insight of the liberal approach to morality that principles to guide our thinking about justice could be discovered by reason, and could be shown to be based on the notion of a common human nature. This human nature was one in which rights to life and to happiness were believed to inhere in the same way for all persons, or in which a sense of obligation to obey the moral law was rooted. The method for arriving at these principles requires the activity of the transcendent consciousness, abstracting itself from particularities in order to identify what was universally and objectively true for all persons. The moral agent is asked in this process to consider, not the unique person who is immediately encountered, but rather those more elusive qualities discoverable by reason which make that person human. To discover these qualities was an exercise of autonomy, of self-legislation, and to direct one's personal life in accordance with their requirements was to act justly. The just society would then be one which provided the conditions in the public world of human interactions for these autonomous rational individuals to flourish.

Recent feminist writers have questioned this method of arriving at decisions regarding justice, for it requires both a formality emptied of specific content, and an isolated moral agent who is asked to put aside all concerns but those essential, and amenable, to rational argument. What is difficult here is that, in the process of abstracting the moral agent from the realm of unimportant contingencies, a clear line must be drawn between this realm and that of the sure and certain principles. In drawing the line, assumptions are made about what is deemed unimportant, and therefore about what may not be open to considerations of justice at all. Discovering the world of concerns to which justice is applicable highlights, at the same time, the boundaries of its scope, and throws into question the nature of the justice so conceived. The person whose full humanness considerations of justice were meant to enhance ends up as a rather stripped-down version of humanity. There is indeed a case to be made that the notion of the human being upon which these principles are purportedly based is a necessary heuristic device which elevates the male, and denigrates the female, aspects of our humanness. Pressing these challenges upon the liberal paradigm, feminists wonder whether this approach to moral reasoning expresses fully enough what may be meant by justice, or whether, as Ruether observed, it offers 'a minimalist rather than an exalted view of the human nature that all human beings share equally'.[29]

Documenting this challenge has been the important contribution of Carol Gilligan, whose interviews with young men and women reveal some interesting features of the acquisition of moral consciousness. These features suggest that the process of development is not the same for both, and that significant differences emerge in ways of thinking and speaking about moral questions. The key point in her discovery of the 'different voice' was that men understand a moral question to put them on the spot as lonely individuals, whose right decision must be based on the correct perception of fairness, according to abstract principles that are applicable in the diverse situations in which they find themselves. The nature of the moral question, as men perceive it, is appropriate to persons who understand themselves to be discrete units, intended to be self-sufficient and capable, with all the necessary equipment and skills to get on in life independently. Moral thinking based on principles gives each individual man the framework for making future decisions, and he has what is necessary to fulfil his moral nature as an autonomous self. A boy thus learns first to distinguish himself from the surrounding world (separation), and then to relate himself to abstract ideals by which he can assess his behaviour, his reasoning, and ultimately his self-worth (perfection).[30] The liberal paradigm, utilising the transcendent consciousness which relates to objective standards of truth and justice, seems to be entangled with the self-understanding of men.

Gilligan argues that this process of development, and therefore the understanding of morality which results, is only one of the ways in which morality and the self may be understood. The processes of moral reasoning and the concomitant understanding of the self as a being in relation to others which women demonstrate is quite different, and is not grasped at all through the imposition of the paradigm of objective justice. Women understand a moral question to disturb the network of relationships in which they are involved, and their right decision must be the one which restores a balance to these, according to the perceptions and experiences of the other persons involved in these situations. The nature of the moral question as women perceive it is appropriate to persons who understand themselves to be connected integrally with other persons, finding fulfilment within good interactions, and seeking to relate as happily as possible with others. Moral thinking centred on consideration of relationships allows woman's interactive self to find its way through the maze of connections that bind people together, and in this way her moral nature as a relational being is fulfilled. The girls who were interviewed using the boys' model of development were judged continually to be morally immature, since their self-understanding never measured up to that of the boys, and since their analysis and resolution of moral dilemmas did not reach the same dispassionate objectivity as the boys'. Most of the girls' answers thus 'fall through the sieve' of a scoring system which is inappropriate to 'the different truth' revealed in their judgement.[31]

Problems with the liberal paradigm concern not only its construction of the self by which it misses significant features of personal experience, but also the formulation of its basic understanding of morality in terms of human rights. Language of rights seriously complicates the lives and development of women, placing a burden of responsibilities upon their behaviour and decisions which does not always allow the fullness of their own distinctive development and contribution to moral issues. In her study of women who approached an abortion and pregnancy counselling service for advice, Gilligan discovered the mismatch between language of rights, positing the abstract notion that such rights inhere in human life itself, and language of responsibility, which was the language used by women in the study. She recognises the ambivalence with which women approach the issue of 'rights', and understands how important such a conception of rights has been for women to participate more fully in 'their fair share of social justice'.[32] However a consideration of these rights as abstractions which exist for their own sake requires women to break into the fabric of interconnected relationships which surround their lives. Thus, in relation to the dilemma of abortion, she writes: 'The attempt to set up the dilemma as a conflict of rights turned it into a contest of selfishnesses, precluding the possibility of a moral decision, since either resolution could be construed as selfish from one or the other perspective'.[33] Considerations of justice construed as rights required women to be more 'selfish', in the sense of the autonomous self described above, than they were comfortable with, and the pull between selfishness and responsibility to others was, for them, the ethical dilemma implicit in the acceptance of the liberal paradigm.

Gilligan's analysis suggests the need for men and women to discover the value of the other's moral perspective, to be able to acknowledge and appreciate the different voices with which they speak in moral dilemmas. In this recognition of diversity, justice may not be able to be construed by one standard only, but may be enriched by the inclusion of other voices. To absorb an 'awareness of multiple truths' is a great challenge to a paradigm which so clearly presents a consistent moral argument, but this is precisely what Gilligan hopes from her study.[34]

A second theme in the recent feminist critique of the liberal paradigm concerns its understanding of power. The emergence of this paradigm coincides with the development of new forms of power: of personal power – in the allocation of human rights to autonomous individuals, of political power – in the establishment of ownership of property as the basis for social contracts and organisations, and of technological power – in the discovery of the means of manufacturing from the natural resources of the earth. The holders of power in liberal society are free individuals, who are believed to have power over their own actions, and who come together for the protection and preservation of their rights through the establishment of social order, to which they accordingly consent. Liberal ideals of liberty, equality, and fraternity are expressions of these new forms of power. The moral principles which ensure them are, in part, an answer to the dilemma of how to meet the competing demands of men, whose freely chosen goals are to be realised if possible, but whose undisciplined self-interest is a constant threat to social order. Power is thus characterised by autonomy, public agreement, and control; it is assured through the exercise of free will, through consent to public debate and justification, and through control of private feeling or sentiment.

Women have looked within this society for 'formal-legalistic equality' with men in the public world, assuming that women could have and hold power as individuals, like men, and believing that changes in the law would bring about major changes in the distribution of power to a wider range of individuals throughout the social structure.[35] However, the challenge of women that they be granted access to this world continually runs up against hidden structures which enforce their powerlessness, and to which liberal ideals are blind. Indeed there appear to be social structures in which these principles are themselves not applicable. Feminists argue that the liberal paradigm is constructed upon foundations which are believed to be the secure and permanent bedrock of social and personal relationships, discovering in liberal thinkers the wholesale importation of ideas regarding differences between men and women, which 'by nature' are believed to establish the necessity for inequalities within the family, in sexual relationships, and in types of work. This heightens women's awareness that they have not been included in the formulation of these principles in the first place, and that to introduce themselves into the terms of reference may exacerbate, rather than relieve, their powerlessness. Such social blindness in the liberal paradigm, by which it is unable to address this foundation with its own principles, leads to a sense of emptiness in liberal claims, and ultimately to a recognition that the scope of power within this framework is limited to the already privileged.

This theme is taken up by Ruether, who examines the theological contributions to the configurations of power in contemporary society. While the work examined in the last chapter demonstrated her commitment to the notion of a transcendent consciousness, by which the universal will of God is known beyond particular forms of human society and moral codes, she also engages in a critique of these assumptions, in so far as they themselves reinforce unjust social structures.[36] In Protestant thinking, there is a recognition that, although humanity was created in a natural state of goodness and of equality between women and men, nevertheless, because of sin, a new order of nature is imposed by God in which man's natural desires are to be controlled, and in which women are to be subordinate to men. This new order comes to be identified

with the private realm of individual self-discipline, in which
submitting oneself to the demands of God controls the desire
for rebellion, and also the realm of family life, in which values
not evident in the public world are imposed. The witness to this
new order is to be the church, in which personal obedience to
God's commands is encouraged, and in which the headship of
men over women is to be modelled.[37] That Protestant Christianity was an important source of support to this division of
public from private, and has reinforced the subordination of
women to men, has led to some difficulty within Christian
ethics of addressing questions of power deeply and critically.
For the very source of transcendence, which previously had
unlocked oppressive situations to bring liberation, is now used
to bar the door against change.

Christian feminism requires an appropriation of prophetic
principles 'in ways the Biblical writers for the most part do not
appropriate them, namely, to criticize this unexamined patriarchal framework'.[38] Still reliant upon the discovery of a
'bedrock of authentic Being',[39] Ruether identifies the 'critical
principle of feminist theology' as 'the promotion of the full
humanity of women' and now turns this against the liberal
paradigm of reasoning inherited from the Enlightenment.[40]
Such an appropriation relies upon an extension of 'the prophetic liberating tradition of Biblical faith as a norm through
which to criticize the Bible', and in this project Ruether knows
that feminism is moving into uncharted territory. There is
nothing new in such a hermeneutic principle as 'the prophetic
norm', but there is something new in 'appropriation of this
norm *for women*'.[41] Implicit here is the recognition that this is
not the way in which such a prophetic norm has been used in
the past, that it has remained strangely silent about features of
everyday social and personal life to which it has not addressed
its critical and liberating message. Thus, while the essential
themes of such a message suggest its applicability to all areas of
human life, leaving no space which can claim immunity or
protection from its demands, nevertheless feminists standing
legitimately within this tradition are at this point risking something quite new in their challenge of power.

What Ruether recognises in this risk is that the tradition of prophecy has become 'deformed' into 'ideology' by which its central themes become 'a static set of ideas', rather than being 'constantly adapted to changing social contexts and circumstances'.[42] The prophetic tradition needs to become alive and renewable in every age, less like a set of empty formulations or principles to be used in syllogistic reasoning for the resolution of moral dilemmas. This reveals a dissatisfaction with the ideology of liberalism which has been so crucial to the birth of modern feminist thinking. While liberalism has sought justice 'socially through equality of opportunity, particularly in education and access to professions', it is nevertheless 'hostile to any economic egalitarianism that touches private property'.[43] Thus this framework becomes deformed 'into the ideology of bourgeois capitalism' which may not bring out its best possibilities.[44] Ruether questions whether the search for equality for women can be accommodated within 'the limits of the patriarchal-capitalist system', and claims that 'consistent liberal feminists come increasingly to recognize the need to transform fundamentally the larger system'.[45] This leads her to understand that the 'logical and social contradictions of liberal feminism lead to its transformation into socialist feminism'.[46]

Against the other-worldliness of so much Christian thinking, which leaves the message of the prophets and of Jesus in some ideal untouched space, Ruether emphasises transformation, for that message to enter dramatically into our present to make things new, and to bring real hope for a different future. This requires speaking out against 'the corrupting principles of domination and subjugation' and bringing into these relationships a new possibility for power.[47] This is the 'creative dynamic of Biblical faith' which must not collude with the status quo, or allow its energy to be anaesthetised by social status or political power. The church throughout history has allowed this to happen, and the present is one of those historical moments in which the choice of prophecy or silence again stands before us. Ruether thus calls for the inclusion of the not-included, or the empowering of the power-less, believing that to avoid this challenge is to collude with injustice, no matter what ideals such collusion is clothed in.[48] It is only the lively appropriation of dynamic prophecy that will embody the richness and the power of biblical transformative faith, thus creating real alternatives to the power which the world offers to us.

The third theme in the feminist critique of liberalism has to do with its understanding of love. There is much to suggest already that justice rather than love has been the major emphasis in this paradigm, and that concern for human relationships as an intrinsic and morally salient feature of human life does not feature prominently within its pattern of ideas. Since love is one of those aspects of human experience which can be relegated to the realm of feeling or passion, it can easily become a nuisance to the transcendent consciousness seeking for objective standards of decision-making. That again it might be understood as one of the expressions of human sexuality raises the problem of its introducing into moral reasoning something men have studiously sought to avoid in such matters. This leaves the impression that considerations of justice, which are objective and fixed universal points of reference, surpass those of love, which are partial, impermanent, and particular. Notions of love expressed by Christian ethicists as *agape*, or self-giving service to others, reflect the anthropological assumptions characteristic of this paradigm.

Feminist writers question whether such an understanding of love is full enough to accommodate the depth of human experience, or rich enough to serve as a distinguishing feature of the Christian moral life. They are critical of the combination of ideas within the underlying anthropology of this paradigm, which makes its understanding of love problematic. On the one hand is a positive assertion that the fullness of human life is possible in obedience to the highest understanding of moral principle and duty. This is accompanied, on the other hand, by a most gloomy portrait of natural human beings, who are selfish, greedy, violent, and aggressive, and whose wills are entirely self-serving. The liberal individual is a self-centred being, concerned for the achievement of its own ends and able to negotiate with others for mutual benefit. Loving human relationships are possible only when the self is sacrificed to the needs or concerns of another, and when the motive for this has been discovered outside the self. By locating what is shared between human beings in the abstract notion of a common nature, sustained in theological anthropology by a transcendent deity, and by giving access to that commonality by means of rational thinking and obedience to principles, interpersonal relationships are of necessity mediated. Feminists ask why that which binds us as human beings to one another may not be our immediate empathy and recognition in one another of shared feeling and desires. That desires have been denigrated to the realm of the arbitrary and selfish is questioned by feminists who propose an alternative understanding of humanness to the one suggested here, with different conclusions regarding the nature of love.

In her careful analysis of the theologies of Reinhold Niebuhr and Paul Tillich, Judith Plaskow identifies the central problem in the understanding of love within this paradigm.[49] Concentrating on the themes of sin and grace, she follows the method of Saiving in setting the alternative of women's experience alongside the anthropology of these two different theological positions. In both theologians, she discovers a common concern regarding human sinfulness as a form of separation from the divine, a separation which can only be overcome by divine action in human life. For Niebuhr, sin originates in the anxiety that accompanies the precarious situation of human life, caught between the limitations of the natural world, and the total freedom of the transcendent. The resolution of anxiety is found by man in forms of sin by which he either identifies completely with the natural world, falling into sensuality, or he attempts to usurp the place of the transcendent deity, falling into pride. Niebuhr understands these forms of sin to be essentially self-love, in which man attempts to secure his own existence through his own effort, and by which he continually misses the essence of his good creaturely freedom. Likewise, for Tillich, the meaning of sin is understood to be estrangement. Again anxiety lies at the origin of sin, since man is confronted with the choice between realising his potential as a free and finite being, and retaining his innocence in essential union with the divine. That man chooses finite freedom now places him in the ambiguous situation of being existentially separated from that to which he essentially belongs, and leaves him with choices that may reveal his longing for union with the divine, but cannot effect his return. These two theological explications of sin reveal an understanding of the dimensions of human life in which love of self arising from fear is a prominent feature.

The overcoming of sin is effected only through the action of divine grace, by which the otherwise inescapable reality of self-love is overwhelmed by its opposite, self-giving love or agape. Since, for Niebuhr, all that man does is filled with pride in his accomplishments and love of his own image, his sinful self must be completely shattered and destroyed for any true love to be possible. His old self must be sacrificed, crucified, so that Christ may live in him, and so that in his new self he may complete Christ's work of self-giving love to all men. The language of the sacrificial love of the cross is central to Niebuhr's understanding of love, for only this love 'completes the incompleteness of mutual love', 'represents a transcendent perfection', and 'reveals the contrast between man's sinful self-assertion and the divine *agape*'.[50] In Tillich, there is a somewhat more positive assessment of human forms of love, as these express and embody man's 'drive toward the reunion of the separated'.[51] However, these attempts at overcoming estrangement are ultimately futile, since finite selves cannot bring about reunion with the transcendent, thus leaving man in even worse despair and frustration. Only in agape, which is not just a higher form of love, but love which 'enters from another dimension', is the human person reaffirmed in the core of his being and reunited with that from which he has been estranged.[52] Loving human relationships are now possible within the spiritual presence, since 'The divine spirit, in ecstatically elevating the individual above her or himself, enables her or him to enter into genuine relations with others and achieve mature self-relatedness'.[53] In both theological anthropologies, the dimensions of human possibilities are contrasted with those of the divine life to which man must surrender if he is to know the meaning and power of love in his life.

In a recent article, Linda Woodhead extends this theological critique of love, by drawing out a composite definition which many Christians would recognise as widely held. Neighbour-love, she suggests, is believed to be 'self-sacrificing equal regard which is indifferent to the value of its object'.[54] The attainment of such love, or agape, is believed to be at the pinnacle of a hierarchy of human loves, ranked according to the degree of human desire involved in each.[55] The teaching of this kind of love pervades Christian life, from catechism to biblical commentaries to historical and systematic theology. Yet, in relation to every word or phrase of this definition, there is something which women find difficult or inauthentic in the light of their values and insights, and thus such a definition is inadequate to accommodate the fullness of human experience in relation to other persons and to the divine. Indeed, Woodhead believes that the ways in which a woman speaks of love can be demonstrated to be the excluded term in the ideal type of Christian neighbour-love defined above. That this definition has been formed against her experience, and that its fullest expression is understood in contrast to her insight, leaves a woman again in an ambivalent position in Christian ethical thinking. A feminist critique stands 'the traditional Christian hierarchy of loves on its head',[56] suggesting another definition altogether of love as 'an active desire for the well-being of the neighbour, and for communion with him or her, based on a recognition of the neighbour's unique worth'.[57] By introducing into a critique of liberalism such an understanding of love based on attentiveness to special details, the underlying assumptions of this model of moral reasoning are exposed more clearly to view.

Two things remain to be said in concluding this critique. The French philosopher Michèle le Doeuff expresses these well.

I am far from being the first feminist to regard the abstract ethics of universality and the law as a liberating point of view. For it enables us to see as morally neutral a great number of things which are required or forbidden by the social code ... It is an important stage of the historical movement of the de-alienation of women to be able to put forward the idea that some things are morally indifferent, as much (to use the old example) as having an odd or even number of hairs on one's head. But the category of the neutral, or indifferent, can only be put forward by a procedure which is itself ethical, which, having located the law elsewhere, can declare that it is not here. It is thus not surprising that for two centuries feminism has been 'moralistic'.[58]

The liberal paradigm has given to women a framework for moral reasoning about which many are now ambivalent. In its own way, this paradigm illuminated the common features of human life that are morally significant, locating these beyond physical, traditional, or social difference. Women were thus given an authoritative voice in which to speak of their concerns and interests in terms that made them reasonable in public discourse and justifiable as matters to be addressed morally and politically. The impulse which informed this paradigm, that ethical considerations drive us on to a universal perspective applicable to all regardless of circumstance, has been shared by women who have used this as a framework for emancipation throughout the world. That one might use reason as a lever with which to prize open unfair practices and oppressive structures has been a significant aspect of the feminist cause, and lies behind its 'moralism'. These points are significant ones in any formulation of a feminist or a Christian ethic and continue to be addressed, as we shall see later, by those feminists who identify themselves as post-liberal.

That women have begun to see more clearly the ethical choice which the use of this paradigm requires, suggests that they are moving into new and deeper awareness of its implications. To locate the moral law elsewhere, to 'declare that it is not here', is to challenge what has come to be recognised as the voice of man, by which his new self-understanding has been expressed, and within which his descriptions of justice, of power, and of love have been formulated. In the process, what is known and experienced by women is displaced from consideration, devalued as the excluded term by reference to which what is good is defined, and rendered mute by increasingly authoritarian proclamations that to be human means what the man says. To take this liberal paradigm completely apart is one of the tasks of the social constructionist approach to moral reasoning. In its critical analysis of Enlightenment humanism, and in its affirmation of the social character of human life, many feminists and Christian ethicists find a more fruitful alternative.

CHAPTER 4

The social constructionist paradigm

Perhaps the best-known and most-quoted line from *The Second Sex* is the sentence, 'One is not born, but rather becomes, a woman.' Having examined throughout the first part of her book the various notions of the determination of women's lives, from biological to economic determinism, and the 'myths' by which these are sustained, de Beauvoir opens the second part with this statement of woman's becoming. 'No biological, psychological, or economic fate determines the figure that the human female presents in society; it is civilization as a whole that produces this creature, intermediate between male and eunuch, which is described as feminine.'[1] Such in a succinct form is the basic thesis of the social constructionist paradigm, upon which an elaborate social, political, and ethical critique has been built by feminists seeking to understand, and to change, the conditions of the lives of women more fully and sensitively. Central to the claims of this paradigm is the recognition of the social construction of values, a recognition that constitutes at many points a challenge to the liberal paradigm, and that provides a distinctive approach to feminist moral and theological issues.

The roots of this way of thinking are to be found among those contemporaries of early liberal feminists who were more revolutionary in their political vision, more militant in political involvement, more socially conscious of the impact of working conditions, class structure, and family life on women, and more radical in the changes they sought in personal, social, and economic relations between women and men. Rather than involving themselves solely in the struggle for equal rights, measures which would include women in society on the same terms with men, these feminists also looked more deeply into existing society, analysing more critically its limitations and possibilities for women, and proposing more drastic changes as the necessary steps towards true and full freedom for women. Their political writings, their stirring public speeches, their styles of life recorded in letters and autobiographies, their attempts at the formation of alternative communities, are all indications of lives dedicated to social change, to fundamental alterations in the institutions which shape women's lives and which were considered oppressive. Their writings reveal an early awareness that beneath the pattern of women's lives lay some kind of social necessity which imposed itself in both subtle and obvious ways, thereby shaping human behaviour and self-understanding. To investigate the nature of this necessity, to describe its shape and its parameters, to discover the openings in which social change could take root, all of these combined in the purposes of the early social constructionists, leaving contemporary feminists with a rich heritage of critical analysis and activist politics.

One of the earliest writers to use this paradigm in relation to the lives of women was Harriet Martineau. Born in England in 1802, she spent two years travelling in the United States, writing her observations of social life there, and using a method of comparative analysis which was to yield many insights into the impact of social structures on human life, and which was later to develop into the discipline of sociology. The work she completed after her visit, *Society in America*,[2] reveals some of the assumptions of social constructionism at work, and begins to set the terms of understanding, and the vocabulary, with which this approach to moral reasoning breaks away from the liberal one. She set her sights on America, as did many of her day, as a land of new social opportunity and of promise, impressed as she was by the idealistic aims of freedom and justice for all. In particular, woman 'is told that her lot is cast in the paradise of women' and 'there is no country in the world where there is so much boasting of the "chivalrous" treatment she enjoys'.[3] Such was the rhetoric of the establishment of American society, reflecting the aura of Enlightenment optimism, and presuming that its mores were a civilized advance on those of the old world. Women should have been able to derive encouragement from the new universalism of the Enlightenment ideal that 'every individual, whether man or woman, has a reason and a conscience' whereby the work of morality becomes something 'each is thereby authorised to do for him or herself'.[4]

Underneath these messages full of hope and opportunity, however, lay 'the injuries suffered by women at the hands of those who hold the power'.[5] Rather than finding women who could look forward to the open prospects of the new society, she found that 'woman's intellect is confined, her morals crushed, her health ruined, her weaknesses encouraged, and her strength punished' through what Martineau identified as 'indulgence'.[6] Women are denied justice, like slaves, 'on no better plea than the right of the strongest'.[7] The messages given to women in this new society needed to be unmasked as a form of social manipulation, by which women were made to fit into a narrative that they had not written, and that was contradicted by the realities of their lives. Exposing this social myth, as a narrative within which women's lives were shaped by, and confined to, the interests of the powerful, uncovered the true state of women in society, whereby they were made into 'the confessors and martyrs of their age.'[8]

Supporting this myth, and ensuring its plausibility as a framework for understanding the meaning and the possibilities of life, were social and economic structures. The condition of women in society was one which gave to them no options for the future but marriage. This 'discipline of circumstance' confined the lives and intellect of women, and was confirmed by educational institutions.[9] To begin to unravel what becomes for women a vicious and oppressive circle of social justification required both courage to expose the myths, and a willingness to be outspoken in locating the problematic social structure as marriage.[10] Martineau found inequalities in marriage, which gave economic independence to men but not to women, and which thus encouraged 'mercenary marriages' as well as forms of 'legal prostitution',[11] again in contrast to the rhetoric of two equal persons joined for mutual benefit and fellowship to one another in love.[12] Her observations revealed both the economic necessity of marriage, since 'it is difficult, where it is not impossible, for women to earn their bread',[13] and the enforced domesticity which that thereby imposed on those who entered into it. That such unwilling acquiescence in structures which were not freely chosen should result in unhappiness and passivity for married women needed to be acknowledged in itself. Martineau also noted the implication which this had for the lives of women employed as domestic servants, and especially for women of colour. The apparatus required by marriage and family life not only was to shape the lives of the husband, wife, and children, in particular ways, but also was a significant factor in the continued subservience of others in the social structure. Its institutional impact was thus not only personal, but political, in its dependence upon, and contribution to, the oppression of others.

What finally emerges from Martineau's work is the recognition that 'the mischief lies in the system' and that only systemic analysis and change will bring the positive future for which women have hoped.[14] Thus she challenged the philanthropic doing of charitable works as a resolution of inequalities of pay and of choices regarding work for women, claiming that 'special methods of charity will not avail to cure the evil. It lies deep; it lies in the subordination of the sex'.[15] Here again her work reveals the basic assumptions of social constructionism that something more powerful than human choice and more pervasive than individual freedom is at the root of the problem of women's lives. In particular, one may not assume that women have consented to their lot, since it has been constructed by, and reinforced in, social practices. Thus 'the acquiescence of the many' in this structure is not a sign of their consent, but rather is testimony to 'the actual degradation of the class'; while 'the burning discontent of the few' testifies to 'its fitness for the enjoyment of human rights'.[16] The ability to criticise the passive collusion of women in the structures of their own subordination, and the ability to muster hope for positive social change, rely upon the thought and the work of individuals acting out of the best motives of human nature. The 'promise of a better time' lay in 'justice to the human nature'[17] which would become possible 'through the efforts of individuals of that class'. Martineau's prescription is thus that: 'All women should inform themselves of the condition of their sex, and of their own position. It must necessarily follow that the noblest of them will, sooner or later, put forth a moral power which shall prostrate cant, and burst asunder the bonds, (silken to some, but cold iron to others,) of feudal prejudices and usages'.[18] Social change will therefore be effected through the emergence of those remnants of positive human virtue untouched by social custom or narrative, especially to be found among individuals who are prepared to be unconventional.

Martineau's work demonstrates in an early form the new approach of this paradigm of moral reasoning which centres on the social construction of value. The tone of her work challenges the note of optimism characteristic of the Enlightenment, which looked to the liberation of humanity from false belief and unjust action through transcendent knowledge. In noting the discrepancy between such hopes and the ways in which social institutions actually function, Martineau began to outline another picture of the nature of the moral project, a picture which she believed more accurately related the realities of women's lives to creative possibilities for change. In the first place, there is a recognition in her work that the words and concepts with which people come to understand their lives are socially given, and thus that the first step in moral awareness is to give attention to the stories people are taught, as these shape human understanding. In the second place, her work reflects the notion that such words and concepts derive meaning from the institutions that are the important functioning units of the society to which we belong. Thus the second step in moral awareness is to uncover the parameters of these social structures and the practical possibilities which they sustain. In the third place, it is at the fringes of these institutions, from among those who may least conform to the given social story, that one might expect to find moral insight. So Martineau's work suggests that the last step in moral awareness is to discover the perspective of the outsider, from whose experiences may come creative vision for change, and whose nobility, away from the crowd, might embody the true goodness of human nature.

Martineau's analysis of social theory and practice was to find an echo a generation later in the work of another English-woman, Cicely Hamilton. A prolific writer and prominent suffragist, Hamilton was to engage in a similar kind of structu-ral analysis, and, in particular, in an investigation of *Marriage as a Trade*, a work which reveals the basic tenets of the social constructionist approach to moral reasoning at work.[19] Like Martineau, she noted the cloak of affection in which relations between women and men are wrapped, and began to suspect both the motives which lay behind it and the social impli-cations which it had. Such false affection both masked and reinforced basic inequalities. Since, in the important tasks of life, women were responsible for 'the unpleasant work in the common division of labour', any deference shown to them became only the 'sugar that attempts to veil the flavour of a pill or the jam that does its best to conceal the noxiousness of a lurking powder'.[20] In this kind of critique, Hamilton both noticed the stories which are told to women to make sense of their lives, and pointed out the disparity between those stories and the realities in which they live. Such disparity gives rise to a systematic use of suspicion, a suspicion that what women were told was in someone's interest, a suspicion that behind these stories lay the concern of men to reinforce their own power and position in society, a suspicion that the function of social structures was to ensure that women believed in, and accepted, the place which had been alloted to them.

Woman is understood here as a creature who has been made, fabricated, moulded to social purposes. This is the essence of Hamilton's analysis of marriage, which is an institution that requires the existence of 'average' women, with 'the character-istics required by an average man in an average wife'.[21] The social structuring of marriage necessitates appropriate training for those who are to fill its requirements; 'it must follow as the night the day that the acquirement of certain characteristics ... had been rendered inevitable for women in general'.[22]

What is significant in this development is that such social construction is purported to be based on the real nature of women, a nature which is claimed to be remarkably consistent even in the presence of very different examples of particular women, but to which, Hamilton argued, women are compelled to conform. Marriage required a number of interconnected assumptions about the nature of women: – that wifely characteristics and duties are what women really want, that their natures really do suit them for this kind of work, that women desire to please others and to serve others' interests before, and in preference to, their own. A social institution thus necessitates the formation of a 'class' of persons who fulfil the required role and function. Speaking of 'The insistent and deliberate stunting of woman's intellectual growth', she indicates that 'woman's morality has been imposed on her' and that, whereas man 'is free to obey his conscience and to serve his God', woman is made to serve the needs of man.[23] The making of woman through the imposition of social necessity is something which Hamilton believed women did not choose, and would not continue to choose, once the spell was broken. Belief in the reality of her 'nature' would then no longer be plausible.

This led Hamilton to protest that such compulsory construction of morality was ultimately false and immoral as a way of life for women. A woman's behaviour, which may appear to be moral according to prevailing social standards, is actually not so, for she has been trained according to 'a code of manners formulated in the interests of her master'.[24] Because of this construction of her morality by others, woman is rendered incapable of true morality, which Hamilton takes to be 'a rule of life which we adopt as a guide to our conduct, and endeavour ... to apply to every action'.[25] Woman lives therefore by 'second-hand virtues', a situation made even more demeaning by the reduction of all of these to the one virtue of 'honour'. That woman's attempts to conform, freely and rationally, to standards set by others should be further distilled into a statement about the physical state of her body, was the final insult and contradiction. She was rendered effectively powerless in her personal and social life by this reduction. The life of woman was thus shaped by the requirements of social institutions which she had no part in formulating, and the virtue of her life was judged accordingly. Her nature was presented to her as in some sense objectively real, while underneath lay determining social and economic requirements, moulding her behaviour and attitudes accordingly. That this ultimately was constraining to her own freely chosen possibilities, and that in the end this undermined entirely the prospect of her own authentic morality, was the result of the social construction of woman's life.

The themes of this approach to understanding and explaining the moral project were to erupt again in feminist analysis with particular significance in the early 1960s when, after a period of enforced social conformity following the Second World War, *The Feminine Mystique* was published in the USA. Acclaimed by its publishers as the work that 'ignited women's liberation', the primary aim of the work was to challenge the social creation of women which had effectively quelled the emancipationist hopes of liberal feminism. Its author, Betty Friedan, set out the nub of the issue in the preface, as her realisation 'that something is very wrong with the way American women are trying to live their lives today'.[26] Examining this more closely she claimed: 'There was a strange discrepancy between the reality of our lives as women and the image to which we were trying to conform, the image that I came to call the feminine mystique. I wondered if other women faced this schizophrenic split, and what it meant.'[27] Looking for the origins of this mystique became the project of the book, in the course of which Friedan examines the prevailing social myths in which women are indoctrinated, and the powerful institutional framework by which those myths are supported and reinforced. Tracing the history of early feminism as the search for an authentic identity for women, she noted with anger the awful joke that was being played on modern women, as they were lured into accepting a role and an image for themselves which virtually enslaved them. Friedan's analysis of this seduction paints a dismal portrait of the making of woman.

There were two steps taken by this work which have been

important to the development of the social constructionist paradigm. Firstly, Friedan offered a contemporary way of examining popular culture, and of considering critically the messages spread throughout a society regarding appropriate behaviour. She saw in these messages the attempt to create a figure who met particular social and economic needs, and who embodied in life the qualities required for the fulfilment of those needs. The purveyors of these messages were manifold, but, in all of them, she uncovered the making and remaking of woman for others' needs as a major focus of attention. In the advertising industry, such image-making took a particularly unsavoury form. Since the primary concern of advertisers was the making of profits for their clients, the selling of products required both careful market research into the kinds of people who would be most persuaded to purchase, and then the subtle creation of those kinds of people through the medium of advertising itself. Examples of such 'hidden persuasion' were typical of the creation of women on a widespread basis throughout popular culture, and Friedan's work encouraged the uncovering of these operations. Secondly, she assumed that behind the workings of popular culture lay power, power which she identified in her work as economic necessity, following the disruption of normal life by involvement in war. She thus had to hand recent experience of the deliberate imposition of social myth required as men returned from battle to resume the places they had vacated to women, in work and in family life. That all sorts of resources needed to be brought to bear on this unusual situation allowed Friedan the broad scope of her own critical investigation, but also provided for future feminists an example of moral thinking based on social and economic analysis.

Opposition to this power was to be found in the 'yearning' women experience in their lives as they confront 'the problem that has no name'.[28] A close consideration of this 'problem' reveals that it is caused by the mismatch between women's own sense of happiness and fulfilment, and that which is offered to them by society. This problem had been explained as a 'loss of femininity', or 'too much education', or 'the demands of domesticity',[29] each explanation suggesting that women have sought inappropriate forms of fulfilling their lives outside the social norms set out for them. Friedan identified the problem as more serious and more far-reaching in its implications than this.

How can any woman see the whole truth within the bounds of her own life? How can she believe that voice inside herself, when it denies the conventional, accepted truths by which she has been living? And yet the women I have talked to, who are finally listening to that inner voice, seem in some incredible way to be groping through to a truth that has defied the experts.[30]

Friedan encouraged the voices of women estranged from social mores to be heard. By setting the yearning of women against the power of socio-economic necessities sustained by cultural myths, she suggested that true moral insight was to come from those who are beyond the pale of social conformity, outside social norms, and discontented with their possibilities. These have been significant steps in the development of contemporary social constructionist feminism as it articulates its hermeneutic of suspicion in our day.

The distinctive nature of this approach to moral reasoning may now begin to be identified. Instead of pointing to a transcendent source of value, in this paradigm, values are understood to be the products of social institutions, within which they serve particular functions. The context for individual insight and choice is the social world, comprised both of structures in which individuals act and interact, and of the language and ideology with which individuals comprehend themselves and the world and communicate with others. This suggests that the social precedes the individual, and therefore that the primary emphasis within the liberal paradigm on personal freedom and transcendence gives a misleading picture of morality. To speak in this second way about morality is to affirm the fundamentally social nature of human beings, and to understand that in all moral deliberation, social realities and language are intrinsic. Indeed the social constructionist paradigm relies upon a reversal of epistemological priority, giving to the social dimension of human life the crucial determining role in moral knowledge, behaviour, and decisions. From the perspective of this paradigm, any approach to ethics which does not begin with this dimension will miss the critical features of lived human moral experience and will, as a result, fail to provide the points of leverage by which such experience may be meaningfully and creatively revised. Moral understanding is constructed, deconstructed, and reconstructed within the realm of the social.

One notices therefore firstly in this approach, the significance of social roles and relationships in constructing moral understanding. The liberal paradigm depended upon the separation of fact from value. Practical decisions were ultimately related to freely comprehended moral principles, recognised or chosen as guides by individual moral agents, and then reassigned to the world of actual things and activities. Any given social role could theoretically be justified, and therefore be challenged, by the knowledge and acceptance of universal principles of human dignity and worth. One transcended the social as a free individual in order to gain critical perspective, and one then re-entered social relations with a clear objective standard of judgement. Within this social constructionist paradigm, fact and value are reunited, in a way that restores something of Aristotelian reasoning to the moral project. What one should do may be derived from a social understanding of who one is; 'ought' may be derived from 'is'. We learn guidelines for our behaviour, not as free-standing individuals, but as members of groups within which differing roles are delineated and rendered meaningful. We assess the value of our work in relation to our fulfilment of these roles, and in the context of the activities by which we relate to others. We describe ourselves in language which permeates the institutions in which our lives are caught up. Values are therefore embedded in the social world, and primary engagement with them, both to conform and to question, occurs entirely within the particular and varied configurations which this context may assume. Moral awareness requires an investigation of this social shaping of human life, an exploration of the manner in which persons are made, a recognition of the

construction of human self-understanding by social requirement and expectation.

There is also a deconstructive aspect to such moral reasoning, however, which looks for some understanding of the necessity for particular roles and relationships, and this is the second
feature of the paradigm. There is believed to be an internal
logic of social life, accompanied by a story provided to justify
and to reinforce its practices and institutions, which it is
possible to explore. Moral reasoning relies both on our ability
to describe the mechanics of social functioning, to appreciate
more precisely how society works, and upon our capacity for
plausible speculation, to arrive at some explanation of why
society works in this way. What has been fruitful in this
paradigm is the Hegelian, and later the Marxist and the
Freudian, explanation, that society is the expression of an
energy which lies hidden within it, an energy which the different forms and structures of the society serve to realise, an
energy which gives meaning to the social world and its
common language. There is thus no need to look outside
society to some independently formed or given human nature,
or to some divine purpose, for explanation, since society and
the morality constructed within it can be understood as an
integral whole. Indeed, such transcendence becomes in the end
unbelievable and unimportant to the social constructionist,
either as an independent realm outside the social, or as a
human possibility for rational freedom from the patterns,
thought, and language of the common world. Deconstruction
depends upon a closer examination of what lies within – a
space of great complexity and depth – a space of many facets
and interwoven textures. It requires a critical consideration of
the expressive function of language and thought-forms, and a
suspicious investigation of the dimension of power in human
relationships.

The third feature of this approach is its encouragement of
possibilities for reconstruction. While the initial impression
given in this model is one of determinism, speaking of human
life passively as something which is constructed in and by the
social world, there is considerable enthusiasm expressed by its

adherents for structural change and for improvement in conditions of living. Room for such activities is provided both by the constantly changing nature of social life, and by the fact that no social order is entirely inclusive. Societies are understood to change over time, to develop through new or different historical circumstance, and thus are believed to be continually in flux. This sense of the historicity of the social world allows recognition of the fact that customs change, practices vary from one place and time to another, words and ideas gain and lose meanings in different contexts, and values are shaped and reshaped accordingly. In each historical form of society, certain values, ideals, and ways of life are promoted to ensure some stability, and are reinforced for the well-being of participants, thus providing a reliable and permanent structure, a network of relationships by which persons may order their lives. The historical dimension of society however implies that none of these will achieve permanence, that formations and transformations are always present, and, further, that attempts to secure society against change are damaging and oppressive to those who are inevitably excluded by existing practices and values. The seeds of reconstruction take root among the maladjusted, the discontented, the dispossessed; they grow in the soil which is cast aside in the normal business of everyday life; they come to flower as new possibilities for social interaction and relationship which are believed to be more inclusive, and thus more authentic and fulfilling to human life. The aim of moral reasoning is social reconstruction.

Feminists use this framework to get a realistic purchase on the social structures which define their lives, to challenge the hidden forces which make these appear to be necessary and inevitable, and to discover the spaces within which new practices, new relationships, and new structures may become possible. There is clear disillusionment with the hopes of liberalism to establish a transcendent and universally applicable moral foundation, as feminists using this second paradigm are suspicious of the way in which liberalism is constructed upon the normatively male human being, and thereby sanctions social structures in which male power is embodied.

Feminists' utilisation of this model helps them to understand the solidity with which this social world presents itself to them, and the powerful hold which the stories accompanying social practices have over human thinking and imagination. To examine the moral force of the roles and relationships offered to women, and the persuasiveness of the rationale provided for these, brings into clear focus what has been taken for granted as necessary or fixed. With this focus comes new insight, and women begin to experience a flexibility of movement, a stretching of consideration, an awareness of impermanence.

Social constructionist feminists look within this creation of woman to discover some explanation, some clue which would help to unlock the stranglehold of endlessly circular reasoning. For many feminists, the explanation is patriarchy, following the definition given by Gerda Lerner: 'the manifestation and institutionalization of male dominance over women and children in the family and the extension of male dominance over women in society in general'.[31] The deconstructive task in describing this phenomenon is to unmask all of its disguised operations historically and in the present. Feminist investigations of the claims of science, the moulding of sexuality and of desire, the configurations of the family, the shapes of social history, the rule of laws, the patterns of language, the orders of the churches, – all lead them to the conclusion that social structures consistently serve the interests of men, while women are secondarily constructed as helpers, deprived of access to power. Much of their work is given to careful investigations of this process, with the hope of discovering, within the parameters of the given social world, the openings for new growth. That women's authentic voices could be heard, that the wisdom of their experiences could be known, that the perspective of their lives could be brought into the foreground, – these are the gaps in the present social order by which its hegemony may be breached, and a revaluing of human life becomes possible. To describe, to analyse, to change what exists are the tasks of this kind of feminism.

This model of moral reasoning has many proponents among contemporary feminists, whose work reveals something of the increasingly complex nature of this kind of investigation, and the areas of disagreement which stimulate present discussions. The New Zealander, Juliet Mitchell, gives an example of this paradigm at work in feminist critique, particularly in her early book, *Woman's Estate*. The liberal social vision she understood to be mere 'egalitarian ideology', but nevertheless she noted its effectiveness in hiding the problems it contains.[32] So long as women adopted this model of political thinking, they would believe that it provided all the depth of social insight needed, and would further be lured on by the possibility of devising a society around its lofty moral principles. Such an ideology may keep women endlessly busy in social reform and disappointed in its failures, but does not actually address the deeper question of radical social reconstruction. For this to occur requires a recognition of the construction of human life around the four necessary social functions of production, reproduction, sexuality, and socialisation, within which women are exploited. In production, woman is denied a role, thus rendering her socially weak; in reproduction, she learns to believe the myth of motherhood and finds herself trapped by the available configurations of family life; in sexuality, she falls in love only to become a piece of private property; in socialisation, her vocation to care creates a new generation of obedient little productive workers from which she herself is excluded. In all of these processes, economic forces are at work, heavily encrusted with stories by which these operations are both disguised and justified, creating what becomes 'an oppressive monolithic fusion'.[33]

These observations lead Mitchell to conclude that 'the liberation of women can only be achieved if *all four* structures in which they are integrated are transformed'.[34] For this to happen will require both careful analysis of their operations in any given time and place, and then an 'attack' on the 'weakest link in the combination'.[35] The resources for this challenge come from the mismatch between these institutions and the personal self-awareness of women which has escaped social control. 'Divided, individuated, isolated – a woman is yet, paradoxically, subjected to the most homogenizing, the most unindividual of ideologies – the nature of her so-called "womanhood", "femininity"'.[36] Woman's intuitions are released in moments of such insight, when the scales produced by this ideological suppression drop from her eyes, and she begins to believe that there could be better and more fulfilling ways of doing things. Each of these functions can then be found a new identity, so that they may express themselves as 'life-giving' to humanity, affirming and sustaining more effectively human social and creative nature. While the experiences and insights of women bring concrete detail to what might otherwise be an 'abstract socialism',[37] Mitchell's hope is for the reconstruction of a more humane social order for all people.[38]

In the work of Rosalind Coward, we find a distinctive use of this paradigm which parts company with the humanist assumptions found in Mitchell. Underneath Mitchell's positive proposals for social transformation lies some notion of common humanness, which she calls the 'bio-social universal' and which provides a foundation for the moral project. Coward belongs to another generation of feminism in which such humanism is challenged as naive, as a form of essentialism that prevents our appreciation of the complexities and the fragilities of human existence. She explores the phenomenon of cultural production in language, images of popular culture, and theoretical disciplines.[39] Here her interest is in the development of social discourses within which human beings understand themselves and their possibilities for behaviour. Her attention is directed at the construction of sexuality, of desire, of gender, each of which is a discourse that interprets the world and human experience in particular ways. Central to Coward's argument is the belief that notions of human nature, and that human persons as subjects, are constructed within such discourses, and therefore that an appeal to human nature, or to personal subjectivity, as if it were outside social construction, cannot be made. It is typically the case that ethics has been humanistic in just this sense, relying upon some understanding of humanness to obtain leverage on present social structures. Coward's work is a challenge to our understanding of the nature of moral discourse. Since we do not have available any unstructured or pure conception of what a human being really is or ought to be, we must come to terms with the limits of, and the openings within, the discourses in which we participate, finding ways in which they may be revised to provide for us new possibilities of understanding ourselves, our society, and our world.

As an example, the deconstructive task in her book is 'to clarify the history of how we think about sexual relations', and in the process to uncover the 'dominant presuppositions' that constitute patriarchal theory.[40] At the heart of all the theoretical discourses available in the human sciences, is a universalising tendency, which brings into the foreground something that can unite diverse cultures and periods.[41] This consistent element has been sexual relations, for 'all these discourses rely on a notion of sexual identity (and therefore sexual regulation) as pre-given.'[42] Notions of the biological, or the natural, have been structured by 'dominant ideological principles', which rarely call into question the 'heterosexual reproductive instinct',[43] and which consistently result in the conferring of power on men.[44] Coward does not, and cannot on her own presuppositions, provide an explanation for this construction of sexuality by relying upon some essential notion of what men or what women are. However, the rejection of essentialist explanations actually allows greater flexibility in relation to possible new discourses, and offers the opportunity for breaking the hold of dominant definitions over subordinate women. Since one's identity as a human subject is also constructed through such discourses, we can detach notions of sexual identity from a fixed relation to anatomical differences.[45] We can then begin to appreciate the great variety of ways in which male and female identity has been constructed, the changing nature of these divisions over time, and the continual process by which meanings are assigned and reassigned within social structures.[46] Attention to the ways in which notions of identity have served to control women breaks the power of these descriptions, and encourages women and men to understand the nature of their collusion in this unequal relation. Such understanding begins to open up new configurations for human relationship, and it is in hope for these that Coward writes.

This kind of analysis has been helpful too in understanding the construction of the discourse of 'race'. Through a number of studies, it has been argued that dominant cultures build their power upon the definitions of those whom they subdue and the assignment of inferior roles to them. The process of domination requires that some group be identified as 'other', as having qualities, propensities, needs which are not merely distinctive, but dangerous or threatening to the dominant group. By believing these descriptions, the subservience of the subject group is justified, and social practices are shaped accordingly. 'Race' is thus described as a discourse, like gender, formed by the dominant culture of western white man as a way of classifying human beings, in order that the interests of that culture might be promoted and rationalised.[47] Women who live at the intersection of a number of these social constructions experience most keenly the problem of the 'colonized mind', and have thus made a significant contribution to the broadening of feminist concern, and indeed to the awareness of 'racist' assumptions within feminism itself. Writing as a black Christian author and teacher, bell hooks expresses the 'yearning' of those who seek liberation, in the hope of 'creating strategies that will enable colonized folks to decolonize their minds and actions, thereby promoting the insurrection of subjugated knowledge'.[48] Cultural criticism is one of the forms available within the context of white supremacy for 'promoting critical resistance' and for enabling 'a practice of critique and analysis that would disrupt and even deconstruct those cultural productions that were designed to promote and reinforce domination'.[49] This project requires the refusal of the definitions of one's nature provided by dominant discourses, definitions in which one's identity and essence as an 'other' is established.

Her goal is to encourage the discovery of 'ways to construct self and identity that are oppositional and liberatory'.[50] Oppositions are expressed when the voices of the oppressed challenge the categories in which their lives are confined. hooks describes the possibility of such an oppositional moment:

One change in direction that would be real cool would be the production of a discourse on race that interrogates whiteness. It would just be so interesting for all those white folks who are giving blacks their take on blackness to let them know what's going on with whiteness. In far too much contemporary writing ... race is always an issue of Otherness that is not white.[51]

To 'interrogate' the dominant culture is to refuse 'participation in the construction of a discourse on race that perpetuates racial domination',[52] and to begin to create a space for resistance. Sustaining this resistance requires 'a fundamental attitude of vigilance',[53] nourished by hopes for liberation. It is in hope that hooks believes we may discover our 'shared sensibilities which cross the boundaries of class, gender, race, etc.', and which 'could be fertile ground for the construction of empathy – ties that would promote recognition of common commitments, and serve as a base for solidarity coalition'.[54] Thus the 'yearning' of her title is understood to be 'a common psychological state',[55] welling up out of enforced silences, and turning marginal places into 'sites of transformation'.[56] hooks considers this 'sweet solidarity in struggle' to be, itself, redemptive, and links the process of liberation to important themes of Christian faith.[57]

One can begin to see through hooks' use of this paradigm its appropriateness as a fruitful model for Christian ethical thinking, and a number of contemporary feminist theologians are working within its terms. The feminist liberation theologian, Dorothee Sölle, has argued that women need critically to examine the construction of their lives and identities within the Christian tradition. Using the notion of theology as *praxis*, she suggests that all theologies are socially constructed communications of, and reflections upon, living encounters with God. Since these always take place in the midst of practical situations and human needs, theology is entirely rooted in history.[58] Accordingly, it is important to ask in what ways particular theological frameworks facilitate such encounters and enable communities of people to live out in their everyday activities the implications of their faith. Theologies which seek a foundation of truth untouched by human history are, she believes, the prerogative of the powerful, so that the supposedly dispassionate search for truth becomes the means by which their right to this position is founded and justified. Thus the portrait of God as a controlling, commanding deity is unmasked as the expression of human concern for power and authority.[59] The primary focus of attention for this kind of theological work becomes the need to convince the unbeliever of this version of truth and to ensure obedience, so that authority becomes a matter of right belief or dogma, moral knowledge becomes knowledge of universal principles and timeless norms, and a good life one which is lived in conformity with these. Discovering the voice of the powerful in this construction of theological knowledge is an important step for women.

Sölle's own focus in theology and in ethics is not on unbelievers, but rather on 'non-persons', victims of exclusion and destruction of the self, and it is from them that social and theological reconstruction will emerge. The importance of feminist theology is that it asks new questions of theology: – who its subjects are, who its objects are, and what its methods are. These, Sölle takes to be questions which will highlight the anchoring of theology in the everyday lives of women, and the real possibilities for liberatory activity which lie therein. Feminist theology seeks for the silent ones, those who need to hear the good news, for whom the encounter with the divine means hope. Thus it recognises that 'Racism, sexism and class society are far more basic boundaries of separation and destruction than so-called questions of faith',[60] and looks for those who are hidden within social situations, the victims of its ways of thinking and valuing, amongst whom criticism of the status quo and new ways of doing things may emerge. In reflecting on the practice and conditions of life of the excluded, a new practical principle emerges which itself becomes the touchstone for future action and thought. The central question becomes whether and how something 'contributes to the wholeness, the well-being, the freedom of women's lives'.[61] This is the appropriate way of linking religious faith to concerns for justice, and it provides a professedly partisan principle by which the Bible itself, the Christian tradition, and present Christian practice may be measured.

The Bible is a resource within this paradigm, not as a book with a thesis to proclaim, nor as a container of abstract principles of judgement, but as a living document, inspired and written in the midst of social and political realities, within which a living God may be encountered and known again in the present. As itself the product of particular social and historical circumstances, its own record is ambivalent, for it both contains the voices of the powerful and witnesses to their undoing through the presence of the powerless. What is discovered within the texts is not therefore a set of the words of God, but rather the word of God as 'movement', as critique and as change in the context and the conditions of peoples' lives.[62] Thinking about God thus 'takes root in the work of liberation', by which communities and personal lives are transformed. This becomes also the test of our language of God, for we must ask the question of the truths about God's being, not as a disinterested enquiry regarding whether or not it is rational to believe, but as a matter of deeply serious personal and social concern. Language of God is thus to be assessed by its capacity to liberate the *imago dei* within us and within social structures.[63] To speak appropriately of God is at the same time to discover the human self anew, a self which is formed in the midst of human interrelatedness. To discover the connectedness implicit in our humanness opens up new dimensions of living that are both practical and spiritual. In this way, words of faith become bread, both to feed the person who is hungry of soul, and to feed the poor and oppressed whom social structures deny by hiding from view.

Such an approach to Christian feminism can also be found in the more recent writings of Ruether, writings in which the construction of human life and consciousness by social structure and discourse is more obviously in the foreground of attention. In *New Woman, New Earth*, Ruether considers the making of women and men through sexual stereotypes, which are 'older and deeper' than other forms of stereotype, and more firmly rooted in a doctrine of 'fixed nature'.[64] She finds throughout history a tendency to conflate sets of dualisms (good/evil, male/female, active/passive), and to project these onto people as a way of ordering their complex natures, the positive part being characteristically assigned to those who have the power of speech and of definitions, and the negative part being assigned to subjugated groups, who are told that their 'natures' require them to occupy that place in the social structure, and that their possibilities for future action or thought are strictly confined. In the process of such a 'false construction of human relations', the real and natural complexity of human beings is denied, and humanity is split into two camps of those who are like us, and the 'others'. This construction is at the root of patriarchy, which has sought to 'elevate consciousness to supernatural apriority', detaching the mind and reason of man from his material being,[65] and has had direct consequences on the life of the planet, since the 'patriarchal self-deception about the origins of consciousness ends logically in the destruction of the earth'.[66]

In theology, as in other human discourses, unequal relations of power in the sphere of social life are extended into ontological categories in which women are assigned symbolic meaning as the less-valued half of a dualism, and into theological categories in which women's place becomes deeply ambiguous. That social relations, and the ideology which justifies and maintains them, are projected onto the divine intention is, for Ruether, a distortion of the truth of the divine will, and an unwarranted misuse of human power. Her explanation of this phenomenon reveals the complex interaction of personal intentions and social structures. On the one hand, such misuse of power stems from 'a basic insecurity that sustains the cycle of dominating violence' and that feeds on 'the unsatiated void of the insecure, ungrounded self, with its unresolved fears of vulnerability and dependency'.[67] There is a reliance here upon some notion of basic humanness, out of whose fears and insecurities these false categories arise. Indeed it seems essential in this kind of explanation to place the blame specifically on the insecurities of men, and to understand sin as man's inability to appreciate the inherent diversity of human nature. On the other hand, she emphasises a structural aspect to this evil, which turns attention away from personal guilt of men or of women, to prevalent social patterns by which our lives are shaped, and in which the church and its theologians collude. Thus, she argues that it is not a chosen pattern, but one into which we are all born and socialised, and, furthermore, 'which we feel powerless to change'.[68] To deconstruct the notion of sin in this way begins to open up new options both for the lives of women, whose identity as shaped within the tradition may now be freed from an inappropriate identification with sin, and for women and men who may be freed from present unhelpful categorisations.

Ruether's hope is based on the persistence of 'intuitive sensibilities' in which the *imago dei* is still located. Thus she believes that 'intimations of healthy and life-giving relationality' remain 'in spite of this ideological and social misshaping', so that better relations may be constructed around this centre.[69] She identifies this centre with the 'eschatological breakthrough in Jesus', who proclaimed the eschaton 'not as a spiritual principle unconnected with social reality', but as 'leaven' which recreates a just society.[70] Because the liberal ideology of 'equal rights' was too individualistically conceived, these new relations will come through a cultural revolution, 'a new culture that gives to all people their human complexity'.[71] Here Ruether suggests that dualisms are not to be reversed, but transformed into a pluralism of shared power, which more truly acknowledges the fullness of our humanity and more creatively expresses the open-ended possibilities for future society. Thus 'we have to reject all classifications of human groups along lines of differences ... based on ontological and moral dualisms'. We need both to recognise our common humanness which such dualisms contradict, and at the same time understand individual human beings as 'complex syntheses within th[e] whole range of human capacities'.[72] Patterning our personal and social lives around these central assumptions will allow many possibilities 'for sustaining just and loving relationality', which are healing to the insecurities and fears of the powerful, and affirming of the full humanness of the excluded. She looks, therefore, for 'a new type of social personality, a "new humanity" appropriate to a "new earth"'.[73]

These themes are taken up in the writing of one of Ruether's students, Rebecca Chopp, whose work in political and liberation theology shares with Coward a suspicion of humanism and a rejection of any foundational beliefs about what is essential to human nature. Her attention is likewise directed to language, to the construction of discourses, which in her second book, *The Power to Speak*, she links to the Christian understanding of the word of God. Chopp's analysis of the social construction of value centres on her view of language as 'both the material and the frame for structural and cultural debates about the role of women'.[74] Language is believed to govern both politics – the place of men and women, and subjectivity – the experience of men and women,[75] and for this reason is the locus of control of human life and thought. Like Ruether, Chopp understands the power of dualism implicit in thought and language, the basic pattern of which 'is the opposition of two terms, an opposition that forces and reinforces the basic couple of man/woman'.[76] To comprehend the power of language in the shaping of human life is essential, both to the task of moral analysis and to the effective proclamation of new life which is embodied in the recovery of the 'power to speak'. We must therefore engage in 'a broad and deep analysis of the ordering of systems and consciousness',[77] to reveal that the governance by language is incomplete, that there are cracks in its framework through which transformation may occur, 'margins and fissures that allow language and thus the social-symbolic order to be corrected, changed, subverted, interrupted, and transformed'.[78] Subversion and transformation occur through a recovery of the power to speak from outside these margins, a power which lies at the heart of proclamation, and of the personal and communal experience of the emancipatory work of the divine.

Such transforming work does not depend upon 'any claim about the essence of woman's subjectivity' and indeed we must 'forego a quest for the identity of "woman" as a universal singular'.[79] To abandon this search is to share in the 'crisis of modernity' in which feminist theologies now exist, and to seek the transformation of 'a social-symbolic order that has been dominated by terms of identity, autonomy, representationality, self-preservation, and presence'.[80] Hope lies with that which 'is not subsumed under the social-symbolic order's terms of equality and autonomous right', and this means that its expression is always particular to the unique situations of oppression in which women find themselves. The 'positionality of women' becomes the locus for the creation of new subjectivities and new politics that will be diverse, unpredictable, and multi-vocal. Here women may express, in the new power to speak, alternatives 'that are both prior to and in excess of the social-symbolic ordering of modernity'. This work will be that of the Spirit which is 'already present in the margins and ambiguities of language, subjectivity, and politics',[81] and which will blow and root where it will. Thus Chopp envisions new things:

It is possible to imagine a new relation to the body and to God, to creation and redemption, to law and to grace, not from a subjectivity that must destroy everything in its path to maintain and establish its identity, but from a subjectivity, a language, and a politics that desires and embraces otherness, multiplicity, and difference.[82]

The fragility of this hope lies both in its open-endedness, and in our inability to capture in language the precision of its terms. 'The hope is not that feminism can give all the answers but that feminism can hold fast to tracing the possibilities of questioning anew'.[83]

Examining the development of this approach to morality reveals the nature of the challenge to Enlightenment humanism which has emerged in feminist thinking as it responds to weaknesses in the liberal approach. Social constructionism contains, at one level, political challenges to the *naïveté* of the liberal social vision, finding in its principles of freedom and equality an ideological cover-up for the unjust, demeaning social and economic practices of advanced capitalism. These challenges are grounded in some notion of what belongs authentically to our human nature as social beings, for whom relationships with one another ought to be fulfilling and creative. Christian feminists will understand God to be the source of this nature, so that to seek to build alternative social structures that complete its possibilities more fully is held to be consistent with, and indeed essential to, obedience to the will of God for the creation. In this way, the divine presence is believed to be actively and practically involved in the daily business of challenging unjust practices and forming better structures of interaction. Recognising that social structures may pervert justice and distort the purposes of the Creator, requires, within this paradigm, not an independently derived set of principles or transcendent knowledge of the divine will, but rather the asking of previously unasked questions. It is precisely this which is believed to be the prophetic gift, for these questions have the power at once to reveal the limitations of an existing order, and to point to the spaces within it upon which new hopes for the future may be built.

At another level, social constructionism contains more far-reaching philosophical challenges both to the notion of human nature itself, and to any understanding of a transcendent authority for morality. As this paradigm becomes more closely identified with a post-modern outlook, it questions the grounding of moral sentiment and purpose in an understanding of the essence, structure, and end of human being. These notions themselves are deconstructed as the necessary rationalisations of the powerful, by which their right to this place is justified and fixed. Religious belief has played its own role in the formation of such notions, providing the ultimate justification for their truth by setting them firmly within the will of the transcendent, whose purpose is believed to be eternal and beyond our reason. At this point, Christian feminists seek to disengage the authentic purpose and will of the divine from human projections and distortions, which are forms of idolatry, making the divine in the image of the human. The social construction of values is a challenge to belief in the untouched delivery of moral principles and values from God, since this paradigm presumes that it is in and through the social dimension, not least through the use of a common language, that the divine is apprehended at all. This paradigm precludes the possibility that any one apprehension by any one group is absolute, since, as the means of our apprehension of the divine come into focus, so also emerges an awareness of their impermanence and their inadequacy. A critical appraisal of the words and images of God prevalent in a society brings out just that recognition, and acknowledges that 'The image of God is subject to change'.[84]

Hope for reconstruction is grounded, not in a closer, but in a looser definition of who and what we are as human, for, in this way, it is believed that the oppression of being defined, and the experience of being fixed as 'other', will be avoided. Thus increasingly, there is reliance upon the deeply felt longing within, the yearning which has no name for itself, the shared suffering of those who are left out of the story. From this source, which in itself is no-thing, comes critique, challenge, and renewal. Social reconstruction thus aims for a recognition of diversity, for the building of structures that allow and encourage the pluralistic possibilities of human being, and for an openness, a tentativeness, that may be self-revising and impermanent. This in itself is a redefinition of what belongs most essentially to our humanness, but it is one which is open-ended, indefinite, and full of surprises. This approach further suggests a dynamic, rather than a static, view of the divine, a God who surprises and upsets by moving in and around the margins of society, to stir up forms of resistance that may ultimately transform this world. This is not a God of whom language of power or control is appropriate, but a God who is understood primarily as the unexpected and unmanageable movement of the Spirit, and it is here that divine authority is located truly beyond human grasping. To affirm the possibility of these hopes is to share with the Creator/Redeemer in the transformation of the social order, so that our communal life itself becomes a prehension of that vision of divinely upheld society in which justice and righteousness are complete.

CHAPTER 5

Critique of social constructionism

The romantic adventure, *The Wizard of Oz*, known to many from childhood, tells of an ordinary Kansas farmgirl caught up in one of the frequent, but none the less legendary, tornadoes which inflict that part of the United States, with often weird and always unpredictable consequences. Dorothy's life is a typical mixture of the material needs of a family living at the poverty line, of good people and bad, and of simple faith in the importance of genuine human emotions. However, Dorothy is herself full of longing for some other place where she would never get into any trouble, and she is thus out of doors when the tornado arrives, having decided to run away from home with her little dog, Toto. Realising the danger of the coming maelstrom, she unsuccessfully seeks entry into the locked storm cellar where the others are sheltered, and, retreating into the house, is struck on the head by a flying window. Knocked unconscious, Dorothy enters into a dream which occupies the main part of the story, until she is awakened by her aunt shaking her to her senses again. In her dream, Dorothy becomes a traveller in a fantastic, colourful world of little people, sad creatures, good and wicked witches, encountering whom, Dorothy seeks advice which would enable her to return to her normal life on the farm with Auntie Em and Uncle Henry, the quintessential midwestern couple.

From the beginning of her dream, Dorothy appears confident about her purposes, so that, however twisted is the path to be followed or unusual are the tasks required of her, she sticks to her goal of beseeching the Wizard of this land for help in returning home. Not only is her perseverance and faith enough to sustain herself through capture, disappointments, and sheer fright, but she is also able to encourage and cajole a scarecrow, a tin woodsman, and a lion, to accompany her to the Wizard, so that their needs also might be met. There is, however, a deep ambivalence about this magical land. Certainly Dorothy has her own utopian vision, wondering initially whether this world was that perfect land over the rainbow sung to her in lullabies, in which all her dreams might come true. It is a land in which she is strong, in which she is physically grown, in which she is an adult, and in which her opinions of things matter to others, and particularly to men. She retains throughout her wanderings a confidence in the power and wisdom of the great master of this fantastic place, the Wizard of Oz himself. It is also true that the story suggests her homesickness, her longing to be back as an anonymous child in the grey Kansas landscape, where at least the people who care about her miss her, and that indeed her return there is effected, not by the Wizard, but by her tapping of the magical ruby slippers three times, whilst thinking to herself, 'There's no place like home.'[1]

In the preface to her reflections on 'constructions of knowledge, authority, and privilege' entitled *Engenderings*, the philosopher Naomi Scheman draws upon the imagery of the Wizard in this story. She explores the notion that the Wizard is the voice of the modern western philosophical tradition, a disembodied voice which 'comes from nowhere in particular', and which, thereby, is able to hold its hearers entranced to its own authority.[2] She calls this Wizard, the 'Grand Canonical Synthesizer'.[3] Characteristic of the Grand Canonical Synthesizer is the tendency to incorporate the experiences and ideas and voices of others into one's own theory, thereby dissolving a multiplicity of differences into sameness, overcoming the need for continuous dialogue through resolution of disagreement, and silencing the authoritative voices of the many through colonisation. In the story, this figure hides behind a screen, operating a sequence of bells, whistles, and explosions which amaze the suppliants, and speaking with amplification through a huge smoke-shrouded mask. For Scheman, this figure is to be found in the authority of the academy, in the intellectual work of those who theorise about human life, in the cultural construction of the knowledge and authority and privilege necessary for participants in the worldview of the modern age. What both puzzles and troubles Scheman is the place and the role of woman in the world of the Grand Canonical Synthesizer.

She can do things his way, adopting his voice as her own and becoming the subject who objectifies all others, and many women do this successfully and well. Indeed Dorothy finds herself in just such a place of privilege – as a worker of miracles, since her house fell upon and killed the Wicked Witch of the East, and as a leader of men, who need her confident approach to life's problems – a place which is sustained by the distant authority of the Wizard. Her expectations are shattered however by her dog, who is not impressed by magic, but who innocently, accidentally, knocks over the screen behind which a very mortal man is hiding. In a frantic exhortation to Dorothy and her companions, the Wizard exclaims, 'Don't look at the little man behind the curtain. I am Oz the Great and Powerful. What I don't tell you is not important to know.'[4] That the person behind the facade of power is a bewildered little man from Omaha, unable to control the flight path of his hot-air balloon, who has set himself up very nicely in a kingdom which does not know him, is the central moment in the dramatic climax of the story. What is intriguing is the residual ambivalence portrayed in Dorothy. She is encouraged by the too-good-to-be-true witch, Glinda, to articulate the meaning of the ruby slippers she has been wearing, and Dorothy complies. 'If I ever go looking for my heart's desire again, I won't look further than my own back yard. And if it isn't there, I never really lost it to begin with. Is that right?'[5] On awakening however, Dorothy seems less convinced of the truth of this homely reflection, since she discovers that no one believes she really went anywhere at all. Her protestations that this was 'a real, truly live place!' are received as the once-again childish fantasies of a little girl. Having remarked at the beginning of her dream, 'Toto, I have a feeling we're not in Kansas anymore', one wonders how she will ever be able to live there again.

To join in a critique of the social constructionist paradigm is to become involved in a lively contemporary debate about the meaning, and the possible demise, of a worldview called modernism. Those who participate find themselves caught up in a whirlwind of stories, images, texts, myths, new discourses that seem to fly past the window randomly, as the house of culture is carried through the air by some stormy force. What begins to settle is a realisation that things may not be exactly the same again, that the ground upon which one has expected to live is no longer firm, and that the shape of the future is quite unpredictable. To work with the critique is thus to be conscious of standing upon a threshold, on one side of which is the ordered world of accepted common sense in which people seem to manage their lives, and on the other side of which is the chaotic excitement of new things in which freedom and playfulness are promised. Such a threshold is crossed within the social constructionist paradigm itself, as it moves from formulations that are critical of, but none the less fundamentally related to, Enlightenment presuppositions, into new territory in which these presuppositions are thrown off altogether. What will be useful in this examination of the paradigm is to consider some of its inner tensions, and some of its problematic implications.

Three main questions can furnish the basis for this assessment, each of which constitutes a vulnerable point in the paradigm, at which its difficulties as an approach to moral reasoning become obvious. Firstly, what happens to the human person, given the challenge to rational agency that lies within this paradigm? Secondly, what happens to any notion of the real world, given that forms of realism are debunked as the neurosis of the powerful? Thirdly, what happens to our hopes for the future, given the difficulty of envisioning some end for life? In each of these three areas, the social constructionist paradigm presents both feminist and Christian ethicists with challenges to moral deliberation and action in the contemporary world. Some of the interdependence of feminism and Christian ethics can be felt at just such points, where consideration of adequate responses to the salient contemporary issues are very much interrelated, and where discernment of the appropriateness of this interpretation of history, as a shift from one worldview to another, is crucial. In an interesting way, the vulnerable points of this paradigm also revolve around understanding power, love, and justice, this time in a world in which the Grand Canonical Synthesizer is believed to be of no help whatsoever.

Feminists have engaged in their own critical response to social constructionism, and this is therefore an important area of present deliberation in feminist theory, from which the resources for this discussion are drawn. Initially, this paradigm was enthusiastically taken up by feminists as a helpful way through the problematic inheritance of the Enlightenment. The historical materialism of Marx and the psycho-social turmoil of personal development documented by Freud resonated with feminist unease about liberal individualism and idealism. The common chord was a recognition of the need for a critique of social practice and of ideology which could unsettle the foundations of patriarchal privilege and create a space for more fulfilling human life. To engage in such a project stirred feminists into the same processes of debunking myths about women's nature, shattering false hopes of happiness, and breaking the hold of cultural assumptions that inhibit and silence women in submission to some greater good. In this process, feminists were searching for that which was more fundamental, more real, more authentic, than social practice and ideology could accommodate. Thus there appear in the paradigm some notions of the real self within, which is struggling to be heard and acknowledged in the world of oppressive structures and relationships, and of the true society, which is seeking realisation through a range of manifestations until its fulfilment. To be able to touch this base, and to ground moral practice in that place, was to offer hope for the reconstruction of the social order in ways that were more fulfilling to the authentic nature of human life. In this form, the paradigm represents most closely a kind of humanistic socialism.

Feminists, however, began to suspect, particularly through the influence of Nietzsche, that this form of the paradigm presented them with a disguised liberalism, still seeking a foundation for morality which transcends everyday practice, and privileging itself as the new authoritative voice of all women. The suspicion that this is so, and that social constructionism is still itself in thrall to the Wizard and dreams of utopia, leads feminists into further considerations. Some feminists therefore describe themselves as postmodern, finding in the works of postmodernists a healthy scepticism about moral ideals, a mistrust of claims to knowledge, and a suspicion of controlling visions of the future. Since some form of these is considered to be essential to the moral discourse of modernity, the underlying question of this later form of social constructionism is whether it has also become post-moral. Some feminists find that their natural ally in this reconsideration of moral and political issues is to be found in post-structuralism which, as a form of critique of modernism, locates the common factor of analysis in language. Attention to the ways in which language constructs individual consciousness, positioning individuals in relation to one another and to ruling ideologies, develops from the assumption of fixed structures of language in the linguistic theory of Saussure, to the presumption of the mutability and permeability of language in the later post-structuralist writings of Derrida and Foucault in particular. Operating within post-structuralist theory, these feminists argue that the means for unsettling the oppressively dualistic assumptions of modernism are to hand, and that the possibilities for women are positive. In this form, the paradigm may be considered more appropriately an expression of the world of late capitalism. The debate regarding the fruitfulness and suitability of the interaction between feminism and both postmodernism and post-structuralism furnishes the context for the treatment of our three issues here, as well as an important source of critique of the social constructionist paradigm of morality.

To take up the first issue, feminists have, within this paradigm, been offering a new view of the human person which is a challenge to the one presented in the liberal paradigm. Human beings are understood here to be social creatures, whose identity is formed through various kinds of interactions, and whose thoughts and actions are shaped by available patterns and possibilities. In its humanist form, this paradigm was sustained by belief that some forms of these interactions and structures were better than others, and that this could be measured by the degree of self-control which people could exercise and by the extent of authenticity which was encouraged. As social beings, people were understood to need and to be fulfilled both through creative participation in the social world, and through the discovery of forms of social practice in which self-expression was received and honoured. Here the human person is assumed to be the source of the awareness and the experiences which can challenge alienation in social relations through the work of authentic self-legislation.

As attention to the construction of subjectivity develops, however, these grounds of judgement become less plausible. In its newer form, this paradigm no longer understands agency in the same way as the independent activity of an individual, acting as a subject upon the material world or other people, as objects of attention. Likewise, it cannot make use of the notion of decision-making as the conscientious reflection on matters of principle which results in a judgement to do, or to choose, or to believe something. Further, the very notion of authenticity becomes suspect, since there is thought to be no given form of the self to be satisfied or fulfilled. The rejection of humanism within this paradigm means that there is no core, or essence, or nature of the human person either lying behind structures, against which these can be measured as adequate, or transcending the structures as a free, thoughtful agent. Instead, the human person is newly understood as a network of various strands of social discourses and practices, intersecting with one another in differing patterns. Such a total revisioning of the human person receives mixed responses from feminists.

Chris Weedon, in *Feminist Practice and Poststructuralist Theory*, investigates the implications of this new alliance, and believes it to be helpful for contemporary feminism to abandon the humanist notion of a subject existing independently of language. 'Humanist discourses presuppose an essence at the heart of the individual which is unique, fixed, and coherent and which makes her what she *is*'.[6] The full impact of social constructionism is to throw this assumption very much into question by proposing a new description of the individual, as 'a subjectivity which is precarious, contradictory and in process, constantly being reconstituted in discourse each time we think or speak'.[7] A fluid understanding of the human agent as a cultural product, reveals that the human subject is subject to changes through historical periods, and through 'shifts in the wide range of discursive fields which constitute them'.[8] This openness to change as a result of fluctuations in discourses is realised as a new openness which the individual can experience and reflect upon, as new recognitions emerge along with new possibilities. Thus, Weedon claims, this 'process of discovery can lead to a rewriting of personal experience in terms which give it social, changeable causes'.[9] The new view of the human subject as open to changing discursive formulations, she believes to be important to the interests of feminism, and echoes Coward's reliance upon the decentring of the self in her deconstruction of sexuality.

What prevents our awareness of this nature of the subject is the prevalence of common-sense notions, by means of which we come to assume such a thing as a human subject at all, using it as the referent by which our decisions and actions may be justified. 'The transparency of language and the fixity of subjectivity, which are central to humanism, are attractive in so far as they offer a degree of certainty about life and apparent access to truth.'[10] Her argument against common sense does not rely upon the presentation of more accurate descriptions, alongside which common sense could be shown to be mistaken. Rather, she claims that such notions are widely accepted because of the assumption that language is a tool used by human subjects, rather than the means by which individual subjectivity is itself constructed. 'All common sense relies on a naive view of language as transparent and true, undistorted by such things as "ideology".'[11] The instrumental view presupposes that persons have free will 'guaranteed by individual rational consciousness' to use language as they choose, the consequence of which must be to blame women for using language which degrades them. Thus, for Weedon, 'Liberal feminism, with its belief in the sovereignty of the individual, is unable to deal satisfactorily with this question of "complicity with oppression".'[12] Feminism needs the post-structuralist critique of these deceptions to create spaces for the liberation of women from false self-understanding.

With cultural discourses at work forming personal self-awareness and consciousness of gender, Weedon believes that the problem of human identity becomes one of constant struggle, not between the public world of values or of ideology and some inward personal authentic self, but rather between the discourses themselves. The struggle in which the life of woman is caught up is a discursive struggle, as different ways of speaking about and understanding herself vie for ascendancy with one another. This Weedon describes as 'a battle for the signified – a struggle to fix meaning temporarily on behalf of particular power relations and social interests'.[13] It is a battle for gendered subjectivity in which reason has no active part, since what the individual thinks or decides is already a function of the embattled discourses. The struggle comes to closure, not when there is a fit between the authentic self chosen by the individual and the social roles given and defined for her, but rather when there is a satisfaction of something Weedon calls 'interests'.

Subjectivity works most efficiently for the established hierarchy of power relations in a society when the subject position, which the individual assumes within a particular discourse, is fully identified by the individual with her interests. Where there is a space between the position of subject offered by a discourse and individual interest, a resistance to that subject position is produced.[14]

What is offered here is not the liberal emphasis on the autonomous subject, but rather 'a contextualization of experience and an analysis of its constitution and ideological power'.[15] For Weedon, these things are more important to feminism, in that 'women's subjectivity will always be open to the plurality of meaning and the possibilities contained within this plurality will have different political implications'.[16] Precisely what these might be cannot be foreseen.

In her consideration of some elements of a postmodern feminism, Susan Hekman argues similarly for the rejection of the modern understanding of subjectivity. The modern age is characterised by a search for certainty, which, with Descartes, is believed to be firmly grounded in 'the rationality of the knowing subject', that becomes 'the self-conscious guarantor of all knowledge', constituting itself in distinction from objects of its attention and agency.[17] Many feminists have argued that this project constructs dichotomies which are inherently sexist, divisive of men from women as subjects from objects, so that a woman only becomes this kind of subject by becoming a man. While some feminists have sought a compromise in this situation, by attempting to 'produce a subject that empowers women to act as agents yet does not embody the masculinist qualities of autonomy, separation and abstraction',[18] Hekman considers these efforts to produce hybrids to be 'an unworkable epistemological eclecticism', trying to graft one thing onto another. She argues that

the subject who has agency, who constitutes a personal subjectivity, is precisely the autonomous, abstract, individualized subject that is the basis of the Cartesian subject itself. It is impossible to retain the concepts of an 'inner world' and autonomous agency and reject the other qualities to which these concepts are so intimately tied.[19]

There is thus no compromise possible, and the sooner the death of this man is complete, the better for women; 'it is only through the death of gendered *and* generic man, that women's inferiority can be overcome'.[20]

This touches deep ambivalences within feminism. It is not easy to accept that, just as women are claiming the fullness of human subjectivity as their own, such subjectivity is believed no longer to exist or to be important, or that, just as women are laying hold of full humanity, the nature of that humanity is dramatically reconceived. That this is still a matter of some reluctance for women is, for Hekman, mere nostalgia at the discovery of the 'bankruptcy of the Cartesian subject'. Feminists should note the making of women into objects who cannot acquire knowledge in the subject-oriented epistemology of modernity, and affirm the need to discover 'an epistemology that does not have man as its centre'.[21] For this reason, Hekman responds positively to the notion of the decentring of the self in which these binary oppositions are unravelled. From Derrida comes the concept of 'woman' as the absent 'supplement', accompanying, but never contained by, language, which may be used both to overthrow linguistic polarities, and to encourage a new discourse that 'speaks in a multiplicity of sexual voices; it is a discourse which has no center, neither masculine nor feminine'.[22] This new destabilised view of the self is the one in which women may find a proper place of equality amidst a wide range of possible identities and voices, avoiding both the fixity and the subordination of the former view.

Hekman believes the role of the human self as a centre of revolutionary consciousness may also be displaced, for its insight into, and account of, alienation is no longer required for political action. Thus from Foucault comes the assertion that 'we can discuss resistance to repression without formulating a metacritique of power; that we can discuss subjects and action without reference to a Cartesian constituting subject'.[23] The political adequacy of this alternative can be found in Foucault's insistence that the 'oppression produces the resistance, no other grounding is required'.[24] Political change does not therefore rely upon the all-knowing subject in its rendering of the big stories of history, nor the subject as active agent, but 'must be guided by a different conception of knowledge that generates a different means of opposition to the subjugation imposed by the discourses that structure societal relations'.[25] Resistance to discourse furnishes the way for the subject to reconstitute itself and 'to fashion new modes of subjectivity', since the understanding of language presented in postmodernism is of something 'fluid and multiple', capable of 'revision and mutation'.[26] This postmodern reconception of the human subject offers to feminism the flexibility required for the avoidance of the sexism that modernist epistemology has fostered.[27]

Some of the difficulties with this revolt against Enlightenment versions of subjectivity have been explored by Kate Soper. She describes anti-humanism as a new enlightenment, which displaces humanist thinking as 'obfuscatory and mythological',[28] as infected with a 'touching faith in truth' that becomes another 'God-surrogate' inserted into western thinking by philosophy.[29] Anti-humanism relies upon the historical materialism of Marx, in which humanism is exposed as merely ideological, as the belief-system of a particular cultural period in which its adherents were privileged, and upon the genealogical critique of Nietzsche, in whose work the pretensions of Enlightenment humanism to replace the divine with man are exposed. As against humanism which 'takes history to be a product of human thought and action', anti-humanism proclaims history to be 'a process without a subject'.[30] Accordingly, the tasks of anti-humanism are to engage in the process of deconstruction, understood 'as a series of *exposés* of lurking "humanist" motifs'.[31] Thus anti-humanism rejects 'any reference to a founding "subject"' by insisting upon the endless proliferation of discourses without guiding reason or purpose.[32] Anti-humanism can thus be understood as social constructionism turned against itself.

Soper argues that such arguments become possible with the shift in the human sciences, from the investigation of the material or economic conditions of living, or of the biological basis of human behaviour, to the process of representation by which we make sense of these human realities and activities. The proper subject for the study of humanity thus becomes discourse, and human beings are of interest as *homo significans*. The process of deconstruction is thus concerned with 'the universal inscription of humankind within language and systems of codification which regulate all human experience and activity, and therefore lie beyond the control of either individuals or social groups'.[33] Attention to signification, to representations of ourselves to ourselves, moves away from the concerns of the humanist in which social structures or forces are typically set over against individual autonomy and agency. Anti-humanism replaces this opposition with the notion of a socially constructed identity, made to represent things through the functioning of discourse, to which the individual is now subject. This gives priority to the power of the process of subjectification, by which persons are made into the particular subjects they are, through the disciplines imposed by political institutions and discourses, a kind of external power that produces individual persons. Soper at this point notes one of the deep ironies of anti-humanism, that it frees us 'from the materialist constraints of biology only by tightening the grip of ideas'.[34] With the 'insistence upon the alien, because symbolically constructed, nature of the self',[35] Soper questions what has been gained through this new project for feminists.

A second concern for Soper is the anti-humanist rejection of the rational determination of life, which has been thought to be the source of revolutionary spirit and vision. Increasingly the source of change is found in some 'natural desire' that is not satisfied by the social order, something not subsumed, which rises up and disrupts existing constructions and discourses. This suggests the power of an inchoate natural desire that lurks beneath social processes, creating pockets of resistance when its interests are not fulfilled, and providing an internal fund of disruptive energy. This no longer holds out the promise of freedom, but only for change, for something different, and in the end the mode of its operation suggests not the exercise of freedom, but its denial.[36] Underlying this rejection of free agency is a rejection of reason as a capacity for distinguishing one kind of thing from another, and for evaluating. Soper discovers, through the loss of this kind of reasoning, the increased victimisation of persons, making them subject willy-nilly to the conditions of society and of language without being able to ask questions of these. Indeed, she claims that, 'it has been the tendency of the "post-structuralist" movement to remove itself from the messy and difficult decisions of everyday politics by transposing all conflict on to the timeless and abstract plane of a struggle between the "cultural" and the "natural"'.[37] We are offered instead 'hypostatized forces and entities' that are extrapolated from real situations to enact metaphysical battles far above the sphere of ordinary human life, interaction, and conversation.

Running through this revisioning of the human subject is the removal of power as a property of the human person, conceived in terms of personal agency, or of self-legislation, or of rational deliberation which issues in action, and its replacement with power that operates beyond and around human behaviour. Power becomes more diffusely understood as that which infuses interactions of all kinds, and which individuals therefore derive by participation within these. The consequent loss of emphasis on the individual person as a clearly defined being, with precise boundaries, makes it difficult to understand how political action or moral evaluation could take hold. If 'every form of resistance, every "freedom" which resists and every desire for liberation are themselves the effects of specific techniques of power',[38] this leaves us with little to choose between one manifestation of power and another, and ultimately means that the postmodern form of social constructionism is post-moral. Yet, hidden within this paradigm are unexplained moral evaluations, which rest 'upon the premiss of an autonomous, natural desire', assumed to be good, set in endless and unresolved conflict with culture, assumed to be universally repressive.[39] Soper suggests the final irony of this rejection of the human subject. 'We must be wary, in fact, lest by focusing on the philosophical "end of man" we encourage a passivity that may hasten the actual demise of humanity.'[40] Her own hope is that feminism will renew its revolutionary roots in humanism.

This on-going debate in feminist theory highlights the need, within a Christian feminist ethic, to pay close attention to the appropriate affirmation of human subjectivity. An issue of central importance to the social constructionist paradigm has been that of the empowerment of human persons through the overcoming of false oppositions and exclusions. In questioning the construction of subjectivity within modernism, feminists have pointed out the inherent dualisms according to which women are rendered non-persons, and thus have recommended a looser description of the human person in which new dimensions are opened out. One of these is the emphasis on the making of personal identity in the historical context of social structure, language, and economic condition. To note this dimension of personhood was to overthrow one dualism, namely the modern portrayal of man as master of history through the use of reason, with woman as subject to nature on account of her embodiment. Social constructionists describe a view of personhood in which change is intrinsic, thus rendering all persons historically formed and subject to construction. In its humanist form, the paradigm recommended the affirmation of human responsibility for these constructions, and encouraged the rebuilding of a better society through attention to issues of wealth, power, and privilege. To do so requires some notion of an ability to stand back, to consider possibilities, and to judge present realities in the light of wider concerns and values. Rejecting humanism has led postmodern feminists to abandon this responsibility as the old dualism in disguise, and this optimistic work for the future as illusory.

Another of these dimensions is the realisation of the thoroughly social nature of persons, which overthrows the dualism of man as autonomous individual with woman as servant. The humanist form of the paradigm sought to emphasise that persons were bound up in a fabric of human relationships, in order that the quality and the nature of those relationships could be understood to be a matter of some importance to the living of a full human life. The moral impact of the paradigm was to encourage the formation of structures in which this communal dimension of the self could be fulfilled, and moral notions like integrity, responsibility, trust, or care, become meaningful in this context. Postmodern feminism takes an altogether more abstract view of this fabric. Discourse becomes the medium through which personal identity is formed, within which relationships are held, and in which persons interact. The human person is conceived as the intersection of a number of these trajectories of discourse, wherein relations with others appear as these lines cross one another. Ways of speaking and thinking in the present can contribute to a greater openness of interaction, but human intersubjectivity seems remote, and the moral notions relevant to this become redundant. The serious dilemma for women is whether the concerns which motivated the critique of the modern portrait of subjectivity have really been met, or have merely been rendered meaningless in postmodern constructions.

The second sensitive area in this paradigm concerns our reliance in morality upon some understanding of the real world, from which moral concerns are raised, and to which moral decisions are relevant. Much that lies at the heart of this paradigm is an epistemological critique of naive realism, in which the world is believed to be reflected by the human mind and represented in the transparent language of facts. Such realism attempts to establish in the world itself a firm grounding for knowledge, by providing objective criteria for the assessment of truth-claims. Descriptions of this real world are taken to be important to the moral project, since it is with this world that morality attempts to engage creatively. Feminists discover through the critical work of the social constructionist paradigm, however, just how completely our understanding of what is real is the product of social concern and interests. Their suspicion that those who describe things have something to gain by the description is fuelled by a recognition that reality-so-called serves an important social function in accrediting the status quo, and in rendering the powerless 'unreal'. Thus, what is considered to be real reveals the interests of the powerful, expresses their concerns, and serves as the rationale for their privileged position. This turns the tables on the hegemony of the realist by giving priority to the work of evaluation rather than description, by suggesting that all forms of realism are ideological constructions, and by arguing for the inclusion of those who have been left out of account. What is problematic within the paradigm is the eventual loss of any fixed base from which to engage in moral assessment, as the paradigm moves from its modern into its postmodern form, and a corresponding accusation that all epistemological claims, in the end, relate and refer only to themselves. This hermeneutic of suspicion takes its lead from the Marxist critique of ideology, from the Nietzchean analysis of the sickness of Enlightenment ideals, and from the Freudian insistence upon the prevalence of neurosis, in each of which feminists have found ways of giving voice to their discomfort with descriptions of the real world, and of the place of women within them. Their enthusiasm for participating in similar projects of uncovering pretensions is a reflection of the deep commitment to the historical nature of morality, wherein freedom to change can be located, as well as to the prospect of creating new forms of life. Beyond this is to be found the very ambivalent inheritance of Kant for feminism. On the one hand, there is a sense in which feminism relies upon the notion of the fundamental unknowability of things in themselves, thereby creating the space within which feminists can challenge definite claims to know exactly how things are. What is less acceptable to postmodern feminists from Kant is the optimistic notion that some unified theory of truth will emerge, or will be agreed, or that indeed such a theory would be a good thing if it were to emerge. Feminists question the search for one overall explanation of the real world, understanding this to be a totalising procedure by which all things are made subject to the wisdom and control of the Grand Canonical Synthesizer. The implications of this suspicion for feminism need closer investigation.

The terms for this debate have been set out in Marilyn Frye's *The Politics of Reality* in which she challenges the supposedly value-free understanding of reality characteristic of liberalism, and uncovers the political motivations in our understanding of reality. She acknowledges that she also began with 'the philosopher's constitutional propensity to view all orderly procedure as beginning with definitions',[41] and tried to provide a definition of sexism, which could be applied to a range of specific situations, using the model of syllogistic moral reasoning central to the liberal paradigm. She became convinced, however, that this was a mode of controlling the world to make it fit preconceived ideas. Definitions of things oppress, since things are moulded, immobilised, and reduced by the restriction of movement and of other interesting dimensions which definitions impose.[42] In just such a way, women have been oppressed, by having the reality of their natures, or the essence of their femininity, defined for them, and they become trapped inside these definitions. Frye's book is an exploration of the defining of reality according to two sexes which, she argues, is basic to the politics of reality.

Thus, she points out the 'Elaborate, systematic, ubiquitous and redundant marking of a distinction between the two sexes of humans' which has become 'customary and obligatory'.[43] This distinction may be taken for granted as obvious, as common sense, as given biological fact, but it is actually the product of interpretation, of man's creation of reality. Indeed, she muses,

It is quite a spectacle, really, once one sees it, these humans so devoted to dressing up and acting out the theory that there are two sharply distinct sexes and never the twain shall overlap or be confused or conflated; these hominids constantly and with remarkable lack of embarrassment marking a distinction between two sexes as though their lives depended on it.[44]

Her appeal is not to some other description of reality which would challenge this one and oppose its terms, but rather is to suggest a serious and all-encompassing form of cultural determination. 'Socialization molds our bodies; enculturation forms our skeletons, our musculature, our central nervous systems. By the time we are gendered adults, masculinity and femininity *are* "biological"'.[45] She recommends that women abandon the controlling politics of reality by which the arrogant eye of the philosopher attempts to establish all the world as his kingdom, and instead become alerted to the possible differences and diversities of human persons. This comes with attention, given by the loving eye, to what is excluded from the system of reality as presently ordered, so that one begins 'to see things that cannot be seen from within the system'.[46] With this new eye, reality becomes much less stable and enduring, and cannot be foundational in moral reasoning.

Marxist analysis has presented to feminism a way of holding oppressive material facts of human social life in tension with ideological pronouncements regarding reality, according to the traditional base/superstructure model. Descriptions of reality can thereby be judged as alienating or as fulfilling against this background of actual human experience, and attention can be given to bringing the two more closely into focus. In particular, women should be able to transform the traditionally limited location, content, and form of political struggle, by descriptions of their authentic consciousness and experience, outside the scope of male constructions of reality.[47] Thus, 'asserting the right of women to define their own identity within political structures'[48] allows them to 'break through the opacity of bourgeois ideology'[49] in ways that are more authentic to their lives. In its postmodern form, however, the social constructionist paradigm gives way to the assertion of the absolute autonomy of ideology from material facts at all, and it is this move which Michèle Barrett finds problematic for feminism, as she examines the anti-realist prejudice lying within this paradigm.

In the first place, the assumption that, because we only know this material base through language, our descriptions of it are inevitably privileged, is questionable. 'It is therefore correct, although tautological to the point of banality, to observe that *our knowledge* of the real cannot exist outside discourse. But it is a very long way from this to the argument that, as Rosalind Coward puts it, to privilege one discourse as reflecting the real is inevitably dogmatic.'[50] While she acknowledges that this form of social constructionism is a critique of epistemological, rather than a rejection of ontological, realism, nevertheless 'the concession of ontological reality is useless if we can do nothing with it in terms of our knowledge of the real world'.[51] Indeed, Barrett finds in this process a kind of 'extraordinary arrogance' by which 'external reality has been conjured away' through the use of the very tools of rationality that previously were valued for their abilities to reveal that reality to us.[52] The irony of this is deep, and leaves Barrett with the challenge that one has thereby returned to a 'phenomenologism', trying to solve the problem of our knowledge by 'dissolving the knowable real world into our discourse about it'.[53] This kind of scepticism Barrett finds unhelpful for feminism, particularly as it may deprive women of the meaning of reflection upon their own experiences.

In the second place, the detachment of ideology from real material concerns is meant to provide more room for feminist reconstructions to manœuvre, but Barrett questions in what context these will make sense or be assessed as better. Feminists have been resisting the argument that gender roles are tied to particular historical social relations which these roles seek to express, impose, and justify, since this would mean that sexual relations were permanently 'frozen' in society. Exposing this as deterministic, post-structuralist feminists argue for an emphasis on discourse as the site of struggle, out of which new and spontaneous things might be produced, which cannot be known in advance.[54] Barrett suggests that these are not the only two choices. She urges feminism to retain some sense of attachment to material realities that shape the lives of women, to real social relations, and to seek to make a real difference there. Otherwise, the political outcome of a rejection of realism is problematic. It is unclear 'that the project to deconstruct the category of woman could ever provide a basis for a feminist politics',[55] not least because no principles are provided for making distinctions between different actions. Indeed, for Barrett, this postmodern form of the paradigm is self-stultifying. 'The feminism enters as an act of ethical goodwill rather than a political practice tied to an analysis of the world; it remains a "self-evident" and unexplained goal which in fact the theoretical consequences of discourse theory must systematically undermine'.[56] Barrett's own argument for some form of 'relative autonomy' of ideology is, she believes, a more appropriate way for feminism to get political and moral leverage on the issues of women's lives.

Further thoughtful reflection is given to these issues by Jane Flax, who explores the intersection of feminism, postmodernism, and psychoanalysis as forms of transitional thinking. The contribution of feminism to this dialogue has been the critical assessment of the category of gender, and, in particular, the delineation of gender as a 'social relationship', 'a category of thought', and 'a central constituting element in each person's sense of self and in a culture's idea of what it means to be a person'.[57] The culmination of the trend to distinguish sex as a biological, from gender as a cultural, phenomenon, is to make the former entirely redundant. What is important from the other two discourses for feminism, in return, is the recognition that any feminist standpoint is also 'partial' and 'reflects our embeddedness in preexisting gender relations', along with the recognition that there is nothing to 'rescue' us from this situation.[58] Human entanglement in social relations and activities is inescapable, and has particular moral and epistemological consequences. Sharing the hermeneutic of suspicion of postmodern feminists, Flax asserts that 'Any episteme requires the suppression of discourses that differ with or threaten to undermine the authority of the dominant one',[59] and it is this logic of thinking which lies hidden in every so-called description of reality. Indeed, Flax argues that '"reality" can have "a" structure only from the falsely universalizing perspective of the dominant group',[60] which then establishes criteria for truth that 'reflect a desire to keep the others out'.[61] Her deep misgivings about human knowledge present problems for feminism by quite distinctly removing certain kinds of discussions about truth.

Flax herself is disturbed by the unusual, even paradoxical, consequences of postmodernism. 'It is ironic for a discourse that so stresses multiplicity that within one of its central concepts – the symbolic – are collapsed activities and organizations as varied as the state, law, production of goods, television, advertising, and literary texts'.[62] Indeed, she understands this also to be a kind of 'unitary approach' in its claim that 'A common logic is said to govern them all'.[63] Thus very different domains are treated as 'isomorphic', leaving the feminist without the discriminatory tools necessary to distinguish the type or the value of the particulars. She recognises the importance to feminism of attention given to the particular lives of women, to women's experiences and activities, especially so that feminists can understand how these 'are partially constituted by and through their location within the web of social relations that make up any "society"'.[64] Here, one notes the use of a more abstract word, 'location', rather than a more personal word, and further, the way in which this process becomes entirely self-referring. The problem, which Flax recognises, is that it can begin to appear as though '"nothing" exists outside of a text', so that everything becomes a play of texts over against one another, in preference to giving 'attention to concrete social relations and the qualitative differences among them'.[65] This carries with it something of 'an aura of inevitability', which may prove incongruous to the interests of feminism.

Yet she believes that feminism can articulate its point of view, can reflect upon our social construction, and can think about how the world 'ought and can be transformed', within the terrain of the postmodern world. Indeed feminists should positively embrace the decentring of the world, and be encouraged

> to tolerate, invite, and interpret ambivalence, ambiguity, and multi-plicity, as well as to expose the roots of our needs for imposing order and structure no matter how arbitrary and oppressive these may be. If we do our work well, 'reality' will appear even more unstable, complex, and disorderly than it does now. In this sense perhaps Freud was right when he declared that women are the enemies of civilization.[66]

Nevertheless there is lingering ambivalence. Flax recognises that 'postmodernism makes it more difficult to discuss questions of justice and power',[67] and, in particular, she is concerned that the oppressed, who have a serious investment in these questions, are not best placed to enjoy the luxury of the speculative postmodern feminism described above. Indeed, she begins to suspect that this is a privilege for those who have confidence in being heard amid the multiplicity of discourses. Having expressed as enthusiastically as she could the collaboration of feminism and postmodernism, doubts still come to her in the form of a recurring 'nightmare'. This, she claims,

> is not unusual among those who reflect upon experiences in the contemporary West. In this nightmare there 'really is' something 'out there' after all – a (Hobbesian) Leviathan at work, content merely to watch while and only as long as we amuse ourselves elsewhere. I leave this dream for others to interpret – if and as they wish.[68]

This question of realism touches quite deeply the need for Christian and feminist ethics to describe the human pursuit of understanding as an exercise of love. Exposing man's efforts at domination by means of controlling definitions or descriptions of reality expresses a mistrust of the human quest for truth as inevitably self-glorifying, and that women should note their own captivity within this quest comes as no surprise. In neo-orthodox theology, such scepticism rested upon a belief in innate sinfulness, a pride in human accomplishments, social structures, and culture. To disclose the parameters and the pervasiveness of this sin was called 'theological realism', so that to be a 'realist' was to acknowledge the sheer unattainability of love in the social arena. Postmodernism has shared in this disillusionment, but, as a form of social constructionism, has located the problem in structures, and then in the logic of discourses, rather than in human nature. This strategy is meant to provide both a way of explaining human entanglement with oppressive structures, within which we are victims, as well as a means of opening these structures themselves to change. Nevertheless, in this form too, there is a deepening sense of the human predicament, as the search for the diverse forms of human pretension is boundless, and as the chasm separating humanity and its deepest concerns from the real world widens.

And love seems equally remote. Feminist writers who grasp this condition are looking for ways of encouraging the loving eye which attends to the diversity and multiplicity of things as they are, rather than as they are misrepresented, or made invisible, in theories about the real. The disruptive character of this love is important, along with its unpredictability, and its power to cast down the mighty from their thrones, particularly through new ways of speaking. What becomes harder to understand within the postmodern form of this paradigm is why such love should be important, how it is to be sustained, and what the work of love might be. Since belief in the reflexivity of knowledge continually turns the thinker back into the categories of thought, the knowledge which love speaks is also understood as the expression of one point of view, no more or less meaningful than others, and equally susceptible to charges of hegemony. In this context, the world becomes a backdrop for competing modes of thinking and speaking, rather than a place within which human attentiveness to the details of daily living present opportunities for empathy and for relief of material suffering. To raise these concerns is to suggest that perhaps too much has been given away in the enthusiasm for unmasking wizardry, and that the postmodern form of this paradigm expresses a need for that which it cannot of itself provide, namely, that the world might actually be known in all of its concrete variety, and loved through actions which affirm its fundamental goodness.

Visions for the future within this social constructionist paradigm revolve around two predominant images. On the one hand is the image of imprisonment, expressed very powerfully by Frye in her lecture on 'Oppression'.

The experience of oppressed people is that the living of one's life is confined and shaped by forces and barriers which are not accidental or occasional and hence avoidable, but are systematically related to each other in such a way as to catch one between and among them and restrict or penalize motion in any direction. It is the experience of being caged in: all avenues, in every direction, are blocked or booby trapped.[69]

Frye compares this condition to life inside a birdcage. Examining one wire of the cage at a time, we may not be able to detect how that one wire in itself inhibits our escape to freedom. It is only when we step back to see the whole network that we can appreciate the extent and the nature of our imprisonment. This image calls attention most powerfully to the construction of women's lives by social forces and ideology, by relying upon the moral force of something being trapped unjustly.

The value of the social constructionist paradigm, in its humanist form, was to provide some perspective on the nature of this systematic oppression, and then to suggest strategies for liberation. Since both the forms of women's imprisonment and the actions required for freedom are structural, the image suggests that personal and social liberation from imprisonment are entwined, the authentic life of the one being tied to that of the other. The central concern is to discover the key, to find the one underlying explanation or cause, in knowing and manipulating which, the cage will be unlocked. So the imprisonment image bears the marks of humanism in its concern for the freeing of that which is presently constrained, in its affirmation of personal agency at present denied to the oppressed, and in its hope for authentic decision-making once the barriers have been removed. This notion of liberation extends the main tenets of justice as understood within modernism, by urging its fulfilment in social structures as the logical outcome of its inherently social character. The image is therefore sustained by a vision of justice as the realisation of the fullness of humanity within the social order, which it is the purpose of moral reflection to refine, and of politics to realise through critique and reconstruction. This justice, rational in formulation and communal in essence, serves as the foundation for a normative ethics.

As the investigation of structural oppression proceeds, however, it becomes plain to the postmodern social constructionist that feminism must 'become a form of resistance to the One',[70] and that underlying humanist assumptions regarding agency, political action, and justice must be decentred. Indeed, the postmodern feminist argues that visions of justice themselves are accomplices in the violence which is the hallmark of modern philosophy and culture, holding us entranced and helpless and silent. A new image of the future emerges here as 'nomadism', and a nomadic ethics is proposed. Rather than finding one place from which to rebuild society, or to root in an authentic personal life, this image suggests 'a set of interrelated "situated knowledges"',[71] in which women give voice to those things that 'are resistant to systematization ... in order to develop multiple, transverse ways of thinking women's becoming'.[72] Rosi Braidotti argues for these *Patterns of Dissonance* as the distinctive 'feminist interventions in philosophy',[73] claiming that this alone will 'undermine the fundamentally aggressive model of thought at work in phallologocentric structures'.[74] Such patterns require risk in developing a 'freer and more disrespectful' discursive practice, and encourage 'a way of being ... which expresses the human being's creative, positive power'.[75] Thus women may disrupt the system by 'remarkable acrobatic talents as they trace mental routes across the void, without falling victim to gravity'.[76]

This nomadic lifestyle, constantly keeping on the move to avoid fixity and oppression, is a journey without end, and is described by Braidotti as a restoration of 'the aesthetic value of thought', as 'the category boundaries crumble away and writing and thought are conjugated together in a new relational mode'.[77] She understands this nomadism to create the very conditions of the possibility of a new kind of subjectivity, in which persons do not realise their own private and individual authenticity, but in which there is interconnectedness.[78] As the various trajectories intersect with one another, the possibility for affirming relational modes of being is opened up, and this, Braidotti understands, is the positive contribution of feminism to the otherwise 'disaggregated universe depicted by the masters of post-structuralism'.[79] To describe this future, she rejects specific visions of 'a new civilization the a priori conditions for which are being laid down today', opting instead for the notion of 'the unbearable lightness of being' as 'the multiple force of all living beings, capable of never-ending shifts, adaptations, and connectedness'.[80] Her hope is that women will be able to carry the baggage of their historical memory of oppression, and, at the same time, be light enough to escape over the fence into a new world, away from 'the noisy vulgarity of the everyday violence of the times, of all times'.[81] Such walking of the 'tightrope stretched above the void'[82] reveals a feminism which is curiously unscathed by suffering, and which cannot provide further description of the new world that lies on the other side.

The decentring of justice removes for the postmodern feminist any substantive understanding of its nature, whereby better decisions could be made and positive steps be taken towards its realisation. As Sabina Lovibond considers the collaboration of postmodernism and feminism, she questions whether this abandonment of the conception of an end for human life is really in the interests of feminism. Without such a teleology, there is encouragement to 'plunge, romantically, into the maelstrom without making it our goal to emerge on *terra firma*'.[83] Not only does this demand 'a *harder*, less wimpish form of subjectivity' than modernism can provide, it is also one which will need to be sustained by the life of the nomad, an image which has a particularly masculine pedigree.[84] Running through the project of decentring justice is likewise 'a loss of confidence in the idea of *false consciousness*', and therefore a rejection of 'the view that personal autonomy is to be reached by way of a progressive transcendence of earlier, less adequate cognitive structures'.[85] One may be able to conceive of political action in this context, as the dynamic view of society and language would suggest constant change, with ever-shifting political realities and contexts, but one would not be able to understand this as purposive in any way. As this form of Enlightenment hope fades away, feminism becomes caught up in a 'terrible pessimism' from which it can only escape in playfulness.[86]

The tension between these images is reflected in present debates within feminism, as the moral and political implications of different kinds of hope are considered. At this point, the sensitivities of the collaboration of feminism and postmodernism become most poignant, and the stakes regarding the outcome are raised. The feminist is torn between interpretations of the new world promised in postmodernism as, on the one hand, the crucial opportunity for unravelling at last the dominant ways of thinking in which her life and identity have been entangled, and, on the other, the elitist option of the articulate for further poetic pyrotechnics beyond the call of sickness, poverty, and cruelty. As the post-moral nature of this collaboration comes into view, feminists again are caught between inner conviction, on the one hand, that some kind of vision is important to the possibility of, and confidence in, the reconstruction of the lives of women, and a realisation, on the other, that specific future hopes are manifestations of the dominance of reason bringing everything into submission to the controlling dreams of the privileged.

This dilemma finds particular expression in the very different conceptions of the divine–human relationship, which the concern for justice finally entails. On the one hand is the humanist version, in which the moment of communion with the divine is both rational insight and affirmation of dignity, whereby the work of justice can take root. On the other, is the postmodern emphasis on the unspoken, the not-subsumed, the unsocialised residue around the edges and exceeding the limits of linguistic structures, which become sites of yearning where the numinous qualities of multi-dimensional human life may be appreciated. In the former, the work of justice always runs the risk of arrogance, distorting the divine presence with human visions, while, in the latter, there is the risk of insignificance, as hope is devoid of specificity. It may be that within the terms of this paradigm, this dilemma is unresolvable, since every form of attempted reconciliation is understood to be the work of the Grand Canonical Synthesizer, and concerns for justice dissolve into either special pleading or fantasy. At this point, one appreciates the sense in which this paradigm crosses a threshold from one worldview to another, and is unable to provide of itself the language or concepts acceptable to both, which would enable the discovery of a way forward. For that, we may need to turn to a different story.

CHAPTER 6

The naturalist paradigm

But men do *not* look at both sides, and women must leave
off asking them and being influenced by them, but retire
within themselves, and explore the groundwork of being
till they find their particular secret. Then when they come
forth again, renovated and baptized, they will know how
to turn all dross to gold, and will be rich and free though
they live in a hut, tranquil, if in a crowd. Then their sweet
singing shall not be from passionate impulse, but the
lyrical overflow of a divine rapture, and a new music shall
be elucidated from this many-chorded world.[1]

In 1843, these words of Margaret Fuller, published in an
American transcendental literary quarterly, expressed something of a vision for the lives of women which is central to the
appropriation of the naturalist paradigm within feminism.
Recognising a situation of unequal privilege between women
and men, she argues that what women most want is 'for that
which is the birthright of every being capable to receive it – the
freedom, the religious, the intelligent freedom of the universe,
to use its means, to learn its secret as far as nature has enabled
them, with God alone for their guide and their judge'.[2] This
call resonates with much that is characteristic of liberal feminism, and suggests hopefully that both women and men will
benefit from the extension of liberty to include responsible
self-determination.

However, the distinctive marks of a naturalistic approach to
moral issues can already begin to be discerned here, for Fuller
was concerned not so much with equal freedom of choice, as
with the discovery by women and men of their own inner

natures, by which a deeper and truer friendship between them could be created. What impeded such friendship was the erecting of an 'arbitrary barrier' between men and women, constructed, and constantly being reconstructed, by male vanity, for man 'wishes to be more important to woman than by right he should be'.[3] The elevation of his own position, and the relegation of women to inferior status, results in false relationships: women try to become like men to gain power and are said to be 'manly' when seeking to exercise their rights; men defend their own position and praise those qualities of women upon which they depend for their own exercise of freedom. To break out of these constraints requires discernment of the true nature of each. Initially, this means freedom for women to develop in themselves. 'What woman needs is not as a woman to act or rule, but as a nature to grow, as an intellect to discern, as a soul to live freely, and unimpeded, to unfold such powers as were given her when we left our common home'.[4] Initially, likewise, this means an end to the 'school-boy brag' of man, the taunts that 'Girls can't do that' which discourage the development of his friend and reinforce the less generous side of his own nature.[5]

Fuller sets her hopes for the emergence of true friendship, both within and beyond the bounds of biology, and her writing is indicative of the dual attitude towards the body which is characteristic of this paradigm. On the one hand is the positive belief that women need to develop the fullness of their own being through a deeper appreciation of their particular embodiment. 'Ye cannot believe it, men; but the only reason why women ever assume what is more appropriate to you, is because you prevent them from finding out what is fit for themselves. Were they free, were they wise fully to develop the strength and beauty of woman, they would never wish to be men, or manlike.'[6] The discovery of woman's own true nature, as a being who is physically and spiritually distinctive, is essential both to herself and to fulfilled human relationships. On the other hand, Fuller argues against the narrow determinism of physiologists, who attempt 'to bind great original laws by the forms which flow from them', for there is an intermingling of female and male within each of us.[7] She urges a spiritual freedom by which women and men may discover the transcendental significance of their bodily distinctiveness, so that they may 'prophesy to one another', by loving 'in one another the future good which they aid one another to unfold'.[8] That moral action contributes to the flourishing of the full human person by its making true in reality what is already true in nature is a characteristic mark of this paradigm. The aim of this self-realisation is, in the end, a transcendent one, expressed by Fuller as the possibility of true love, such that women can become 'good enough and strong enough to love one and all beings, from the fulness, not the poverty of being'.[9] That she was in the early stages of exploring the dimensions of this through her own somewhat unconventional marriage and motherhood, added to a deep sense of loss at her untimely death by shipwreck in 1850.

The appropriation of a naturalist paradigm of morality is one of the most highly charged and controversial issues within feminist thought. There is a deep ambivalence running through feminist debate about this paradigm which, for those who support its use, is evidence of its importance and unavoidability in some form within feminism, and for those who despise any form of it, is indicative of the desperate collusion of women in their own oppression. In the development of modern feminism from the eighteenth century, this paradigm has been forged in the midst of controversy, in dialogue and dispute with significant male thinkers whose reliance upon its terms constitutes much of the central core of their understanding of humanness. From Hegel, to Rousseau, Darwin, Freud, Levi-Strauss and Lacan, some understanding of what lies in man's and in woman's nature has been proclaimed as the framework for our lives, decisions, and actions, and has been used both to explain and to justify particular social arrangements. Feminists have engaged with each of these thinkers in turn, some to find in their arguments the epitome of all that feminism opposes, others to find within their insights new ways of appreciating distinctive values of and for women. The focus of discussion has been a set of interconnected beliefs: that women and men are by nature fundamentally different, that a distinctive psychological development attaches to each, that the social roles within the family and the wider society are determined by these differences, that women and men live by naturally distinct sets of values, and that these differences in some way attach to the distinctive bodies of women and men. Accordingly, it may be said that biological sex is believed to shape gender, and thus the movement of argument within this paradigm runs counter to that in the social constructionist paradigm.

Added to this more recent debate is the recognition that this also represents one of the most enduring of paradigms of moral reasoning, so that it may be found in the earliest days of philosophical and theological reflection as a useful way of considering contemporary moral questions. The paradigm thus may be labelled 'traditional' by those who would claim that it has provided the most consistent framework for decisions regarding women, 'traditional morality' referring to gender-specific behaviour justified according to its terms. The ambivalence of feminism is part therefore of a larger issue concerning the relation of feminism to tradition in general. Nevertheless, some form of this paradigm has made an important contribution to the development of modern feminism, particularly by those feminists, often called romantic, who turn it to women's advantage. The debate has once again been heightened in recent years with the emergence of new French feminisms that use in various ways its basic terms.

A controversial figure in feminism has been 'Red Emma' Goldman, a native Russian who lived in the United States, who was not only an ardent campaigner for the right to birth control, but was at the same time a purponent of traditional commitment to love and motherhood. She was opposed both to the naive hopes of liberal feminists, who believed that, with the right to vote, things would improve for women, and to the enthusiasm of Marxist feminists, who looked for an end to traditional women's roles in a new social order. The most important aim of emancipation was for women 'to be human in the truest sense', by rejecting the artificiality of their lives.[10]

Her article, 'The Tragedy of Woman's Emancipation', written in 1911, explored the failure of liberal feminism, which contributed to 'a slow process of dulling and stifling woman's nature, her love instinct, and her mother instinct', until 'the majority of women have become mere professional automatons'.[11] Believing that the modern emancipated woman had become 'a compulsory vestal, before whom life, with its great clarifying sorrows and its deep, entrancing joys, rolls on without touching or gripping her soul', she urged women to explore this depth of soul so that they might recover their own springs of action.[12] The special moral knowledge of women could not be satisfied by nor fully expressed in the ideals of intellectual autonomy and moral independence that Goldman believed to be central to liberal society and feminism. To continue to aim for these was self-contradictory, for it pandered to the values of male self-sufficiency. Women should reject the 'artificial stiffness' and 'narrow respectabilities' of liberal emancipatory ideals, producing 'an emptiness in woman's soul that will not let her drink from the fountain of life', and seek instead to make that special contribution to humanity of which women alone are capable.[13]

As an anarchist, Goldman believed that human life flourished best when individuals were free of domination and authority in social and personal relations. Her arguments for individual freedom are not like liberal ones, in that they do not assume the stability of social relations in the context of which rational transcendence may be exercised. Rather, her arguments reflect an integrated humanism in which social and political structures must be challenged ethically from within, out of a concern for the implications they have for human relationships and development. Thus property relations are inherently unethical, enforcing upon human interactions a concern for ownership that is alien to the works of love, and that introduces the damaging consequences of jealousy into human affairs. One discovers this, not through reflection upon principles, but through closer examination of human experience. Thus also Goldman sought to demonstrate that the social regulation of marriage cramped the full possibilities of love which, when acknowledged, have the power to restore the dignity of autonomy and authenticity to the persons concerned.[14] Indeed, Goldman suggested that the ruling of reason as it sits in judgement over individual action was paralleled in forms of social control that prescribe, regulate, and coerce individual behaviour. Instead, we should recognise that 'good and evil, moral and immoral, are but limited terms for the inner play of human emotions upon the human sea of life', and accordingly 'rise to the lofty heights of the true humanitarian'.[15] Her notion that a person is 'a small cosmos' affirms the wholeness of the human being, and looks for the flourishing of love between persons, for 'It is glorious and poetic if these two worlds meet in freedom and equality'.[16]

Virginia Woolf may also be placed within this paradigm for her emphasis on the distinctiveness of women's writing and of women's insights into political and personal living. Troubled by the exclusion of women from the academic tradition and from political life, she sought both to explain, and to make creative use of insights that this position uniquely afforded them. Behind their exclusion lay the needs of men. 'Women', she wrote, 'have served all these centuries as looking-glasses possessing the magic and delicious power of reflecting the figure of man at twice its natural size'.[17] The subversion of this positioning had already begun with those early women, who appeared on the surface to be fulfilling social expectations, but who were all the while keeping their writing and their insights hidden away in secret places.[18] What was now to be encouraged was for women to make this secrecy explicit, firstly by the setting up of *A Room of One's Own*, where women's insights and values could be explored without constant and invidious comparisons, and secondly by the overt political involvement of women in challenging a social order framed out of the purported superiority of man's values. To take positive advantage of their special knowledge was the first step in women's moral awareness, and for Woolf to open the door of this room has been of enormous influence in the development of women's writing and political action.

Woolf's description of the moral reasoning of women

demonstrates the alternative moral epistemology of this paradigm, which engages in a continuous process of deepening reflection upon what is the case, in order that more appropriate forms of social role and of human relationship may be created. The process of moral reflection is both a mirroring of what exists, and a forming of new ideas by which to exist. She imagined women attaching to their wrists a 'psychometer', which 'would look something like a thermometer', and which would register in its quicksilver 'any body or soul, house or society in whose presence it is exposed'.[19] The sensitivity to both public and private morality which such a meter would record was a metaphor for Woolf of the ability of women to be attuned to the essence of things. Through such means they are able to judge truth from falsity, and to encourage the development of authentic ways of living and of relating to others. Touching this base, women are able to break the vicious circle of endlessly dancing round the mulberry tree, in which they faithlessly and insincerely chase after values and roles that are not theirs.[20] In this refusal, the spell is broken, and new action becomes possible, action which is more authentic and nourishing to the fullness of human life.

She introduced the figure of Antigone who embodies in a significant way the kind of moral reflection Woolf herself recommended. Woolf understood Antigone to be a person who used her relegation to the status of 'outsider' to challenge the laws by which her father sought to rule the city, with reference to a notion of the true law. She believed Antigone's vision of this law evoked a higher loyalty and purpose which challenged the laws of men, and further that this was discoverable within women's nature. This law could not be said to be laid down by 'God', since Woolf understood such notions to be essentially tribal and patriarchal, and it could not be set by 'nature', since this is an inconsistent and now humanly controllable reality. Rather, law is 'discovered afresh by successive generations, largely by their own efforts of reason and imagination', which are in turn 'to some extent the product of our bodies'.[21] Antigone's claim that 'Tis not in my nature to join in hating, but in loving', is born of the depths within herself, and its proclamation is not an abstraction but a lived feature of her daily existence.[22]

In her understanding of this phenomenon of women's uniqueness, Woolf acknowledged the important development of a literature of self-consciousness, which women are now to take up, to fill the empty shelves with their reflections.[23] For, not only do the lives of women reflect the ridiculous and shallow character of much that happens in society, but they also bear in their own lives and bodies the impact of these false ways of living. The insights of women thus challenge social practice and values from within, not by reference to principles, but by the embodiment of their consequences in human life and relationship. Woolf exposed the pomposity and competi-tiveness of men's lives, to demonstrate an awareness of the 'half-human' nature of social and political life, and to seek to bring people together in better ways, in order that persons may become whole. That Woolf's reflections were initially stirred by the sight of a tail-less cat 'trespassing' over the college lawn, a sign for her of the anomalous and unnatural place of women, who then discover the fullness of human being within them-selves, is an indication of the paradoxical character of this moral reflection.[24]

It is possible now to describe three distinctive features of this paradigm. The first feature is the notion that there is a natural basis for moral behaviour, which is in some way a given feature of being human. Something in this natural basis is presumed to be consistent across different societies, and furnishes the means by which human beings recognise one another, and communi-cate their common concerns and problems of living. This con-sistency extends also through history, so that by reference to its terms, judgements about the past and suggestions for the future may be made. In some way, this natural basis for morality is linked with embodiment, so that the consideration of biology affords especially privileged access to it. The major figures who use this paradigm thus both describe the physical parameters of life and indicate the psychological, moral, and spiritual impli-cations these parameters carry with them. Statements about the physical make-up of human beings are understood within this paradigm to carry dual logical force, both as descriptions of facts about persons which can be observed and measured, and as prescriptions of values regarding human life which can be obeyed and fulfilled. To discover what is morally good is thus to know oneself better as a natural being, and to seek to be good is to obey the law established within one's nature as human.

The outstanding figure in whom this paradigm is to be found is Aristotle, whose scientific claims have been the major source of western assumptions in biological investigation, being seriously challenged in the biological sciences only within the last hundred years. Aristotle's naturalism with regard to human life was formed from the convictions that the existence of two sexes, male and female, was of obvious and unavoidable significance to the proliferation of life, and that the ordering of human society came to rest in the end upon this functional necessity. To be human was to be able to identify oneself as male or female, and to be completed as human was to engage in personal and social relationships that affirmed this embodiment. This naturalistic basis for morality left room for individual considerations of application and degree, while at the same time providing a reliable general pattern to which reference could be made in decision-making. To be morally good was to be what one was born to be.

In Christian theology, this naturalism has been given theological justification as the will of the divine Creator, who made human beings male and female, and, who gave to them the ability and the desire to be fruitful and multiply. To grasp this natural fact of life was therefore to be in touch with the intention of God; to be what one was created to be by God was to be obedient to the divine will. Upon this foundation, social roles could be established and personal relationships entered into with some degree of assurance. For this foundation is understood to be unchanging, being established in the very structure of life itself, and forming something of a natural knowledge of the divine available to all living beings. To participate fully in the good creation made and blessed by God was the purpose of human life, and in important ways, the natural is identified with what is good.

Feminists who work within this paradigm seek to place moral recommendations for the lives of women within a consideration of their natures, in the context of what are believed to be the distinctive gifts and attributes of women. In order to do this, several critical points need to be made about the traditional form of the paradigm. Firstly, it must be said that the descriptions of women which have so far been offered within this paradigm have not been made by women themselves about their own natures, but are rather imposed upon women by men. There is thus a point to be made about authenticity, which relies upon women's own description and assessment of their lives and experiences and relationships, and it is on this basis that a proper naturalistic feminism must be built. Secondly, it must be argued that forms of naturalistic morality have served to benefit the privileged position of those who write its terms, in some cases through the portrayal of hierarchical relationships which presume the subservience of the woman to the man, in other cases through a dualism which defines women as the negative, the lack, or the absence of what characterises men. Again, a proper naturalism must be seen to be even-handed in its positive portrayal of the natures involved. Thirdly, and critically for its appropriation by feminism, the traditional form of the paradigm has tended to be deterministic about the role and behaviour of women, so that they were understood to be subject to a particularly strict biological control in a way that men were not. Again, if naturalism is to work for feminism, then it must explore the way in which biology determines destiny, and the impact of this on the nature of rationality, for both women and men.

That questions were already being raised in the nineteenth century about the appropriateness of naturalistic thinking in the case of people who had been made slaves, helped to strengthen the feminist case that this paradigm also needed drastic revision in relation to their lives. To challenge it was to insist that women become themselves responsible for the presentation of what belongs to woman's nature, and to recognise that their portrayal of this nature would need to be a significant undoing of the generally negative and demeaning portrait of women in the western tradition. All of this is fraught with difficulty for the naturalistic feminist, who finds that a whole range of possible positions are available, from gradual revisionism to complete reversal of the tradition, and who is challenged as much by those occupying the next nearest position as by those within the tradition itself. To recognise this within naturalistic feminism generally is to become sensitive to the special problems this presents to the Christian feminist, faced with the difficult task of arguing within a tradition of theological naturalism to which she is herself either an outsider or a second-class citizen. Her challenges may be thought by fellow Christians to be unacceptable revisions of a purportedly unchanging created order, and by fellow feminists to be an inappropriate form of collusion with the weighty moral forces of male dominance. Something of this debate can be found in the works of contemporary feminists.

A second feature of this approach to morality is to be found in its understanding of moral reasoning which offers an alternative moral epistemology to that found in the other two paradigms. While the liberal looks to reason as a form of transcendence, leaving considerations of matters of fact to one side while judgements of value are formed in relation to universal principles, the naturalist understands reason as a process of deepening awareness of what is already the case, so that its many facets and possibilities are opened to the increased sensitivity of the moral consciousness. The liberal seeks a foundation for morality in principles, established and upheld for the Christian by divine will, and believes its form of moral reasoning to provide a straightforward conclusion derived syllogistically from a set of rational premises. Compared with this, the naturalistic form of reasoning appears circular, consistently committing the naturalistic fallacy by relating what ought to be the case to what is the case, and making no attempt to stand outside, to transcend, to find the Archimedean point of reference. While the social constructionist questions the work of reason as a cultural formation which can only operate within the tramlines laid out for it, and looks instead to the irrational eruptions of the unsubsumed for moral insight, the naturalist sees the creativity of reason working with its given materials in imaginative ways. The social constructionist calls for disruption in moral reasoning, so that one is on the lookout for the excluded terms which, when spoken or made manifest, can unsettle the status quo and overturn its self-confident hegemony, in a way that Christians believe characterises the in-breaking reality of the kingdom of God. Compared with this, a naturalistic approach seems only to be playing a set of variations on a theme and, being dependent upon the very terms it seeks to revise or overturn, is rendered incapable of the genuinely new.

Through all of this, the naturalist paradigm understands moral reasoning to be related closely to the realities of lived human experience, to be both an expression of that experience and a means whereby persons may seek better and deeper and fuller forms of experience. The paradigm aims to provide for the moral agent more fortunate ways of behaving, and it is in this sense a teleological approach to moral matters. What is of concern is the development of the potentialities which lie within the human person, which may come into the fullness of their realisation through appropriate decision-making and careful actions. The point is therefore to give attention to the development of character, both with reference to the kind of person one is becoming as an individual, and with reference to the kinds of relationships one is forming with others. This process of deepening sensitivity to the possibilities of one's own becoming is central to moral development into the fullness of being. The paradigm therefore necessarily relies upon some claims about the nature of persons, some anthropological affirmations which are tentatively grasped from experience, with more or less detailed specification, and which are then refined in and through the process of moral reflection and action. For the Christian, this theological anthropology is the systematic representation of those insights derived from the encounter with the divine in the context of human life. In its claims, it draws attention to the deep structure of humanness at the centre of moral reasoning, which provides reference points for the guidance of daily living, in the hope and expectation of growing into the fullness of human being.

Feminists who work within this paradigm are concerned to illustrate this process of moral reasoning in the lives of women, as women come to terms with their own lived reality, and seek appropriate ways of developing their separate individuality and their styles of human relationship. What is inescapable in the paradigm, and what constitutes one of the critical points of conflict in its appropriation, is some reference to general statements or beliefs about women's nature in the context of which this development is to be set. Some generalisations need to be made, tried and tested, and revised, in order for deepening moral sensitivity to be encouraged. This means making claims about the nature of women, in the context both of natural sciences that devalue the feminine, and of a tradition of metaphysical assumptions, which feminists deeply suspect of being entirely and implicitly male-centred. Many feminists find in this paradigm a most helpful way of affirming and encouraging the development of the unique, special nature of women, but, in order to do so, new paths in science and metaphysics may need to be broken.

A third feature of this paradigm to be noted is its understanding of the human person as a unity of mind, body, and spirit. Paying close attention to the integration of the human person as a whole being suggests something of the personalistic end towards which moral considerations aim. For the naturalist, this contrasts with the notion of the human person at the heart of the liberal paradigm which, by so emphasising the freedom of the rational mind, has difficulty reattaching this capacity for transcendence to both bodily reality and the interrelational world of other persons. If some form of mind–body dualism is characteristic of liberalism, and if its outcome is an individualism revolving around the independent self, then this naturalistic approach appears to be both more integrative in its psychology and more communal in its description of the self. Since the dualism of the liberal paradigm was criticised as contributing to the misunderstanding of women, by identifying them with the lesser-valued half, a naturalistic humanism holds the promise of a more wholistic, and therefore egalitarian, view. Likewise, this emphasis on the personal within the naturalistic paradigm contrasts with the de-centring of the self increasingly emphasised in the social constructionist paradigm. If the social constructionist answer to the enforced dualism of western metaphysics is a shattering of the logic of identity altogether, leaving the human person as a fluid and continuously changing phenomenon, naturalism appears as a return to the common-sense notion that there is a core of personal identity which may be known and developed through moral consideration. Since the de-centring of the self leaves many feminists either frightened or hopeless with regard to the future, naturalism offers some vision of a social and personal goal of moral action.

The integrative approach of this paradigm means that moral reasoning focuses on the development of character through the function of the conscience in its growing sensitivity to the significant features of different life situations, and in its capacity for affecting positive changes in social arrangements and relationships that are more conducive to the flourishing of life. What is discovered in this process is the basically social character of the human person, whose selfhood is never a purely individual and private matter, but who is a communal being, formed in, and challenged by, relationships. Moral reasoning is therefore a process of 'thinking with', a dialogue between participants in a shared process of moral clarification and practice. Certain aspects of the social constructionist paradigm can be found here too, since the relationship of persons in, with and to social structures is a significant feature of the integrated approach. In what senses the material conditions of living and the historical changes of society have an impact upon, or interact with, the fundamental structures of humanness is a key question, still unresolved, within this paradigm.

For feminists, this paradigm has been particularly helpful in highlighting some of the features of the moral life which are believed to be most distinctive and most helpful to the full development of women. For many women, the process of full moral awareness begins in the work of consciousness-raising, whereby a closer consideration of the features of daily life for women is encouraged, and a critical look at ways of revising these is begun. In this process, the wholeness of the person is confirmed, since feelings and sensitivities are taken as seriously as thoughts and speculations. Indeed, it is important in this process that women are encouraged to trust their feelings, since these are believed to carry insight and to offer access to truth. The point of developing moral awareness in the feminist appropriation of this paradigm is that women will be able to grasp the distinctive morality which characterises their nature as women. Here again, an area of controversy emerges as feminists debate the extent to which this distinctive morality is exclusive to women, the necessity of separatism as a means of enhancing its full potential, and the problem of making sense of the exceptions to these generalisations about women.

Influential in the thinking of many contemporary women, and outstanding for her use of this paradigm, is Mary Daly, whose prolific writings have addressed women's consciousness of the desperate state of the world, and of their special task within it. Her sense of the importance and the power of human nature in determining our values and relationships and visions is profound. The problems of the world and of human society are caused by the self-serving values and arrogant behaviour of men, for it is characteristic of man's embodied nature to seek domination and control, to be anxious to protect its power, and to make woman into 'the Other'. This 'phallic morality' is socially expressed as patriarchy, and it is the major determining force in world affairs throughout history to the present day. The importance of feminism is to offer a genuine alternative to this morality, and it is one which can only be created by another nature altogether. Acknowledging her debt to Woolf, Daly produces a feminist ethics that is written completely from women's experience and insight. The task requires women to reclaim their own natures, so that entering 'the realm of the wild reality of women's Selves',[25] they may develop the fullness of their own being. Daly affirms this nature of women as fundamentally good, since it is the place where women discover truth,[26] where the radical bonds of friendship are formed, and where women may 'mend and create unity of consciousness' for the healing of creation.[27] It is hard to overestimate the impact of this call for the release of women's strengths and the affirmation of their natural values, for many feminists believe that it completely reverses traditional naturalism in a most positive and challenging way.

The process of moral reasoning Daly calls a journey, a spinning, a voyage, into a place of pure insight and value, untainted by the language, culture, presence, or expectations of men. For this, a meta-ethics is necessary, an ethics which is 'postpatriarchal', 'situated behind' patriarchy, and transforming patriarchy.[28] These nuances of the prefix 'meta-' indicate the distinctiveness of this moral approach as a form of thinking within a phenomenon until new features emerge and an entirely different reality begins to appear. Daly's technique is to gaze so intensely at patriarchy, as a woman situated outside its terms and yet bearing its consequences, that the contours of phallic morality emerge in all of their horrific and gruesome detail, and the new possibility of feminist morality suggests itself. This new morality exists 'in the Background', behind the 'Patriarchal Pleasure Park', in which women are perpetually trapped in the preserve of the past and domesticated to serve the needs and pleasures of man.[29] It is discovered by a process of 'exorcism' in which the false circularity of male mystifications is broken through the imaginative and innovative use of language. Daly's invention of words serves to upset the baggage of assumptions that accompanies everyday vocabulary, and, by using alternative words, she conjures up new pictures of what is the case.[30] Implicit in this process is the belief that language reveals nature, and therefore that women's reclaiming of language is necessary to the expression of their own true natures. Since the essence of moral reasoning is partisan, generalisations about the natures of women and of men appear continuously in Daly's approach, and there is no suggestion that a common ground may be discovered on which both may stand to grasp truth.

The morality discovered by women is 'deeply intuitive', and it is an important purpose of Daly's writing to stir up and fan the flames of this fiery wisdom. Women's confidence in these intuitions and commitment to their truth are encouraged through reflection on experience, by which women develop a 'new organ of the mind'.[31] This reflective consciousness surpasses the knowledge of good and evil as defined and delineated by men, and challenges men's ethical theories, 'in the sense of masturbatory meditations by ethicists upon their own emissions'.[32] Daly understands women's moral consciousness to be inclusive, overcoming the pretensions of phallic morality in its 'boundless boringness', by giving primary attention to 'the powerful and multidimensional gynocentric symbolism of the "O"'.[33] Women's recognition of 'the power of our moving, encircling presence, which can make non-being sink back into itself', can be understood 'to represent our aura, our O-zone', within which life-loving feminists have the power to affirm the basic Gyn/Ecological principle that 'everything is connected with everything else'.[34] Her hope is for the recovery of a deeper truth, 'beyond, behind, beneath the patriarchal death march – an unquenchable gynergy'. Thus women will engage in a process of alchemy, and 'transmute the base metals of man-made myth by becoming unmute, calling forth from our Selves and each other the courage to name the unnameable'.[35] This truth is apprehended within and amongst women, and is nurtured in separation.

In a work of a completely different tone, Carol McMillan uses this paradigm without the adventurous reshaping of life as envisioned by Daly. McMillan is troubled by the anti-naturalism she believes to be intrinsic to feminist ethics, challenging the liberal paradigm for its dualism of reason and emotion, its attack on 'the tyranny of nature', and its outcome in the individualistic free-for-all of postmodern social constructionism. Her belief is that both feminism and sexism, as products of the Enlightenment, rest on the same 'spurious contrast ... between rationality and intuition', a mistake which undervalues women's distinctive nature.[36] Thus the moral reasoning of women must find its place within the context of modern emphases on a rather limited kind of rationality and on the prestige of science. The greatest tensions are likely to be felt at these points, since, in the recovery of instinct, intuition, and unity with nature – all of which have been said by men to characterise the special gifts of women – there is the risk of accepting the accompanying devaluation of these gifts as second-rate forms of reason. McMillan struggles with this too, for she cannot see how women may join in the exercise of reason as transcendence of the physical, without accepting what to her are some of the great mistakes of the Enlightenment. To reach a new apprehension will require two things.

Firstly, women will need to reject the language of biological determinism, which presumes that physical realities have a simple causal relationship to personal feelings or behaviour. This presumption is based on a reduction of the natural world to measurable reactions of a mechanical kind, and is common to the naive materialism of modern science. Women know a more sophisticated embodiment than this, and realise that issues of their nature may not involve 'an inquiry into the nature of a physical entity' or be 'something that could be decided by science'.[37] She claims that those feminists who have uncritically adopted the notion of agency as control over their bodies reveal a rather restricted view of personhood.[38] Indeed, she finds this assumption of power over the body to be implicit in feminist demands for 'rights', and questions both the personal and social consequences these have. The implicit assumption that what is passive is bad, while what is active is good, suggests a psychology that is not plausible in a full human life, and is indicative of a society which cannot handle powerlessness and suffering. Thus the technological control of women's bodies at all stages of life is the sign of a society ill at ease with pain, and of women colluding in the mechanisation of their bodies.[39]

Having said this, McMillan urges women, secondly, to understand the internal relationship between social arrangements and biological realities, for 'the natural facts of human existence play a central role in the structure of our ethical institutions'.[40] Against social constructionism, women ought not to be misled into thinking that all connections between biology and society are arbitrary conventions established out of male vanity.[41] 'The salient point is that while natural facts do not determine our institutions in any absolute sense, we are likely to get into trouble sooner or later if the structure of our social institutions is such that it ignores, consciously or unconsciously, the passive givens of human existence.'[42] These givens of birth, death, and sexuality are implicit in the human condition, though differently shaped and understood, and it is with reference to them that women will find their role most meaningfully explicated.[43] Thus she encourages women to think within 'the human condition' from their special embodied position and social responsibilities, which include the ability to give birth and to nurture the young.[44] Women's distinctive 'mode of being in the world' needs the recovery of motherly reason, and a reconsideration of virtue ethics.[45] Obedience, humility, and patience, she argues, can be reclaimed from the prejudiced attention to their unnecessarily male-biased presumptions and be released to develop the fullness of their contribution to human social life.[46] This will most especially be the responsibility of women.

A fuller description of this reclamation is given by Nel Noddings, who offers *Caring: A Feminine Approach to Ethics and Moral Education*, as a corrective to the male bias in ethics. Following the arguments of Gilligan and others, that men learn morality through the experience of separation and judgement, Noddings believes this ethic of 'Logos' is at the root of the problems of violence in the world.[47] She makes no apology for describing a radical alternative, for what is 'the more natural and, perhaps, stronger approach ... through Eros, the feminine spirit'.[48] She means by this, 'feminine in the deep classical sense – rooted in receptivity, relatedness, and responsiveness',[49] asserting that 'relation will be taken as ontologically basic and the caring relation as ethically basic'.[50] In her description of this natural base, Noddings suggests the possibility of 'a form of caring natural and accessible to all human beings', which furnishes the irremovable subjective core of morality.[51] However, these are aspects of human nature into which women have privileged access and insight through their biological capacity for mothering, for it is in mothering that the basic relationality of our humanness is formed.[52] Thus, caring is central to the self-image of women through 'biologically facilitative factors' that are not available to men.[53] This form of naturalism is believed by many feminists to be irreconcilable with a religion constructed by men around a righteous and distant Father-God, and illustrates one of the areas of tension between feminism and Christian ethics.[54]

Caring requires an alternative form of moral knowing that does not centre on the discovery of general principles, or on obedience to external commands, but rather on an apprehension of the reality of another person. Intrinsic to the activity of caring is the 'displacement of interest from my own reality to the reality of the other', which Noddings describes as a kind of receptivity not quite the same as empathy.[55] This kind of moral attentiveness develops from an initial apprehension of the other's reality into a fellow-feeling, into a commitment to act, and then into a continued renewal of commitment when the feelings have faded. Noddings describes this as the process by which the ethical self is formed, as our capacity for judgement, and our openness to expanding circles of care are developed. An ethic of care affirms the importance of particular individuals, expresses the joy of relationships, and celebrates the concrete details of everyday living in which and from which the toughness of caring needs to be fashioned. In all of this, Noddings seeks to describe a 'faithfulness to the fundamental relatedness that induces caring', for she considers this to be central to human growth and flourishing, and the very heart of a feminine approach to ethics. [56]

Noddings' appropriation of the naturalistic paradigm owes much to those moral philosophers who have stressed the role of sentiment or feeling in ethics. Through their appreciation of the non-rational in human life, Noddings is encouraged to develop an analysis of emotions as both receptive and intentional, rather than as merely private internal states. Revising Hume, she argues that morality is based on two sentiments, both 'the sentiment of natural caring', which is innate in each of us, and a responsive sentiment, by which this first is kindled and remembered.[57] In common with other naturalists in ethics, she argues that 'natural caring – some degree of which each of us has been dependent upon for our continued existence – is the natural state that we inevitably identify as "good"'.[58] This experience gives rise to the 'I must' of ethics, an obligation which 'arises directly and prior to consideration of what it is that I might do'.[59] From this instinctive origin comes the hard work of conscience that must now develop the will to be faithful, and encourage those intentions that are true to this relational context.[60] Against the abstraction of universal love, this is an ethic which recognises that the 'imperative in relation is categorical', and also that a careful pragmatism is required to sustain caring relationships.[61] Thus an ethic of care encourages the development of personal character in all its fullness, as well as the preservation of 'the possibility of future caring', the details of which she presents as a feminine approach to moral education.[62]

In the work of Lisa Sowle Cahill, we meet a form of feminist naturalism rooted in Roman Catholic moral theology, which she believes is 'particularly hospitable to the assumption that investigation of human experience will contribute fruitfully to normative ethics'.[63] Since our human nature 'can be known and appreciated at least in its fundamental outlines by well-intentioned persons thinking rationally', the task of deriving theories of natural law from these basic and shared human realities is central to Christian ethical theory.[64] Therefore she claims that 'a thorough feminist revision',[65] of the ethics of sexuality is both compatible with, and indeed required by, the logic of this tradition. New information and insight from the experiences of women, as well as continuing empirical studies of gender in the human sciences, will challenge a reconsideration of what has in the past been considered normatively human, and of what has been derived from scripture. Affirmations about human nature within scripture suggest that both gender differentiation and embodiment are central, rather than peripheral, features of full human life. Not only is this distinction between the sexes 'necessary for humanity's completion but also ... part of the human creature's good, appropriate, and blessed finitude'.[66] What is not intrinsic to such claims is any notion of subordination of one gender to the other, any sense that the characteristics of one are inferior to the other, and any implication that sexuality is purely utilitarian. These assumptions are the consequences of sin, and therefore do not belong in a description of what is normatively human. It is the particular critical and innovative task of feminism to challenge precisely these assumptions, and thereby to offer to Christian ethics a more appropriate understanding of humanness.[67]

The task of doing so requires precisely the kind of reasoning which is distinctive in this paradigm, namely a willingness to participate in a continuous dialogue between the various sources of Christian ethical insight, accompanied by both tentativeness and realism. There is no sense in which knowledge of human nature forms a permanent, abstract, unchanging, or ahistorical foundation for morality, and neither does Cahill believe that such is required in Catholic moral theology.[68] Thus she argues that 'the project of defining "human nature" no longer depends on establishing *clear and distinct*, as well as *culturally transcendent*, ideas of "uniquely" human characteristics shared by all the species' normal members'.[69] Instead, we must enter into constructive conversation with the empirical sciences which offer descriptions of real human situations, in a way that 'gives us a "window" onto the normative',[70] and allows inductions from 'concrete elements in human experience' to what is 'hypothetically universal'.[71] This process allows us to make some meaningful contextual assertions about human nature, while at the same time recognising that these constructions 'are to an extent human fabrications within a given socio-cultural perspective'.[72] What such 'empirically based generalizations' may provide is some notion of 'the range of possible human properties and of the arrangements into which they are likely to fall', without determining in some fixed way exactly how those will be realised or expressed.[73] The whole Christian community is involved in these 'processes of recognition', whereby both the signs of the presence of God may be seen and understood, and the church may be 'true to its own historical experience as covenant people of God'.[74]

Cahill indicates her own integrative approach to moral issues in her investigation of the nature of sexuality. Understanding sex to be a 'language' which has 'unitive and communicative powers', she considers the important contribution which feminism has made to a properly relational view of sex. The experience of women, in 'both its biological and its historical contours', gives a window 'onto the elemental meanings of human sexuality', and points to the fullness of the human person beyond biological determinism and unrestrained freedom.[75] Feminism seeks an understanding of sexuality in which 'Biology is not destiny. Neither is freedom disincarnate'.[76] The wisdom of women regarding sexuality has not only complemented Freud's connection of sex 'with the deepest reserves of the personality', but has also linked sex with 'the heights of human communion, and even with the transcendent'.[77] To claim that the body is 'the locus of our full personal existence' is to place women and men within the same interpretive framework, and thereby to challenge all forms of dualistic thinking that degrade the body and identify women with its lesser status.[78]

This exploration of the importance of relationality to our understanding of human nature is further elaborated by Carter Heyward. A priest in the Episcopal Church of the United States, she came out as a lesbian in 1979, and continues to challenge the church with questions regarding the imposition of gender identity and the practice of sexual relationships. She argues that biblical texts regarding two sexes should not be read, as Cahill does, as imposing gender differentiation, but rather should be understood as insights into the relational character of human being. It is our human nature to be made for relationship, with one another, with the earth, and with God, and to participate in honest, just, and empowering relationships is to fulfill our humanness. Women have particular insight into, and experience of, relationship through their own bodies, as ones capable of bearing and nursing children, as ones who know sexuality in a special way, and also through their experiences as outsiders to structures of power. Heyward's relational ethic is an attempt to affirm the wisdom of women, and the longing of women for relationship, which have been ignored, feared, kept to the margins, or rendered insignificant through the Christian tradition and the institutional church. It is the special task of Christian women today to live in the contradiction between the truths of their humanness, which are good and trustworthy insights into the will of the God for the whole creation, and the teachings and practices of a church which is frightened of, or undervalues, these. She does not, like Daly, believe that this requires an exodus from the church, but rather the 'prerogative to trans-valuate traditional Christian or religious norms', which is the continuing task of Christian feminism.[79]

This means that feminists will be constantly probing behind the surface of moral claims and ideals to ask questions about their implications for relationship. Since the point of moral thinking and argument is actually to participate in the loving work of God in the midst of the world, the fundamental issue in moral teaching is whether or not obedience to the imperatives brings about loving transformations in the world. To search for this kind of truth means that the moral person is attempting to be realistic in different situations, recognising the potential ambiguities of judgement and decision, and experiencing the tensions between the relational imperative and unjust struc-tures. Gay and lesbian Christians are particular examples of this kind of reasoning, for Heyward understands them to be challenging the assumptions of 'natural' heterosexuality with concerns about the quality of relation between the persons involved. The threat that this poses to bring down the whole sacred canopy under which 'normal' sexual relations have been preserved, is also the promise of a much richer under-standing of love, and a more inventive kind of creativity than the procreation of children alone may suggest.[80] To dispute what has been considered natural with a new description of the natural, Heyward admits makes her feel a kind of 'craziness', and she holds before herself the very serious question of whether she is 'concocting a reality' to suit herself.[81] That this should be troublesome is indicative of a paradigm in which there is no place ultimately to stand to determine this once and for all. Thus Heyward understands that moral disagreements will be conflicts of vision from within embodied experience, and her hope is that, amidst these disputes, we will encounter the transcendence of God, not as a disinterested otherness, but as a 'crossing over' of power, as a breaking down of barriers, as the making of connections, through which human life may be sustained and enriched.[82]

Once again, we meet an integrative view of the human person in her description of sexuality as both a bodily and a spiritual reality. Women's knowledge of sexuality is special here, for it speaks to, and longs for, the interrelation of all things in a way that approximates divine creativity and love. Indeed, human bodies are more than flesh, they are also the presence of God in the world, so that as we act, and love, and suffer, and enjoy, we are actually 'bringing God to life again, and again'.[83] Thus, 'our bodies *are* ourselves ... And it is as bodies that we share creative power: intellectual, moral, emotional, spiritual power. As physical beings – we come to know ourselves, and one another, and we come into a power that moves among us, between us, within us, inspiring, encouraging us toward the realization of what may be best for all of us.'[84] To know this is to take more seriously our responsibility for our bodies, and to appreciate more fully the significance of our relationships with others. Such knowledge demands the work of love as 'making justice in the world', and the commitment to be faithful to the love of God, as it demands also the work of criticism when right relation is denied.[85] Living in the fullness of the body is therefore not, as the inherited fears of the Christian tradition would have us believe, a revelling in a self-indulgent licence to do whatever one wants, but an expression of the compassion given to us by nature, known to us in our inmost desires, and attuned with the divine compassion through which the world is made whole.

These uses of the naturalistic paradigm by different feminists demonstrate the variety of ways in which it has been interpreted and applied to the lives of women. Grounding its recommendations within some broad understanding of human nature, this paradigm has provided a framework that directs attention to that which is universal, as well as to that which is immediately experienced by individuals. As a way of understanding feminist ethics, it has much to commend itself as a positive expression of the distinctive contribution of women to moral knowledge and behaviour. To get hold of the conception which women have of human nature has been important, not only for the authentic expression of women's experiences and values, but also for the broadening of our general understanding of what it means to be human. This kind of feminism raises questions about the supposed gender neutrality of accounts of the human, and argues that the category of the human needs now to be inclusive, to take account of what may have been overlooked or denied in previous formulations. To be able to recognise the limitations of naturalism within the tradition is a courageous step, for it requires a willingness to understand that what is given is also grasped by human consciousness and interpreted through embodied experiences. The outstanding contribution of a naturalistic feminism has been to require a greater thoughtfulness and self-awareness on the part of those who would present such a form of ethical reasoning today.

Within the application of the paradigm, however, lie difficult and unresolved tensions regarding its political implications, and its consequences for those who have once been or still are within the Christian community. The extent to which a tradition is revisable is one of those issues, for there is a tendency within this approach to moral reasoning to make broad generalisations about what has always been the case, or what is true everywhere. Feminists who seek to question those generalisations on the basis of new ones can find themselves in deadlock, struggling against a framework which digs itself even more firmly into the ground of what has previously been said, and shrinking both its own understanding of humanness and its awareness of human responsibility for the tradition beyond all reasonable belief. To find themselves in this place has led many naturalistic feminists to seek separation, and traditionalist institutions, like the church, to claim a hollow victory. Again, the outstanding contribution of a naturalistic feminism is its serious desire to meet the tradition in discussion of a subject that matters intensely to all concerned, with a shared interest in its social implications and practical applications. A careful critique of this paradigm will be helpful as a way of highlighting some of these issues more explicitly, and of considering its potential usefulness for the dialogue of feminism and Christian ethics.

CHAPTER 7

Critique of naturalism

Few works have described so vividly the renewal of a naturalist paradigm in society as that by Margaret Atwood, in *The Handmaid's Tale*.[1] Published in 1985, this novel presents an anti-utopian vision of the future, unfolding some of the problematic implications of trends and ideologies in the present world. At one level, the story demonstrates the consequences of a politics of scriptural fundamentalism, which in this case takes certain passages of the Bible to be unquestionably authoritative and applicable directly to disconcerting contemporary situations. Thus, in the setting of 1980s New England, major concerns are developing around the breakdown of traditional family life, the campaigns of feminists for equal rights, the legal practice of abortions, the prevalence of same-sex relationships, unprecedented levels of environmental pollution, and the uncontrollable spread of sexually transmitted disease. All of these suggest a society which has lost its basic social units, through a combination of individual freedom of choice and successive short-term relationships, and which is now worried about the health and the future of humanity. The solution to these concerns appears to lie in a tightly controlled form of ascetic discipline throughout the public and private realms, which the political revolution violently imposes, supported by the straightforward use of biblical texts. The land is returned to the rule of the Fathers, modelled after the Old Testament patriarch, Jacob, for whom wives and concubines are provided to propagate the species, modelled after Rachel and Leah, and who may once again worship their God in the cleansed and promised land of Gilead. Atwood presents in this novel a stripped-down version of naturalism which has little sophistication or subtlety, but a chilling sense of plausibility.

The storyteller is a young woman, raised by a single and actively feminist mother, who has been to university, held a responsible job, and had an affair with a married man whom she later marries and who is the father of her daughter. She is typical, in that her life is a composite of recognisable features of young women we know, and her joys and sorrows, decisions and mistakes, are ones with which we too are familiar. Under the new regime, she is taken as a Handmaid, whose function it is to allow herself to become impregnated by the Head of a Household in the presence of his Wife, whose function it is, in turn, to raise the child and to create an air of social respectability within the domestic domain. These women, as indeed all persons in this new society, are kept in their places by forms of surveillance and by armed Guardians, for they have particular socially necessary functions to perform that are meant to constitute their complete identity. Their lives are strictly circumscribed by these roles, through which they contribute to the welfare of the body politic, and ensure the survival of the human race for another generation. Social control of human beings is sustained through rituals, regulated language, uniforms and names to identify function, and strict training. The new society has abolished freedom of choice altogether, as it has outlawed the confused variety of alternative life styles, both of which are believed to have contributed to the widespread violence, and to the abuse and degradation of women and children, characteristic of the former society. This new one presents itself as a rational alternative, truer to the best potential of human nature, and justified by sacred texts.

On another level, this novel expresses one woman's struggle to understand herself and the meaning of her life in the context of a major shift in political and moral thinking. It is true that her memories disturb, and that wondering what has happened to those whom she has loved consumes much of her time and emotional energy when alone. Under the new system, these memories would presumably no longer be problematic, for she would not understand the anguish they present. It is true that she still knows and uses the former names of her friends, and has not yet accepted the new names of Handmaids – Offred, Ofwarren, and so on, which name the Commander whose temporary possession they have become. So it is also true that her decision-making has not quite adjusted to the new values, as she continues to look for companionship. These values will disappear as personal names do, and as language to describe friendship, and indeed love, becomes no longer available. It is true that her hopes are confused as the context in which to realise them has so drastically altered, and as the very real option of suicide presents itself vividly to her. Hopes will be shrunk into expectations in a social order of monotonous regularity, and the boundaries of her life will be defined by fear. In all of these things, the narrator lets us feel the turmoil of social change, and her 'limping and mutilated story' reflects the fragmentation of her life.[2]

Through the changing scenery, however, are some very real questions about this new life, questions which are left as ghosts haunting the text long after the reading of it is finished, and which lead us into the deeper implications of this paradigm. Something has happened to language in the new society. The regulation of social intercourse is facilitated through the imposition of a strict formality in everyday conversation, and through the return of naive realism to language. Handmaids greet one another by saying, 'Blessed be the fruit' and 'May the Lord open',[3] formulae which serve the dual purpose of confirming them in their appropriate social function, and of directing their attention to that part of the body which is most necessary to this. Similarly, it was 'decided that even the names of shops were too much temptation for us. Now places are known by their signs alone',[4] signs which picture the things on sale within. So too the computerised prayer factory, 'Soul Scrolls', receives orders for prayers by telephone, to be mechanically printed and voiced on behalf of the purchaser. To pray in this new society is to order the production of words, as to have 'faith' is to believe that God records all of this literally in 'listening'.[5] By a renewed insistence that language describes things in the common world, and more specifically tangible physical reality within that world, a process of reification takes place. In this process, language is believed literally to refer to what is 'there', and what is 'there' serves as the foundation upon which the new society is structured. That the naive realism of language becomes the necessary tool of an authoritarian political ideology is the haunting question left by the text.

Something has happened also to women in the new society of Gilead. Women become objects here, defined and used by men, for purposes which men have determined are important. The narrator, Offred, describes her encounter in the doctor's office receiving a gyneacological examination. Following a custom familiar in some parts of the world, she is screened from the doctor by a sheet dropped from above, falling just at her neck-line, so that she appears to him only as a torso without a head. She knows her body to be 'poked and prodded' by a 'rubber-clad and jellied' cold finger, while the doctor calls her 'Honey', without any intimacy of relation, but only the assumption that she too is generically a 'wife'.[6] His masked voice offers to impregnate her illegally, under the guise of concern for her welfare, lest she be sent away as an Unwoman through suspicion of infertility.

This total identification with function allows only a limited kind of friendship, as a few days later her Commander falteringly seeks a different approach. Requesting that she come to him after lights out, he asks her to play Scrabble with him, and offers her forbidden magazines and books to read. Offred knows the potential dangers of the encounter, since Handmaids are merely 'two-legged wombs ... sacred vessels, ambulatory chalices' in relation to which 'there are to be no toeholds for love'.[7] The pornographic nature of their relationship is the outcome of his freedom contrasted with her necessary obedience, and of the pleasure he derives in watching her 'enjoy' the things that his regime has forbidden. Her first evening with him concludes in her own experience of 'the wandering womb ... hysteria', as her body erupts in 'laughter boiling like lava in my throat'.[8] Atwood suggests that a restoration of naturalism necessitates an unbalanced dualism of dominance and sub-

mission, which is in the end demeaning of women, and this is
the second haunting question of the text, illustrating a further
area in which this paradigm of moral reasoning is problematic
for feminism.

The third issue concerns vision, for something has happened
to imagination in the new society. It comes as no surprise in the
story to learn that the strict gender roles required under this
regime are supported by the existence of brothels, in which
men can enjoy the forbidden and non-reproductive pleasures
of sex, and can realise in any bizarre form their personal sexual
fantasies. Offred is herself taken to Jezebel's illegally by her
Commander, who dresses her in an old satin costume with
mauve and pink feathers, and purple sequins that are 'tiny
stars'.[9] There she discovers other women dressed in a wide
variety of costumes, so that the atmosphere is something like a
masquerade party, each woman representing some man's
dream of woman. Offred is told not to give herself away by
staring, but to 'act natural', and so she tells herself to 'keep
your mouth shut and look stupid', all the while questioning, 'Is
there joy in this?'[10]

By contrast, Offred's time alone can be spent in full
awareness of her self, in a different sort of imagining altogether.
'I sink down into my body as into a swamp, fenland, where
only I know the footing'.[11] The impact of man's vision of her
self has been that 'I used to think of my body as an instrument,
of pleasure, or a means of transportation, or an implement for
the accomplishment of my will'. Alone, and away from this
company, she enters a new realisation.

Now the flesh arranges itself differently. I'm a cloud, the shape of a
pear, which is hard and more real than I am and glows red within its
translucent wrapping. Inside it is a space, huge as the sky at night
and dark and curved like that, though black-red rather than black.
Pinpoints of light swell, sparkle, burst and shrivel within it, countless
as stars. Every month there is a moon, gigantic, round, heavy, an
omen. It transits, pauses, continues on and passes out of sight, and I
see despair coming towards me like famine. To feel that empty, again,
again. I listen to my heart, wave upon wave, salty and red, continuing on and on, marking time.[12]

These words reveal to us the hidden and often unvoiced vision of woman, carried within her as 'pinpoints of light . . . countless as stars', accessible only when the categories of gender associated with naturalism are transcended altogether. The third question which haunts this text is therefore whether this paradigm can really allow the spiritual wisdom of women to be expressed in all of its distinctive fullness. The uncertain outcome of Atwood's novel suggests not, as the Handmaid sits in her room at the ending of her tale, awaiting an unknown future, holding her costume in her lap – 'a handful of crumpled stars'.[13]

The three points emerging from this story can be used to demonstrate the continuing discussion amongst feminists regarding the use of a naturalist paradigm. In these considerations, the interweaving of assumptions from the three different paradigms can be noticed more fully, as feminists from within each perspective debate with one another the implications of a naturalistic approach to morality. Similarly there are theological assumptions interwoven and entangled in this debate, which can begin to be distinguished and considered, as the intrinsic relation between feminist and Christian ethics begins to become more plain.

What has happened to language in Gilead illustrates one of the problems in the appropriation of this paradigm for feminism, for the language in which this paradigm represents moral reasoning makes credible a kind of foundationalism in ethics. The novel illustrates the power of a belief in biological imperatives, which drive this political revolution, as the basic necessities of life for reproduction and survival impose themselves with supposedly undeniable force, even as Darwin and later Freud had foretold. That these drives should somehow inevitably translate themselves into patriarchal social structures that establish man's law and order, and use women as vessels for the germination and nurturance of new life, suggests that in the end, however it is dressed up and presented, naturalism means that biology determines destiny. The fear of feminists is thus that the paradigm resists revision, and that the easy route to its acceptance is to believe that nature is a permanent base on which social life and moral decisions are to be founded. Such a foundational approach is however a diminished version of the possibilities of this paradigm.

The naturalist approach has genuinely sought a kind of sympathetic realism in ethics, discerning moral value within the world in a way that seems responsive to reality, believing the world itself to exceed any social construction of it, and to be rich with meanings that our free choices encounter. In claiming this, naturalism touches the precise point of convergence of arrogance and humility, and these qualities become part of the argument between traditional and feminist versions of the paradigm. The question of how to distinguish the humble receptiveness to meaning, by which what transcends human choice or perspective is acknowledged, from the arrogant imposition of meaning upon the world, by which advantage is gained for those who name this reality, is a constant feature of the debate. However, the circular logic of this paradigm means that no authoritative value-free place is available from which to confront a 'mythology' of natural law with a demythologised version of it, from which definitively to expose arrogance and humility, and thus this critical point, and any feminist critique of traditionalism, or vice versa, cannot be resolved by taking an outside viewpoint. The logic of this approach means that nature is not known as an uninterpreted reality, since our attempts to discern fact and value within it are indicative of a continuous process of rational engagement with what is there. What is described as, or believed to be 'given', cannot therefore be taken for granted, but is something which we struggle to understand, since the natural is altogether more elusive, more interesting, and more surprising than many descriptions of it would suggest.

Since this paradigm has been thought to embody a faithful appreciation of the creation, and of the Creator whose will is impressed within its structures and operations, this becomes also an intensely difficult theological matter for those engaged in Christian ethical thinking. Here the qualities of arrogance and humility take on the dimension of responsiveness to this Creator, in the form of obedience or disobedience to the pat-

terns and possibilities of life which are given for human fulfilment. Once again, feminists who challenge the Christian tradition believe that the easy route to the acceptance of naturalism
within Christian ethics is through the assertion that the will of
the Creator is physically scored as a single pattern of life on
each creature, and plainly recorded in certain biblical texts.
One possible Christian form of naturalistic ethics is thus a
foundational one, and this may indeed be its most popular
form. However, the challenge to it is not necessarily from those
who wish to avoid nature by simply making everything up, but
from those who are more conscious of our human responsibility
in making sense of it, and more alert to the difficulty of
understanding exactly what it is that God has created and is
creating. There may thus be a form of Christian feminist
naturalism which seeks to be faithful to the Creator's will
written within nature, in the context of serious and deep
wondering whether we have ever got it right. And so long as
this remains a burning question in the human soul, it cannot
be, and never has been, extinguished by fiat.

This paradigm has been entangled with studies of the
human body in the natural sciences, and it is in examining the
history of these studies that the problem of foundationalism can
be further illuminated. For what is plain in this history is that
proclamations regarding sex and its meaning in human life
have been made by one group at one time, to be altered or even
completely contradicted by another group at another time. To
seek a basis for moral decision in the study of biology may
therefore be more of a risky business than the upholders of this
paradigm might suggest, and is an indication of the continuing
task of interpretation of nature while we are living within it. As
an example, Londa Schiebinger has traced the debate within
the biological sciences regarding the sex of the human mind.
During the development of the new science of anatomy in the
sixteenth and seventeenth centuries, several important break-
throughs seemed to suggest and to prove a fundamental
equality of women and men, which early liberal feminists were
keen to seize upon and to utilise for social change. The Cartesian scientist, Francois Poullain, pronounced in 1673 that 'the

mind has no sex', a statement based on scientific evidence that 'Women have sense organs similar to men's and brains with the same power of reason and imagination',[14] and in addition Buffon suggested that 'the male and female contribute equally to generation'.[15] It therefore seemed reasonable to believe that 'sex is only skin deep',[16] and this was reflected in the the drawings of the human body in early textbooks.[17]

What fascinates Schiebinger is the way in which the new science changes from this initial enthusiasm and support for equality, into a fierce and highly charged assertion, and proof, of 'difference'. Indeed, science becomes through the late eighteenth century, the institution by which, and anatomists the spokesmen for, a reinstigation of the body as a site of difference of men from women, a development which points to a complex interaction of political ideologies, social changes, theological assumptions, and continuing improvements in new investigative techniques. This is noticed in relation to studies of the uterus which, in the midst of debate and uncertainty regarding how to classify it, began to focus on this organ as something wholly unique and incomparable, *sui generis*, its distinctiveness so marked from anything belonging to male anatomy, that the implications were held necessarily to be significant. This was one step in the process of a 'resexualization of the body', whereby it was to be demonstrated that sex was 'more than skin deep'.[18] Sexuality then began to be understood, not as something which resided in reproductive organs only, but as written throughout the whole body, in a way that was heavily laden with cultural values. The whole life and consciousness of the female human being was thus believed to be influenced by the presence of a womb, which imposed important social and educational requirements upon her. In the process, subtle or ambiguous aspects of anatomy were hidden within generalisations about what was 'ideal', and these ideals themselves were now reproduced in the anatomical illustrations of textbooks.[19]

Schiebinger notes that this process of demonstrating the natural basis of the complementarity of the sexes is much more than a matter of discovering facts in the natural world through observation and experiment, and then stating them in text-books and lectures. The history of this subject suggests that, although there is clearly something there to be discovered in nature, our grasp of that is entangled with many other things. It is interesting to her that beliefs about gender differences are part of a cultural history, in which notions of maleness and femaleness generally were changing quite significantly. An earlier, more metaphysical science made use of rich metaphors of male and female, in poetic language and imaginative illus-tration, understanding these to be symbolic pointers to higher truths. A whole cosmology in which the feminine was an icon of science and of truth struggled with, and lost to, a newer materialistic cosmology, so that modern science has been char-acterised by the progressive loss of this feminine imagery, replaced by the man in a white lab coat. With this shift in the meaning and self-understanding of science comes an exclusive focus on the empirical, quantifiable, and observable, and the need then for these to bear the weight of demonstration and belief regarding women and men, and indeed of sexuality in general. The idea that we might be able to appeal to facts, and more than this, the attempt to state as simple facts, the details of the male and female bodies upon which certain moral claims and social responsibilities will be constructed, is to minimise the complexity of the language of the body.

A different kind of analysis of the tendency to foundation-alism is undertaken by Sabina Lovibond, who presents a closely argued logical critique of aspects of the new realism in ethics. Recent moral philosophy, in response to the anti-authoritarian individualism of the liberal paradigm, has been emphasising the submission to reality at the heart of moral thinking in a new form of naturalism. Such an approach attempts to recover the moral meaning of nature and the embeddedness of moral language in the natural world that had been lost with the Enlightenment. Following Wittgenstein, Lovibond argues that this approach is community-dependent, since the language forms available through which the world is conceived are public ones, established within forms of life in the context of which they make sense. Within this new naturalism is thus a pull towards objectivity, not merely because the world itself pulls us towards it, but because this morality is a communal project of discovering that world. One finds therein 'the logical link between *objectivity* and *intellectual authority*'.[20] There is a shared interest in developing the common standpoint which can become the basis for a life together and the reliable grounding of decision-making, as the centre of judgement moves from the individual to the community. Since those of common viewpoint trust that what they believe in and commit themselves to is objectively real and important, the dynamic of community life becomes a feature of the logic of moral realism. Lovibond thus understands the new naturalism to be a form of social constructionism, a 'mediated' realism.[21]

There is a spurious conservatism in this approach, which, Lovibond suggests, is supported by, and manifested in, a tendency to reify the objects of value for purposes of universal agreement, to create fetishes of certain things and actions, and finally 'to conceal the role of human activity in maintaining order within the language game', for the purpose of social cohesion.[22] Much of this is characteristic of McMillan's critique of feminism, as she seeks to ground social practices in 'the human condition', which increasingly in her writing takes on a definite shape and character as 'demands of life'.[23] A community that establishes this foundation is able to adopt an authoritarian style in resisting alternative viewpoints, different perspectives on truth, and dissent in general, which would undermine the common standpoint. Thus the consensus will throw up various forms of mystification to 'segregate dissent',[24] by claiming that dissent is 'a peculiarity of isolated individuals', that it is recommending what is 'unnatural', or that the views of dissenters are 'non-traditional'.[25] All of these are types of reification, in which for example, the 'tradition' is made to seem a 'thing' that is monolithic, a fixed reality, a solid block of data, and dissent is made marginal. These manœuvres reflect a loss of confidence in the naive realism of language, and the political need to establish authority.

A naturalism that tends to foundationalism, whether of the traditional or the feminist kind, is not only unhelpful to feminism, but reduces our appreciation of the complex interpretative framework needed in response to the impingement of the physical world upon human life. Essential to the appropriation of this paradigm within feminism will be its capacity to be accepted as constituting a hermeneutic of nature, rather than a law of nature imprinted on the mind or the body, and, in so far as it is a hermeneutic, to be able to participate, women and men together, in delineating its outlines and implications. Within that interpretative exercise, descriptions of the balance between what more regularly underlies human behaviour and what is historically changeable and socially constructed, as between what is instinctual and what is rational, are crucial, both to the self-understanding of women and men, and to the entire vision for human life which the paradigm upholds. This is a major undertaking for ethics, but it is one with which a naturalistic approach ultimately challenges us to engage.

The objectification of women is the second problematic area within this paradigm. Atwood's novel demonstrates the ease with which the exploitation of distinctive natural interests of women reasserts itself, in the face of what were considered the temporary and superfluous eruptions of feminist egalitarianism. No matter how feminists may think they are turning this paradigm to women's advantage, it relies upon ahistorical generalisations about women, and colludes with the descriptions which have traditionally been given of their receptive nature and nurturing potential. When these qualities are introduced into social patterns and economic life, they are found to be structurally subservient, and logically secondary, to the ones characteristic of men, and thus the old inequalities of dominance and submission are reintroduced in a new guise. Feminists therefore challenge this paradigm for affirming values that insulate those on top of the social hierarchy, while facilitating their access to the resources of those underneath, so graphically illustrated in the doctor's examination. The complementarity of woman and man sought by naturalism is thus a snare and delusion. The reaffirmation of a double standard of moral virtue appears to be implicit within this paradigm, pointing not to the liberation of women in the future, but rather to their continued participation in an oppressive past, as the Handmaid is virtually imprisoned in her tiny room.

The advantage of a naturalistic paradigm for feminism has been the attempt to ground itself in women's experience, and both to affirm and to make creative use of the moral wisdom which comes through women's consciousness. Such a positioning is fraught with ambiguities, in that it is rooted within the context of structures that are experienced as oppressive, and of values that are unequally distributed and determined. Furthermore, to build a distinctive ethic here is to develop some notion of an ideal person, and of ideal forms of behaviour, on the basis of different human experiences. The question central to a critique of naturalism is thus twofold. The first aspect of the question is to enquire about the status of claims regarding difference, and to ask whether these are so fixed into ontological categories that the separation of human beings into two types becomes an essential feature of this paradigm. Whether naturalism necessarily entails ontological dualism is one consideration. The second aspect of the question concerns the implications of this separation, for it can be argued that things are divided into two by means of contrast and opposition, and that this division logically gives priority to the first term. Whether naturalism necessarily entails a relation of superiority and inferiority is another consideration. Forms of ethical naturalism have tended to box women in, while giving men the freedom of the universe, and whether a form may be found in which this is not the case is the challenge from feminism.

Feminists have made different kinds of responses to these dilemmas of naturalism, which, as indicated in the previous chapter, is one of the reasons for the intensity of debate regarding this paradigm. Some will argue for giving priority to the female term in a dualism, and will seek to unsettle the traditional relationship by means of reversing the valuations given. This has the advantage of placing women first, and can be clearly identified as a feminist stance in promoting women's interests. Others will argue for the abandonment of dualism altogether, in favour of a recognition of the diversity of human beings, within which all kinds of persons can be located. This has the advantage of avoiding any preferential identification of some human beings as the standard by which others are judged. Each of these responses also has disadvantages, for the first can captivate women with a set of expectations for their lives just as much as it can stereotype men, while the second can render women invisible once again in the general category of the human. It has been precisely the dilemma experienced in having to make this choice which constitutes much of the attraction of a postmodern approach to ethics that abandons humanism altogether. What will be important for a feminist appropriation of naturalism is a more flexible and open-ended description of human nature.

For the Christian feminist, the critique of naturalism touches some problematic areas of the doctrine of human nature that are still the subject of continued debate. The matter of the division of humanity into two categories calls for careful biblical exegesis as well as close investigation of the theological tradition, but Christian feminists are not convinced that dualism does justice to the real and the potential diversity of human beings. In addition, they have borne the brunt of the oppositional nature of these categories throughout the history of the church, and are therefore unhappy with a male/female dualism as the purportedly ideal form of human relationship. Feminists are pressing for further consideration of what constitutes the *imago dei* in which human beings are created, by challenging some of the assumptions carried through the tradition regarding both the inferiority of women in relation to this image, and the compulsory complementarity which has been considered essential to its embodiment. In making these challenges, feminists are expressing a critical awareness that descriptions of human nature are implicated in unjust social structures, and caught up in ongoing failures of human relationships. Such a keen sense of the consequences of sin in our human understanding of ourselves expresses also the longing of feminists for a description of aspects of humanness which can provide a context for the works of justice and of love.

Jean Grimshaw takes up the problem of the validity of an

ethic constructed upon ideas of feminine nature, arguing that, in this form at least, naturalism will not be helpful to feminism. Much of the plausibility of belief in a separate women's nature and insight has been derived from the lived discrepancy between existing moral theories, ideals, and language, and women's experiences. The idea of women's distinctiveness has therefore also been established in opposition, and built upon beliefs about the nature of men and of men's morality. She questions whether women in fact have a really 'autonomous' nature on the basis of which an alternative ethic can be founded, underneath which is her concern that this separation of female and male natures, which also establishes two distinct sets of ethical requirements, can be politically defeatist. The claims of a separate women's morality can amount to stating the obvious, in a way that affirms women in the things they are already doing and thinking, and provides a positive identity for them as a group. However, unless these values can be reattached to something of our common human life, they become irrelevant, leaving a divided society no better off than before.[26]

Since many naturalistic feminists clearly do seek to engage in social challenge and change, Grimshaw argues that descriptions of human nature must be set within an analysis of existing power relations. Without a thoroughgoing critique of social and economic structures, feminist descriptions of the special qualities of women's nature will both repeat and strengthen the ideologies that have been considered unhelpful and oppressive in the past. With reference to the work of Gilligan and Noddings, she finds a tendency to affirm the more 'nebulous or unfathomable' nature of women's moral reasoning, which dangerously colludes with male prejudice.[27] Thereby the particular emphasis placed on the 'different voice' of women not only repeats some of the prejudices about women against which liberal feminists fight so hard, but will so remove women from discussion of general moral principles that their participation in wider political debate will become problematic. In addition, feminist insistence upon this distinctiveness becomes itself a kind of ideal by which women also judge one another, a new ideology which exercises its own control over the lives of women.[28] That this can and does become easily linked to new forms of economic exploitation of those who care, and to the isolation of those for whom relationships are important into private spheres of activity, is an indication that naturalistic feminism can serve the interests of those already in power very well. Indeed, stressing women's virtues as care, or as concern for relationships, can actually give a society and its dominant institutions greater access to women's loyalties by relying on those very things which she too believes are her strengths. The best society in which the complementary approaches of women and men can be given full scope for appreciation and development may turn out to be Gilead.[29]

Finally, Grimshaw is doubtful about the generalisations made regarding women and men, which become ahistorical and simplistic, and which tend to lift the reasoning that is meant to be characteristic of this paradigm out of the complexities of human life, and the varieties of human experience, in which it is most meaningfully set. Cultural and linguistic differences make the classifications of women difficult to sustain in any universal sense, because what counts as caring, or concern for relationship, can differ so widely. The consequence of generalisations may be that we miss the subtleties of decision-making which are a feature of everyday life, and which require us to understand what would constitute care in particular circumstances. This process of seeking to understand is what constitutes reasoning, a process in which women and men alike engage in complicated and overlapping ways. Thus, she claims, 'there is no non-contested or isolable paradigm of female values or priorities which can be seen as a source for feminist philosophical thinking'.[30] Rather feminists can contribute to a thorough 'reevaluation of concepts, theories and priorities' which will provide a better framework of understanding for the whole of human life.[31]

A different version of the problem of dualistic thinking in this paradigm is given by Susan Brooks Thistlethwaite, who explores the theological implications of the fact that naturalistic feminism has been primarily articulated by white women. In their concern to reappraise the relationship of women and nature in a positive way, naturalistic feminists have left the implications of class and race out of account, reproducing unhelpful generalisations about all women which are inaccurate, and which serve to strengthen and to hide the social and economic oppression of black women. The sense of unity amongst women which is developed through appreciation of common experiences and insights carries 'the distorted freight of one's own social location', from which women claim privileged access to ontological truth, and seek to disturb patriarchal falsehood.[32] Black women argue that their own different experiences of life do not fit the descriptions given, and furthermore that, when their experiences are introduced, naturalistic feminism is shown to be colluding in, rather than reversing, existing racist prejudices regarding the natural world, difference, and evil.

Many feminists who appropriate this paradigm for moral thinking have rejoiced in the belief that 'female is to male as nature is to culture'.[33] All that is wholesome and life-giving is believed to reside in nature, in creation, where connectedness and bodiliness and goodness can be affirmed and celebrated. Black women's experience of nature does not on the whole affirm this naive 'biophilia', which indeed may itself be the product of the privilege of white women's lives, protected from the harsher realities of nature by the work of slaves. Similarly, naturalistic feminists presume that they have affirmed difference, by positively evaluating the skills and insights of women neglected or undervalued in the tradition. This affirmation is however dependent upon universal statements about women which ignore their cultural and racial differences, which indeed show a disrespect for boundaries in an enthusiastic concern for connectedness, and which in the end find differences problematic.[34] Black women are thus made to bear the burden of really being different, since they cannot even identify with what is being called 'woman'.[35] Further, there is an affirmation of the unambiguous goodness of women's nurturing and caring, which tends to assume that women are unaffected by the Fall, and that the overcoming of evil is possible through identification with the untainted nature that is dormant within them. The writings of black women indicate an awareness of the ambiguities of the human situation, and a familiarity with violence, aggression, death, and suffering, that makes the writings of feminists seem idealistic and one-sided. Unless good and evil are understood to be intertwined, and the powerful spiritual forces in the universe recognised as both creative and destructive within women's lives, again the prejudice that blackness is associated with evil is reinforced, and 'racial conflicts among women' are hidden.[36]

Thistlethwaite's analysis reveals the influence of Tillich upon feminism, particularly through the work of Daly, and her critique suggests some of the ways in which his theology may not be helpful to Christian feminism. In an interesting way, Daly shares Tillich's understanding of existence as characterised by separation, for we live with distinctions in daily experience that alienate persons from one another. Thus, she argues that in the foreground of human life, the world is divided up by men for their purposes and pleasures, social structures are invented to sustain these divisions, and these are confirmed and worshipped in various forms of false religion, or idolatry. Daly's intention is to describe the background, the realm beyond mere existence in which separation is overcome, and unity may be celebrated. It is in this place that the god beyond God is discovered, and a life-sustaining ethic may be established on pure ground untouched by male-factors. Thistlethwaite is rightly critical of the search for purity in a pre-lapsarian state of oneness, and of the inevitable abstraction required to remove oneself from the messy ambiguities of life. These points serve to suggest that a form of feminist naturalism which will be helpful to the lives and experiences of real women will need to accommodate diversity much more than some forms of this paradigm do, and will need to take realistic account of the politics of dualism into which a female ethic may unwittingly feed.

The friendly game of Scrabble between Offred and her Commander concludes with her eruption of laughter, as she collapses into the wardrobe back in her room in inarticulate hysteria. Something has happened to the imagination in

Gilead, leaving women to play controlled games of words with men, or to perform men's fantasies in the now seedy hotels at the fringes of the official social order. The concern of some feminists is that the dimensions of human nature, which this society incorporates in dualistic form, are not wide enough to accommodate the imaginative flights of vision and of possibility of which women are capable. To remain within the bounds of humanness leaves only the predictable options of doing what supposedly comes naturally to women – reading fashion magazines, helping one another in natural childbirth, or looking after relationships – these changing of course with different cultural manifestations. The spiritual insight of women may exceed these bounds, in ways that have been known to be dangerous and anti-social, since they express what cannot be formulated or embodied within any given order. To a certain extent, these insights are anti-humanist, in that they disrupt settled assumptions about human nature, and express something of a divine madness that sweeps away the dross of personal identity. However, these insights are also fully human, in that they are incarnate in women, manifest in the bodily sensitivity of women, and uttered through women's constantly displaced desires. It is the paradox of this imagination which the naturalistic paradigm seems inadequate to render meaningfully, and therefore the hopes this paradigm can formulate are constrained by the obvious.

This critique of naturalism may be traced also to the work of de Beauvoir who, in yet another appreciation of the richness of her writing, is believed by many to have changed the course of feminist argument with *The Second Sex*. Her investigation of the process by which the 'feminine' is created, moved feminist debate into a consideration of the inadequacy of all systems of thought to address 'the woman question'.[37] Without claiming that these systems were biased by being expressions of male embodiment or perspective, she argued that their limitations were the result of the fact that 'Otherness is a fundamental category of human thought'.[38] Since women are defined and conceptualised as 'the Other in a totality of which the two components are necessary to one another', they are not only always understood as beings-in-relation, but cannot be understood as they are in themselves within existing forms of thought.[39] For de Beauvoir, therefore, 'The drama of woman lies in this conflict between the fundamental aspirations of every subject (ego) – who always regards the self as the essential – and the compulsions of a situation in which she is the inessential. How can a human being in woman's situation attain fulfillment?'[40] Such thoughts, and the breadth of investigation by which de Beauvoir demonstrates them, proved inspiring to a cluster of new French feminisms, which have taken up the challenge of finding woman as she is in herself.

While much of their work is considered to be 'essentialist', in seeming to imply that particular women are instances of a general type that precedes and determines their individual existences, the writings of these feminists attempt to give voice to the woman who exceeds categorisation, who slips away from definition, who lives around the borders of human thought. In this sense, the challenge they present to a naturalistic paradigm is to insist that its terms may be too limiting for women, and that the full nature of woman will not be grasped simply in opposition to that of man. Similarly, their challenge is to the circularity of logic characteristic of this paradigm, for the insight of women is understood to challenge what language and culture represents as fact – what is the case, not with some statement of principle, but with what comes from outside culture, from the repressed that has been set outside existing language forms. What women know is what has been absent from culture and language, and to express this is therefore to speak from a transcendence that is out of this world.

Finally, the work of these feminists is a recovery of the language of the body, in a way that distinguishes it from Anglo-American feminist thinking. While the latter have used the word 'sex' to mean a set of anatomical facts about the body, and the word 'gender' to mean cultural constructions of bodily identity, French feminists do not use this dualism. In so far as the naturalist paradigm has been an attempt to get back to the basics of anatomy, which are held to be more fundamental to human nature than changing ideas about gender, it has missed the point about the uniqueness of women, re-placing women in categories that are insufficient to their distinctive being. The emphasis of French feminists on 'writing the body' is on morphology, a term that incorporates both physical and social realities. Women are encouraged to speak from the wholeness of their bodily experience, to express political and moral realities that are there embodied, and to make present in the world the absent wisdom about which the world itself cannot speak.[41]

These ideas are especially interesting to Christian feminists, for whom the reality of women's lives on the boundaries of culture is no new phenomenon. Throughout biblical texts, and in the history of the churches, women have been the absent or the silent figures on the fringes of stories and events, whose presence has been noted in order to confine it to expected responses or necessary actions. Attempts to recover what women themselves were thinking, feeling, or doing has been an important work of women's biblical studies, so that women imaginatively reproduce what the lives of Hebrew women were like during the Exodus, what Bathsheba would have spoken about in her relationship with David, what the woman who anointed Jesus' feet believed she was doing, or how women understood themselves in the early communities of Christians. These are matters about which the texts are silent, and for women to begin to give voice to these things is a challenge to the cultural construction of the Bible, in which women rarely speak directly. To engage in this work is to affirm that the wisdom women may utter is another kind of expression of divine truth, which constantly slips away from the captivity of a patriarchal tradition and a male-centred theology. For this reason, feminist theologians draw strength from the understanding that the divine Spirit is a feminine noun, so that the movements of this Spirit throughout creation and in everyday life, and the possibilities which this Spirit can make real in the future, may have direct connections with the imaginations of living women, whose existence is precisely at these margins. The fact that women may envision a new heaven and a new earth from this place is a bold proclamation that from their bodies they may even give birth to God.[42]

In her brief essay, 'The Laugh of the Medusa', Helene Cixous makes the contributions of new French feminisms clear, and from her piece we can draw out the implications for the naturalistic paradigm. Firstly, she emphasises the limitations of woman's nature when she is understood to be the 'Other', constructed in the image of man as his opposite, made into his other half. She has been drawn into this role through man's 'enticement machine',[43] which has lured women 'with flashy signifiers' and 'sells them the same old handcuffs, baubles, and chains'.[44] Accordingly, woman has 'constituted herself necessarily as that "person" capable of losing a part of herself without losing her integrity', and in this role has understood herself to be 'a giver'.[45] A feminist naturalism which writes of women in this way, and evaluates positively the contribution women can make to the complementarity of the sexes is, for Cixous, presenting a person who has chosen what 'she can merge with, without annihilating herself', but who is not as she might be in the fullness of her being.[46] To begin to challenge this limitation is to unsettle all human relationships, for 'her liberation will do more than modify power relations or toss the ball over to the other camp'. Hers is a dream of liberation which 'does extend beyond men's imagination',[47] and requires us to 'defetishize' as men and women together, by rendering 'obsolete the former relationship and all its consequences'.[48]

Cixous understands the source of these imaginings to be the bodied experience of women beyond all cultural and linguistic constructions. A woman is 'a moving, limitlessly changing ensemble, a cosmos tirelessly traversed by Eros, an immense astral space not organized around any one sun that's any more of a star than the others'.[49] From this cosmic identity, women write the imaginings of their displaced desires, their repressed but never sublimated libido, expressing the potential for the fullness of being, rather than its partial segments.

If woman has always functioned "within" the discourse of man, a signifier that has always referred back to the opposite signifier which annihilates its specific energy and diminishes or stifles its very different sounds, it is time for her to dislocate this 'within', to explode it, turn it around, and seize it; to make it hers, containing it, taking it in her own mouth, biting that tongue with her very own teeth to invent for herself a language to get inside of.[50]

Such language comes from the future; it is written in anticipation, and for Cixous, 'Anticipation is imperative'.[51] Thus she understands that women have 'come back from always' to speak of the happiness and the love that is possible but not yet here.[52] Contingencies of the present do not 'prevent woman from starting the history of life somewhere else'.[53]

The imagination of woman as she writes her body speaks a love that does not 'need'; it is not constituted by a lack which has 'to be filled out'. Her love expresses the fact that 'living means wanting everything that is, everything that lives, and wanting it alive'.[54] Her inexhaustible imaginary[55] writes in a language that 'does not contain, it carries; it does not hold back, it makes possible',[56] and in this form she manifests the power of 'the song: first music from the first voice of love which is alive in every woman'.[57] Cixous' vision for this love is of a transformation, which has 'far more radical effects of political and social change than some might like to think'.[58] Its embodiment is in women who give:

> She doesn't 'know' what she's giving, she doesn't measure it ... She gives that there may be life, thought, transformation. This is an 'economy' that can no longer be put in economic terms. Wherever she loves, all the old concepts of management are left behind ... everything we will be calls us to the unflagging, intoxicating, unappeasable search for love.[59]

Here the distinctive possibilities of women's imagining are described as love without end, which 'rejoices in the exchange that multiplies' and speaks from an anticipated fullness of life.[60]

In her studies of the Old Testament, the feminist biblical scholar, Phyllis Trible, has shown in quite remarkable ways the presence of such imaginings and voices in the women of an ancient patriarchal society. Her analysis of four *Texts of Terror* tells the sad stories of women who are used and abused by a system set up for the advantage and promotion of men's interests, sexual needs, and concerns for male progeny to continue their lineage. In the stories recorded about Hagar, Tamar, an unnamed wife, and the daughter of Jephthah, Trible describes terrifying events of rape, murder, sexual abuse, and exploitation that are uncomfortable to remember, and that have no happy ending or moral lesson. Her suggestion is that these stories have another kind of meaning, in that they reveal dimensions of religious faith not usually spoken about or represented theologically, that slip through the spaces of the text. Although minimal words are spoken by these women themselves, within the language and the construction of the stories are new and hidden riches of faith that come from women who are victims of the system. Thus Hagar, exploited and expelled, is the first woman in scripture to hear an annunciation and to dare to name the deity, while Jephthah's daughter, killed by her father in fulfilment of a pointless vow to God, is a reminder of the assertive determination to love in spite of death. The intuition of women that life is more than this, and their courage to live as powerless and abandoned women, are the absent truths of faith haunting the text and the tradition around its fringes.

In each of these texts, the male figure is remembered and celebrated in the tradition as an exemplar of faith, and the woman is forgotten, so that the task of interpretation is one of recovering 'sympathetic readings of abused women', and of discovering the redemptive possibilities around which the stories hover.[61] There are other texts however, examined by Trible in her *God and the Rhetoric of Sexuality*, which make more explicit the link between the divine nature and women's embodiment. In a poem which has particular relevance in our contemporary world, the prophet Jeremiah speaks through the voice of a woman a message of divine compassion and of redeeming love, which the woman herself has made possible by her life.[62] The poem opens with a woman's voice heard in the land, a voice which is identified as that of Rachel mourning for the death of her children and for her empty womb. 'Directed to no one in particular, and hence to all who may hear, the voice of Rachel travels across the land and through the ages to permeate existence with a suffering that not even death can relieve.'[63] Her lament receives consolation from God, that out of suffering will be brought hope, words which come to focus on a man, who represents the people of Israel, and who repents and implores God to restore him to right relationship. At this point, God speaks directly from the divine womb, from which the remembrance of God's own children draws forth compassion and the fullness of love.[64] The poem comes 'to the inner recesses of human existence where the physical and the psychic unite to convey the depths of divine love'.[65] God becomes mother.

It may be suggested that the times of the eighth century prophets bear some striking resemblances to our own, that the shifting intellectual framework which accompanies postmodernism, the fragmentation of social and political life, the impossible gap between the rhetoric of free choice and invisible management at a distance, and the desperate starvation of basic human needs which cannot be fed from the trinkets of late capitalism – all of these combine to shape a world that is in exile. The kind of foundationalism which the naturalist paradigm seeks to reintroduce is one response to this metaphysical alienation, that grips us in a strange land where we cannot get our bearings. Its ontological dualism seems such a common sensible way of handling human affairs, and of directing sexual desire. Its search for security in the firm ground of nature as God has created it is understandable in a context of rootlessness and nomadic wandering. But still, another song is heard. So it is that a poem from Jeremiah should echo today in the writings of feminists, speaking as those who embody the world's deepest sufferings and tragedies. So it is that women know this world to be in exile, and speak to it across time and space, from a place that is not yet.

Jeremiah concludes his poem with the astonishing words, 'For God has created a new thing in the land: female surrounds man.'[66] Indeed, he suggests in the final verse that 'the bitterness of Rachel has become guideposts for the return home', and thus that the voices of women are precisely those which are indicative of the way of redemption.[67] Trible herself is aware of the ambiguities of these claims, and of the ease with which they may distil into mere conformity with women's typical role, or into passivity with things as they are. This constant tension of present reality and future possibility is obvious in the story of Ruth, whose leap of faith surpasses that of Abraham, who reverses sexual allegiance, and who wills to become an alien in the land to redeem its emptiness and despair.[68] That her actions are described by men in ways that subordinate her own self-understanding to their prerogatives, making her simply a child-bearer in the line of 'Rachel and Leah who between them built the house of Israel', is a sign of the impossibility of capturing women's spiritual truth and significance in the categories of man's reality.[69] Trible concludes her study by suggesting that women are 'working out their own salvation with fear and trembling, for it is God who works in them'. The voice in which they challenge culture is itself 'a legacy of faith to this day for all who have ears to hear the stories of women in a man's world'.[70] Whether there is room within a naturalistic approach to morality to comprehend this meaning of the work of women, or whether its categories will always reduce women to their utility in the natural processes of life, is the third challenge from feminists to this paradigm.

Through a critique of the naturalist paradigm, new insights are opened up, and some of the deeper theological implications of the morality it represents can begin to be seen. In questioning the tendency to foundationalism within this paradigm, feminists are raising the possibility of a dynamic understanding of nature and its laws, which would be open to the changing cultural contexts in which we find ourselves throughout history, and which could include women's imaginative participation in the formation of cultural ideals and values. In questioning the objectification of women as fixed kinds of human beings, feminists are concerned about the political implications of affirming what is distinctive to themselves within the context of unequal power, in which they also are implicated and indeed have gained from a certain relative privilege. Finally, in questioning the limitations of the notion of what is human within this paradigm, feminists are wondering whether its terms in the end can include what is most distinctive about their embodied spirituality and hope for the world. In these questions, there is a challenge to the voice of man in this ethical tradition, and a real concern that continuing to work within this paradigm will involve women in collusion with what is not in their interests. This brings us full circle to the emergence of liberal ways of thinking, which grew precisely out of recognition that there is a shared human nature lying beyond the reach of gender. The extent to which this voice of man has also been accepted as the voice of God raises a further problem of the theological implications of a paradigm that does not have a reputation for being prophetic. Whether women's contributions will render it so remains to be seen.

Transition: picking up some threads

Having examined in some depth the three major frameworks of moral understanding which have been found throughout the history of modern feminism, the complex relationship between feminism and Christian ethics can perhaps be appreciated more fully. Feminists themselves have used different sets of assumptions in order to investigate the lives and the positions of women in all kinds of societies. Because these assumptions can take feminist thinkers in quite different directions, there is now a very diverse body of literature scattered throughout a range of academic disciplines, as well as in political and popular writings, which attempts to illuminate and express feminist viewpoints. Sometimes the work that has been done within one framework sits comfortably with that of another, and much collaborative work can be done to develop clearer understanding of the social and moral issues of women's lives. Perhaps one of the clearest illustrations of this comes from those feminists who identify with the social constructionist task of investigating the impact of structures upon the shaping of human consciousness, but who at the same time believe with liberals that there is an authentic nature within us, shared in common with men, which can only be fulfilled through a just social order. In other cases, the work of feminists is contradictory, seemingly running at cross-purposes in discussions of the priorities of feminism. Here the obvious example is of those feminists who work within the naturalist paradigm, believing there to be a distinctive nature of women which feminist ethical thinking can enunciate, which exactly runs counter to the postmodern feminist claim that there is no such thing as a given nature, and that a feminist ethic must shatter, rather than complete, personal identity. Feminism is itself a diverse phenomenon, and has come to value its own poly-vocality.

Contemporary feminism may be understood to be grouped generally around the three clusters of assumptions, or paradigms, labelled liberalism, social constructionism, and naturalism. Each paradigm forms a reasonably clear set of interrelated notions through which a moral stance can be identified, and each one has frayed edges that make the stance less distinctive away from the centre. One of the things which a book like this could do is to seek to argue persuasively for one or other of these clusters, and to insist that it offers the best framework within which to understand and to develop feminist thinking and activity. Thus a comparative exercise would come to an end by evaluating and choosing the best of the paradigms for future work. This, it was suggested in the opening chapter, sets up an unhelpful rivalry between alternative ways of understanding, and in addition makes it difficult for those feminists who actually find something valuable in each of them. Thus, for example, the work of Rosemary Ruether may be found both within and across the different paradigms, as she follows strands from one and then from another, tracing their implications and possibilities. This is not an indication of confusion, but of struggling to discover what resources there are within the philosophical and theological traditions that are actually helpful to women. In addition, each of these paradigms may be in need of serious revision with the inclusion of women's insights, and the extent to which they are open to this, and flexible enough to incorporate new ideas, needs to be discovered in further work. Therefore, it is not clear that a decision to opt for one paradigm can be made at this stage, nor even that it would be desirable to do so in the long term, until we have examined more closely some of the common themes that run between and across these clusters of ideas.

Since each cluster is made up of interwoven strands of belief and commitment, similar strands may be identified within other clusters, where they may be used in exactly the same way, or with slightly different nuances and consequences. It may be helpful in the remaining chapters to consider a few of these similar strands, to follow their implications, and to search out the openings towards which they point. Three moral concerns may be found to emerge from feminism, and they are instances of problematic areas with which each paradigm is explicitly engaged, or which are implicit within its assumptions. In concentrating on these concerns one at a time, in drawing them out for special attention, something may be shown of our appreciation for the insights that are unique to each cluster, and for the special way in which this concern is illuminated therein. Likewise, this exercise may help us to acknowledge the critical thinking with which feminists from the different clusters have challenged one another, seeking to refine more carefully what the key issues and actions of feminism are or should be. So this exercise can, through conversation between the paradigms, begin to draw attention to those areas of further study that may be helpful to feminism as we move into a new century. Lastly, each of these concerns may be shown to involve implicit theological claims, which make feminism more than a secular phenomenon, and which draw its insights onto shared ground with Christian theological work. To bring to light this implicit theology of feminism will serve to illustrate its intrinsic relationship with Christian ethics.

Already it has been mentioned that the interaction of feminism and Christian ethics is characterised by the same diversity and interweaving of strands of belief. The same paradigms which are used in contemporary feminism are also to be found amongst Christian ethicists as they too search for moral understanding. In similar ways, responses to this diversity have also been considered, and some ethicists may be found who argue for the priority of one paradigm over another, while others embrace the diversity with which they believe the Christian community now must live. In the midst of this diversity, common problems and questions are emerging for Christian belief and practice, which form the core of a new apologetics that has become significant in recent decades, and particularly noticeable in the discipline of ethics. It is the thesis of this book that these moral concerns emerging from within feminism are not unlike those that emerge within Christian ethical thinking; that those who are attempting to clarify, and to make appropriate response to, these concerns are working within a context of challenge and critique in which descriptions of the moral project available from the tradition are believed to need reappraisal in the light of contemporary questions; and finally that attention to the theological dimension of these areas of common concern will demonstrate the value of collaborative work. Both feminist and Christian ethical thinking may step forward more confidently and more wisely by engaging with one another in this serious way. The interdependence of feminism and Christian ethics may thus prove to be fruitful, and some quite creative developments in theory and practice may take place.

To complicate the matter of diversity further, the context for these considerations is the rupture experienced throughout society between modern and postmodern ways of understanding the dimensions of the ethical project. Feminism and Christian ethics now occupy a new and a strange terrain, which unsettles some assumptions that might once have been taken for granted, and presents new problems that can be both disturbing and creative. Christians are not of one mind about how to understand postmodernism, and neither are feminists. There is some indication that postmodernism extends to the furthest extreme the implicit presuppositions of modernism regarding individual liberty in a socially managed context. If this is the case, we are witnessing the logical outcome of Enlightenment ideas about liberty, equality, and fraternity, without any of the idealistic frills which once inspired revolutions. That there is now a new sport of hunting liberals and mocking their concerns as mere political correctness is an outcome of this view. There are other indications that postmodernism radically reverses modern notions of the human person and her capacity to reason about truth. If this is the case, then the human project of knowledge, and the person around whom it has been centred, needs an entirely new language, and the politics of reality becomes problematic.

While the first interpretation might incline towards the redis-covery of an earlier form of society in which these modern pretensions were not to be found, the outcome of the second is less clear. Whether and in what form we should be colluding in the demise of liberalism, whether we ought to be reshaping society in the form of some traditional alternative, or whether the possibilities of postmodern pluralism are the exciting new venture of the future, are the common questions.

In the midst of the discussion of these is the difficult matter of reassessing the nature of the moral project. In so far as the feminists investigated here have been concerned with that task, their insights and questions may inspire new considerations relevant in this new context.

CHAPTER 8

Towards an appropriate universalism

In her recent contribution to consideration of *Prospects for a Common Morality*, Margaret Farley writes that 'Feminists have understandable reasons both to reject and to promote belief in a common or universal morality'.[1] So many of the ethical writings of feminists, their stirring speeches and declarations, as well as their carefully detailed analyses of the lives of women, rely upon universal claims regarding what is the case about the world as it is, and what ought to be done everywhere about it. Feminists have made use of ethical universalism as a framework within which to grasp more clearly the problems that need to be addressed by women, so that some general description might be given upon which all could agree, and to judge moral and political priorities, so that actions might be undertaken to make things better. In this sense, universalism has served feminist ethics well. There is also, however, a growing recognition within feminism that such universal claims require a methodology in ethical reasoning that is increasingly understood to be itself unethical. Feminists are thus beginning to doubt their reliance upon universalism, and to ask whether it is actually compatible with feminism, and helpful to the lives of women.

That this is one of the significant threads to be taken up from this analysis is becoming increasingly obvious, as feminists seek to understand the full implications of a gender critique of ethics, and to discern the openings which lie ahead for exploration. It will be helpful in this chapter to set out some of the conflict which lies now very much at the centre of feminist debate, so that the dimensions of the problem with universalism can begin to be seen. Much of this discussion is conducted between those liberal feminists who are still seeking the full extension of the Enlightenment project to include women, and those post-liberal or postmodern feminists who have abandoned this project as an entirely fruitless effort for women. In this debate lie some important theological implications which take us into the midst of similar discussions within Christian ethics. However, this debate between two forms of feminism is not the end of the story. For what is now emerging amongst feminist thinkers is a critical examination of the terms in which this conflict itself is set, and a corresponding search for an appropriate universalism that will sustain and nourish a feminist ethic. It may be that here are the signs of a new feminism, which is neither postmodern nor liberal, out of which some important new ethical considerations may develop.

To speak first in general terms, it may be said that the search for the universal in ethics has called forth a stretching of the moral consciousness for the farthest reaches of reality. The most persistent definitions of ethics as a discipline have emphasised, at its core, the discovery of some ultimate points of reference, in relation to which the rest of human life might come into perspective and be valued appropriately. To be able to consider what extends beyond one's own circumstances or condition, to be able to reflect upon one's social mores and tasks to ask whether something should be done, has been taken to be a central ethical concern, reaching out to connect with those things that lie at the heart of life as it ought to be. In so doing, the ethical thinker was also connecting with those values or principles which were believed to be relevant more widely, not simply to one's own situation, but also to that of others, so that ethical debate was inspired by the need to understand these moral truths in the different circumstances that a variety of people bring into consideration. The element of the universal in ethics has brought the ethical thinker into touch with ultimacy, has stirred new feelings about, and responses to, lived realities, and has sustained individual efforts to move forward positively through moral decision and action.

Such a search for the universal has been taking place through the revolution in human consciousness and in political structure that occurs with the Enlightenment. For a new group of people to be able to grasp hold of political power, and to challenge existing authority, required imaginative work to establish new foundations for decisions about what is just and unjust. One type of exploration of the universal begins to be shaped here, and it is one which has become central to contemporary understandings of justice. The significance of Descartes' grounding of certainty within the thinking self, and his proof of the existence of a God who is logically necessary to sustain its truth, is profound. For thereby a new world of possibility and of meaning opened up, a world available to the thinker, within which principles could be discovered for the governance of nature, the ordering of society, and the patterning of personal life. Here it was believed a true justice could be established, which transcended existing forms of society and, at the same time, was widely available to any who engaged in its methods of reasoning. As a response to the turmoil and confusion of the times, this establishment of a new kind of objectivity in reasoning, and in moral reasoning in particular, was a major breakthrough, providing universal standards of judgement that could be grasped as fixed points on the horizon by all men of reason.[2]

Already at this time, women began to get hold of the possibilities this presented for the reshaping of their lives, and, through the years, this way of thinking has exercised a powerful hold upon feminist moral imagination. Important to this developing rational understanding of justice has been its universal implications and applicability, regardless of particular situations and conditions. Through all of these the conception of justice drove the moral thinker on to consider what was logically required of the moral agent, and to discover there a very powerful form of human unity. To see through the mind's eye the essential qualities of the human being that were really of moral significance, to be able to base one's decisions regarding particular persons on that consideration alone, and to be able to envision a society in which such persons could live together under just rule, fairly and equitably, was a profound affirmation of humankind in general. Here was to be a project which human beings themselves could mould in accordance with universal principles, and in which, from all around the globe, they could be full participants. The society so shaped would know no bounds erected through personal loyalties or attachments, but would be nourished by the common allegiance of all participants to the universal vision. For theologians to portray the divine being as the upholder of this vision, by whose will it has been established from the creation, became a further expression, and indeed a confirmation, of its universality, as well as an affirmation of man's role in carrying out the divine work of justice.

It has been the liberal form of universalism which has been available to, and primarily used within, feminist thinking, for it has offered a framework for ethical insights into the lives of women, and a vision for the future, in which something within those lives might be set free and fulfilled. To be given the critical tools for measuring and reshaping their lives in accordance with right principles, lies at the heart of feminist reconstructions of social orders in ways that are more just for women. Within Enlightenment universalism lies considerable reliance therefore upon Kant's elaboration of a metaphysics of morals for an age sceptical of our grasp of natural value. Kant's description of the categorical imperative as that logically necessary principle, in obedience to which a good will might be become truly moral, not only gave new expression to the concern for human unity, but also presented the shape of this new type of reasoning about justice, by which the dignity and autonomy of women might also be affirmed. Many feminists are still persuaded that decisions regarding justice for women are best formulated in relation to the principle of treating persons as ends in themselves and never as means to an end, and have affirmed the notion of personal autonomy upon which that principle relies.

In her recent study of *Justice, Gender and the Family*, Susan Moller Okin argues for the 'considerable potential' of the liberal tradition to provide 'a fully humanist theory of justice',

believing that within its terms can be found the framework for
treating 'women, as well as men, as full human beings to whom
a theory of social justice must apply'.[3] Challenging a liberal
society to reshape its social structures, she urges the use of
Rawls' 'veil of ignorance' as a heuristic device, so that a
'potential critique of gender-structured social institutions ...
can be developed by taking seriously the fact that those formulating the principles of justice do not know their sex'.[4] What
this would mean in contemporary society is a thorough critique
of practices relating to the family, for family life continues
to be protected from the strict requirements of justice, that
each individual is an autonomous and responsible person, and
in fact, establishes and reproduces an inequality between
women and men which '*makes* women vulnerable'.[5] Her vision,
that 'A just future would be one without gender', expresses
exactly the scope of this application of universal principles, by
which 'one's sex would have no more relevance than one's eye
color or the length of one's toes'.[6] Within a work such as
Okin's, there is a most impressive searching for consistency of
judgement throughout social institutions and practices, and a
concern that the daily lives of women also be practically
affected by the application of universal principles of individual
equality and fair treatment. Something in this kind of universalism is deeply compelling within liberal humanism generally,
and liberal feminism particularly.

Now, however, universalism has come under scrutiny by
feminists, casting doubt upon this particular form, and revealing a deep ambivalence about this approach to ethics. On the
one hand, as Okin rightly argues, the respect for individual
self-legislation, and for the dignity of persons whose work and
commitment are essential to social well-being, has not yet come
about in society. Furthermore, there are institutions like the
family, which have been resistant to these requirements of
justice, and indeed seem to reinforce the impossibility of these
ever being realised. Thus the formulations for arriving at
decisions of justice, which she describes, and which have been
central to liberal feminism, seem to be exactly what feminists
ought to work to effect. On the other hand, there is a dissatis-

faction with this understanding of justice, and with the universalism in which it is enmeshed, since its terms seem not quite to capture what it is that women want to say about the human person, the methodology by which they reach moral decisions, or the vision which can any longer sustain a just society. Combined with the Cartesian thinker, the Kantian moral agent has become a kind of composite human being, which feminists, following Genevieve Lloyd, have called the Man of Reason, and his identity lies within the terms of liberal universalism. It is claimed that this form of universal reason hides the masculine voice in which it has been conceived, and that its terms are formulated in the absence of, and indeed as protection against, women.

Throughout its history, this universalism has been the project of the autonomous self, the quest of the solitary individual for the dimensions of consciousness. As Grace Jantzen has argued, the notion of personhood presumed here has been of a being unhindered in the free exercise of its choices, existing in a fundamentally competitive, and a potentially hostile, relationship with other such beings. From such an understanding of persons, central in modern libertarian democracies, comes an ethic of rights, which grant an entitlement to private self-legislation, limited only by the possibility of harm done to others.[7] Justice becomes the system by which rival claims can be adjudicated, and antagonisms between separate sets of desires can be resolved without war. What lies at the heart of its universalism is the notion of separated selves, whose independence needs to be held in check by an impartial framework of moral principles. There is reason to believe, from the writings within this tradition, that its continued emphasis on separation is indicative of beliefs about what it means to be a man, rather than to be fully human. These 'configurations of masculinity' suggest that underlying this first approach, and essential to the development of impartial frameworks of principles by which to make decisions, is a mistrust of women, an anxiety about relationships, and a generalised fear of being subsumed into non-differentiated unity once again.[8] Accordingly, this form of universalism presumes the separation of persons from one another, which a common adherence to principles is believed to overcome.

While the kind of justice proposed by Okin requires a blindness to one's own particularities, it is argued that this methodology draws one away precisely from those features of the situation which make it moral at all, namely attention to the actual individuals involved, their needs, and the qualities of relationship in which they are caught up. Something of this lies within Woodhead's concern for attentiveness to detail, and it is also to be found in the work of those who describe an ethic of care. Sara Ruddick argues that maternal thinking responds to demands from others, and, in that sense, it does not allow the privilege of standing back to think hypothetically, to draw over one's face the veil of anonymity in order to be completely fair, nor the necessity of waiting to determine whether one's response to need is legitimately required by a categorical imperative.[9] To care is to make concrete response in the moments and particular situations in which one is caught up. In so far as moral knowledge has consisted of abstract principles, the acceptance of, and ability to apply, which are characteristic of the morally knowledgeable person, this is a form of universalism which feminists may find unsatisfactory. As Iris Young argues, 'The theory of justice is intended to be self-standing, since it exhibits its own foundations ... It is detemporalized, in that nothing comes before it and future events will not affect its truth or relevance to social life.'[10] Such a foundation of truth takes one out of the contingencies of living moral situations, and devalues the knowledge which may be gained therein. To say that one knows because one understands the principle is only one form of knowing, and some feminists argue that it may not be the one most critical in moral knowledge. If universalism requires increasing abstraction, it may not be entirely helpful to a feminist ethics.

Sharon Welch has expressed this as a challenge to the abstraction of persons central to universalism. One must surmise, in this kind of ethics, that other persons are like oneself, using the arguments from analogy that Jantzen has so neatly mocked, and then ascribing to these others the same sets of characteristics given to oneself. Welch describes this as the belief that 'the partners in moral dialogue ... are assumed to be fundamentally the same; each individual is seen as "a rational being entitled to the same rights and duties we would want to ascribe to ourselves"'.[11] In this process of reasoning, persons are generalised through being identified as holders of common attributes, and on that basis a decision is made regarding what considerations to give to them. Thus Welch understands moral decision to be guided by 'norms of *formal equality and reciprocity*; each is entitled to expect and to assume from us what we can expect and assume from him or her'.[12] No real interpersonal encounter takes place in such reasoning, since the individual is protected by the distance which such abstractions impose between persons. That this form of universalism sustains the separation of individuals from one another, confirming this separation as appropriate in moral decision-making, is, for Welch, not only reason to question the ethics of this methodology, but further to claim that it is entirely unsuited to the Christian life.

That the social and political consequences of this kind of universalism are divisive is by now also well documented. Seyla Benhabib notes that 'the neglect by universalist theories of the moral emotions and of everyday moral interactions with concrete others has everything to do with the gender division of labor in western societies subsequent to modernity'.[13] To make justice 'the core of collective moral life' limits the sphere of the private household to 'mere reproductive units whose function is to satisfy the daily bodily and psychosexual needs of their members'.[14] It is this, she argues, which lies at the root of the neglect of women's activities and insights in moral matters. Indeed, it may be said that this reinforces a process of the shrinking significance of family relationships and life together in ways that many women have found disturbing. That this process continues into increasing divisions within the public realm too, is cited by Young as further evidence of the unfortunate consequences of a universalist approach to moral concerns. She argues that the 'ideal of impartiality ... legitimates bureaucratic authority' in which the tasks of management are separated from other tasks, 'making managers oversee the different and partial perspectives on the organization'.[15] The really 'professional' person in the social structure is therefore the one who can take an objective point of view and use impartial reason in making decisions. Again, the consequences of this for the lives of women within the public realm have been to require of them that they become like men to exercise this kind of authority, or else not make progress through existing structures. This form of universalism is especially blind to its own assumptions regarding who counts as a person in the first place.

In all of these challenges, feminists have been contributing to the death of the Man of Reason, whose exploration of the universal does not entirely connect with women's moral sensitivity, and may indeed have been a journey away from the influence of women altogether. So there are serious questions amongst feminists regarding the continued application of a methodology for arriving at just decisions, that seems to draw them away from what matters to the distinctive experience and insight that women can bring to bear in moral considerations. In many ways, the feminist critique brings us to the heart of the ethical project itself. For feminists are wondering whether universalism in any form is ever appropriate, or whether we have simply not yet arrived at an appropriate form, which can sustain an understanding of justice that can do justice to women. It may be that these considerations point to the need for a new conceptualisation of justice, as full as the one emerging with the Enlightenment. It is to this project that many feminists believe women can make a special contribution in speaking of justice in our world. Such new considerations may be deeply informed by Christian insights.

Postmodern feminism has consolidated two important questions regarding the nature of the search for the universal in ethics, which require us to ask quite seriously what it is that feminists are doing with ethics at all. Firstly, it is argued that ethics requires the discovery of ultimate categories into which all things can be fitted, and it is this which the quest for the universal has accomplished. Its claim on the territory of the absolute is effected through the vision of the critical eye, which discovers the principle of classification, and which may now control reality accordingly. The work of Frye in describing the politics of reality has been of considerable significance in emphasising the oppressive consequences which the classification of gender has for human life. There is deep mistrust of this unifying quest of reason, which believes in its own powers of identification for, as Young expresses it, 'The logic of identity denies or represses difference ... it flees from the sensuous particularity of experience, with its ambiguities, and seeks to generate stable categories'.[16] Universal thinking in ethics eliminates differences through thought, so that uncertainty may be resolved, and security provided against the unpredictable. The territory of the universal is thus considered to be a realm which transcends the confused variety of the everyday, and from which only the monologue of the voice of truth is to be heard.

Judith Butler argues that the appropriate feminist response to this is to disrupt gender categories in unexpected and imaginative ways, so that they do not become solidified into permanent truths.[17] Deliberately causing 'gender trouble' is the special political and philosophical importance of lesbians, who refuse the categories by which persons are classified and controlled. The project of feminism thus comes to embody, in constantly disturbing ways, the fact that human life exceeds the bounds rational man has sought to impose, and to remind us of the sheer complexity and indefinability of human identity. With this emphasis, postmodern feminism is deeply anti-ethical in its rendering of all categories as unstable, and in its insistence upon allowing the full diversity of human beings to be appreciated. There is theological significance in this, for something in the nature of divine judgement has to do with the Word of God that smashes human realities, breaking them up into fragments, in case we are inclined to give them too much credence in the living out of our human lives and relationships. That our secular sisters have often been ahead of us in noting the fragile nature of these categories, and the foolishness of our trust in them, is reason for Christian feminists to embrace their courage in this rejection. It has expressed for many Christian feminists exactly the kind of freedom which is given in Christ to live beyond the confinement of the law. Postmodern feminism calls us to recognise diversity that defies categorisation.

Secondly, it is argued by postmodern feminists, particularly in their appropriation of Foucault, that universalism in ethics requires some overall account of reality, in the context of which actions that accord with right principles are effective. Scepticism about such accounts comes from the belief that all of them are written by the privileged, in order to exercise and to maintain their control over reality. Thus Enlightenment universalism has been a kind of western liberal conquest of the world, by the telling of a grand narrative, into which the lives and actions of all humanity can be woven. This quest for the universal is operating 'under the spell of presence', under the illusion that its ultimate reference points are real, and have been described accurately by those who know them. The meta-narrative which emerges with the Enlightenment has assumed its universal relevance and applicability, without knowing the particular persons or situations involved, and so it has seemed to be the most logical framework for the establishment of a common morality for modernism. As Young has described it, such universalism supports a belief that moral agents are impartial, and are therefore best placed to make decisions about universal justice, when in fact they are the privileged speakers of the ruling interpretations of reality. 'The ideal of impartiality legitimates hierarchical decisionmaking and allows the standpoint of the privileged to appear as universal. The combination of these functions often leads to concrete decisions that perpetuate the oppression and disadvantage of some groups and the privilege of others.'[18] Accounts of reality carry authority, reinforced in structures, which 'silence, ignore, and render deviant the abilities, needs, and norms of others'.[19] Universalism is thus deconstructed as parochialism.

Feminism has played its own part in this story, in the arrogance of white western women that their account of oppression and liberation is universally the case amongst women. Their own attempt to establish human unity by means of rational agreement to a set of principles has met an angry response from particular local groups of women throughout the world, whose different stories have not been heard. The attention of postmodern feminists is directed to what is absent from the big stories, to what has been overlooked in the progress towards truth, to what has been relied upon but not acknowledged in making the journey. The sad recognition of the failure of liberal political vision has been, in this account, not a matter of its inconsistent application or even its male bias, so much as an expression of a deeper disenchantment with controlling narratives that necessarily repress the particular, and create those who are outsiders. What feminism is to do with this awareness is problematic, for this knowledge cannot itself become part of a new story without losing its own distinctive perception, and therefore seems consigned to the role of permanent outsider. This intensifies the dilemma for feminists, since postmodern feminism appears again to be radically anti-ethical in its insistence upon speaking the meaningless truths that stories cannot accommodate.

Once again, this is of deep theological significance, for Christian ethics has been set in the context of a grand narrative of the divine–human relation, and moral insight was a way of understanding what roles we each have to play in the story. Trible's insistence upon telling the stories of those women whose lives are unaccounted for in the theological narration of salvation history is an example of this concern, and it draws us towards the mystery of what has not been explained. Indeed, her attention to the texts of terror compels an acknowledgement of the more astonishing transcendence of God, which, so far from being captured in our theological stories of the covenant relationship, is actually constantly haunting and disrupting them from outside. So also Welch takes up the theme of the theological privilege which claims access to truth, while hiding those voices that cannot be heard in that context.[20] In the process, the differences that are really present are dissolved into universal concerns, and resistance is hampered. The declarations of what is universally true actually set up an unacknowledged battleground in which those who are hidden and oppressed must struggle for voice. How else are women to explain the absence, so often, of Ruth and other significant women of faith from theological and liturgical recitals of the story of Christian faith. Thus universal discourse elides oppression, hiding its own exercise of power, and creating pockets of subversive memories that rise up to disturb and to challenge the status quo with new ways of being and thinking. Postmodern feminism disrupts ethics, as Chopp suggests, with surprising eruptions of the Spirit freely dispersing its power to speak.

Yet it must be said that feminism is not entirely at ease with postmodernism, and that discussion regarding the compatibility of the two is being heard more widely. The nature of the dis-ease has to do with four crucial areas of concern. The first of these is the removal of a framework in which concerns for justice can be meaningfully set. On the one hand, it has been encouraging to be able to knock down the idols and to proclaim the death of the formalist approach to justice, as one which does not take the human person in all her fullness seriously. To break up this kind of universalism has been a healthy exercise of the moral consciousness in the affirmation of difference, and so it has been important for postmodern feminism to be understood as an ethical disagreement with liberal feminism. This means, on the other hand however, that postmodern feminism, in deconstructing all frameworks, has left itself without one in which to understand its own concern for women's lives, and in which to make sense of its own ethical arguments. In her analysis of the relationship of *Foucault and Feminism*, Lois McNay expresses her anxiety that feminists may overlook possible points of conflict with postmodernism. In particular, she is concerned that there is a 'false polarization that the debate on modernity and postmodernity has established between theory and practice, metanarratives and action, the general and the particular'.[21] In the context of a Christian postmodernism, to this we may add the further polarisation of law and grace. McNay's concern is that feminists rush in too quickly to abandon theory, just at a time when some theoretical framework is exactly what is needed to comprehend gender issues more fully.[22]

This has left feminism open to the challenge that it may be entirely reduced, without remainder, to some form of pragmatism, for this seems a good way, perhaps the best way, in which a concern for situations and concrete individuals may be realised in an ethical form. Here there is no need for universalising statements, or abstract talk of rights and equality, since the right thing to do emerges from the discussions amongst those who happen to be involved, and since the agreement which is reached for the next step forward is a tentative one, able to be questioned and undone at the next meeting. In the place of 'transcendental concepts of justice' are provisional recommendations and working hypotheses. Whether feminism resolves itself finally into a version of pragmatism may be understood as one of the implications of the antirealism within later forms of social constructionist feminism. However, this conclusion does not rest easily with feminists. As Catherine Wilson expresses this, 'We have to conclude that if ... they must give up their analytical work, their effort at laying bare and morally evaluating the actual operations of their society, the bargain is a poor one for feminists.'[23] The necessity for a framework within which to reflect ethically is crucial, so that women may continue to raise questions quite specifically about sexual difference, which otherwise will disappear among affirmations of difference – generally speaking, and feminists will be 'left holding a sadly empty bag'.[24]

A second concern about this alliance is expressed so vividly in Flax's nightmare scenario. Feminists are questioning whether the new world-view of postmodernism is really an opposition to modernism, a social alternative to liberalism, or whether, on the contrary, it is individualism run riot. In many ways, emphasis on what is specific, local, particular, and concrete is evidence, not of something really different, but of a continuing process of fragmentation into smaller and smaller units. As the personal subject is also decentred into a being with interests, social units become the place in which these interests struggle with one another for recognition and fulfilment, and ethics becomes the management of these battles. This is not dissimilar to the supposedly impartial rule of principles of justice, but a lot less kindly. Feminists see the connection between this way of thinking as an extension of *laissez faire* economics, and the increased growth of mega-institutions, of multi-national corporations, of the media, of medical technologies, all of which exist as superpowers to control and to manage rampant individualism. There is nothing encouraging to women in this, for, in expressing the extraordinary manly effort to live beyond illusions, the every-day world is left without meaningful interactions. And women bear the consequences.

Lovibond has engaged in a feminist critique of Nietzsche on precisely this issue, in pointing out 'the phallic, or "masculine protest" character of Nietzsche's philosophy, and of post-modernist theory in its more overtly Nietzschean moods'.[25] She cautions feminists to be wary of the alliance. 'Turning upon the Nietzscheans their own preferred genealogical method, we might ask: *who* thinks it is so humiliating to be caught out in an attitude of "nostalgia for lost unity", or of longing for a world of human subjects sufficiently "centred" to speak to and under-stand one another?'[26] This question haunts the dialogue of feminism and postmodernism. If women are once more to be left looking after the daily business of life, while their brothers zoom around in the intellectual hyperspace opened up by the postmodern imagination, then the hope which is celebrated here is too otherworldly to be meaningful to feminism.

It leads into the third concern of feminists in the postmodern rejection of universalism, which is the effective removal of language of normativity. In its concern to deconstruct the 'view from nowhere', in favour of the endless interplay of discourses in which we find ourselves entangled, postmoder-nism has rendered all ethical stances as 'standpoints', from each of which, reality looks somewhat different. This affir-mation of different points of view is intended to prevent the domination of the One, the single understanding, the unitary will of God, so that each diverse interpretation and experience is valued in and of itself. However, it must be asked in what context these multiplicities are valued. Postmodernism presents feminism with the strange combination of emphasis upon the specific, alongside the possibility of a 'view from everywhere' in which these specificities are enjoyed. The imagery of the dance is used to suggest the playfulness of the scene, in which, as Bordo says, we may 'celebrate a "feminine" ability to identify with and enter into the perspectives of others, to accept change and fluidity as features of reality'.[27] Chopp has encouraged these multiple and shifting expressions as the gift of the Spirit in glossolalia. However, there are reservations about a postmodern feminism which refuses 'to assume a shape for which they must take responsibility'.[28] As Soper argues:

In the absence of any clearer sense of what is entertained under the notions of the "multigendered" society, or the society of 'proliferating gender' or 'bodies and pleasures', one inevitably tends to conceive these as designating either a melange or blurring of existing sexual distinctions – which they therefore do not transcend – or else an alternative so devoid of specificity that it can hardly qualify even as fantasy.[29]

A reluctance to speak normatively about human life, and about gender, can have unfortunate consequences for feminism in actually obscuring the hierarchies which their emphasis on heterogeneity is meant to overcome.[30]

There is thus within feminism a real question about whether women may do without some generalisations about themselves and their situations, and a framework in which these may be discussed, distinguished from one another, and evaluated. Without such a theoretical perspective, and indeed some meta-narrative of justice, it is difficult to understand how conflicting interests can be balanced and alternative possibilities considered. McNay argues that, 'Whilst feminism has to guard against the dangers of generalization, it nevertheless rests on the fundamental assumption that the inequality of the sexes is indefensible and unjust.'[31] Exactly how we could express this in a postmodern world is difficult to comprehend, for it has deconstructed precisely those categories in which injustice could be diagnosed and remedied. This is the point at which Benhabib finds postmodernism 'baffling', in its positing of 'those hyper-universalist and superliberal values of diversity, heterogeneity, eccentricity, and otherness'.[32] She argues that,

In doing so they rely on the very norms of autonomy of subjects and the rationality of democratic procedures which otherwise they seem so blithely to dismiss. What concept of reason, which vision of autonomy allows us to retain these values and the institutions within which these values flourish and become ways of life? To this question, postmodernists have no answer.[33]

It is important that postmodernism has taught us 'the theoretical and political traps of why utopias and foundational thinking can go wrong', but she urges women to retain the exercise of an enlarged imagination, by means of which norms of human interaction may be established, and concerns for moral value expressed and debated.[34]

A fourth area of concern from feminists appears in the work of Sharon Welch, who raises the important theological dimensions of this debate. Her feminist ethics of risk combines insights from the postmodern critique, with Christian affirmations of a compassionate God. Acknowledging her debt to postmodern thinking, Welch suggests that the critique of universalism is useful for Christian ethics, which is otherwise in danger of losing the impact of the specific and timely focus that is essential if God's presence is really to come alive in particular situations. What sustains liberal universalism, she argues, is a language of utopia, of the better world which is to come if only we do this or that. This language and the universal vision of which it speaks, carries with it assumptions of a final and complete victory, which those who do good will be able to effect, to make the world a safer place for democracy, or for the flourishing of basic Christian values, or other forms of positive change. She writes,

The aim of a final defeat of all evil forces, or the aim of finally meeting all human needs, does not appear as anything but praiseworthy on the surface. It is indeed surprising to find that such utopian goals as the defeat of evil and meeting of all needs can have, and often do have, highly dangerous consequences and that these constructions make peace less likely and justice seem less likely.[35]

Welch's argument here, and her illustrations of such utopian thinking within American politics of nuclear deterrence, may be heard as a condemnation of pride in human works.

Within this is a deeper realisation that such an ethic has been, and continues to be, believed by good people, who think that, out of their efforts, the world will more closely approximate the kind of place it ought to be. In theological terms, this is an expression of being able to share in the good works of bringing in the kingdom, so that God's will may be done on earth as it is in heaven. Human participation in this divine work is predicated upon an ethic of control, described as 'the assumption that it is possible to guarantee the efficacy of one's actions'.[36] An ethic of control is constructed, in Welch's view, out of a particular notion of what constitutes responsible action, so that to be responsible is to *do something about* what is wrong in the world. Welch writes her study in the context of what she calls 'cultured despair' about this ethic of control, a despair which is due partly to a loss of idealism, partly to the failure of the utopian vision to come true, and partly to the guilty conscience of those who think they have simply not yet done enough to save the world from its pain and its warfare. So far, this kind of analysis shares in the postmodern debunking of liberal universalism, as a control of reality, through acceptance of a grand narrative of world events. It also shares in a certain Christian awareness that life under the law is a vicious treadmill of seeking to work out one's own salvation and that of the world, whilst constantly failing adequately to do so. In her reflection upon the futility of life under law, Welch is participating in a recognisably postmodern attack, and is encouraging a renewed emphasis upon life under grace, living by faith alone.

She does not leave us, however, with the suggestion that such graceful life cannot actually be manifest within this world and its institutions. To do so would be to accede authority to those structures that most press down upon the lives of women, and to abandon the creation as a place in which divine grace is encountered and known. She does not therefore collude in the polarisation of law and grace. Rather she encourages a positive acceptance of finitude, in which two theological discoveries are made. There is firstly a recognition of finitude as the providential limits which life in the natural world sets upon human possibilities. This is important to Christian ethics, for these limits serve as a 'check against the idolatrous reification of any particular human project'.[37] There is secondly a recognition of the interdependence of created things in which human life is embedded, also important, for these provide ever-changing possibilities for loving relationships. It is in the context of a new affirmation of creaturely life that a feminist Christian ethics suggests a framework for an appropriate universalism, sustained by the compassionate presence of God, and continually offering opportunities for this love to be interwoven into relationships with our fellow human beings and the natural world. Welch offers this as an alternative to the otherworldliness of a utopian ethics of control. In the context of our considerations here, it may also be understood as an alternative to the otherworldliness of postmodern subversions of any rational ethics of justice. Her encouragement is for women to engage in the kinds of interactions with the world and other persons that may both embody the tenderness of God towards the creation, and also transform human life in the context of that creation into the beloved community.

The feminist critique of universalism in ethics has manifest many of the common themes of ethics after modernity, at the same time as this critique has been giving preliminary pointers towards a new way forward in ethical thinking. Such pointers are indicative of an unwillingness to abandon the ethical project, and a desire to discover a form of reaching out to connect with what is ultimate, through the exercise of our moral reasoning. As feminist writers explore an appropriate universalism, there are a number of dimensions which they would seek to ensure in any new approach, which would allow their practical concern for the lives of women, their analysis and critique of women's conditions of living, and their hopes for women's greater and more complete fulfilment, to be understood and expressed. That liberalism may no longer furnish the framework appropriate for this kind of ethical critique and reconstruction, may clear the way for another approach to be considered, tried, and tested, in the light of feminist concerns.

Four dimensions would seem to be crucial in the feminist search for an appropriate universalism. What is required, firstly, is a framework in which sensitivity to the concerns of women may be diagnosed and evaluated, so that matters of sexual difference are not elided into more general considerations, or do not disappear under the guise of falsely inclusive terms. An appropriate universalism will take gender issues, and the difference gender makes, seriously. This will depend upon some affirmation of the goodness of the everyday world of human interactions and embodiment. An appropriate universalism will emerge from within these, and not be a new form of controlling them, or limiting their influence. Thirdly, feminism requires a rational framework for the consideration of moral norms, within which women can engage with men in the crucial process of ethical reflection upon social and personal dilemmas. An appropriate universalism will need to reconceptualise justice, in a form that is responsive to the diversity and the wholeness of human persons. Lastly, an appropriate universalism points us with renewed interest towards the importance of theological affirmations regarding the sustaining matrix in which human welfare and flourishing is nourished and inspired. That belief in God, and serious consideration of the divine nature and activity, continues to be a matter of discussion amongst feminists of all kinds, is one of the hopeful and potentially creative signs of the dialogue of feminism and Christian ethics in a postmodern time.

A step towards this appropriate universalism has been taken in feminist considerations of life in community, and to these we now turn.

CHAPTER 9

Towards a redemptive community

A second thread running through the different forms of feminist moral thinking has been that of individualism. To give priority in moral reasoning to the individual, to allow individuals the discovery of meaning in life, to affirm individual fulfilment, to provide the structures for individual expressions of authentic life, have been persistent themes of feminist writing. That feminism should have emerged with the encouragement of Enlightenment individualism, and that it continues to press for the recognition and treatment of women as individuals, has meant that some attention to what it means to be an individual self is a key issue for debate amongst the various paradigms. Indeed, there is now considerable re-evaluation of the nature and the requirements of such individualism, both within feminism itself, and more widely in political and moral thinking. Sensitivity over this issue has heightened in recent years through a renewed emphasis on the nature and significance of communities, and indeed on the priority of the community in shaping the moral project itself. In these new considerations, there is a good deal of reassessment of the implications of individualism, along with concern that expressions of individuality, particularly in the unhindered exercise of free choice, are not so happy a prospect for human social life as once may have been believed.

Feminists are deeply entangled in this current debate, as those who have both shared in the critique of individualism, and yet invested a great deal in urging individual freedom, at last, for women. Feminist writers have challenged the notion of the separated self, while, at the same time, seeking some kind of separateness for individual women; just as they have questioned the political implications of autonomy, while, at the same time, urging women to exercise greater choices in their own lives. Thus there is not a small measure of ambivalence about these new developments in communitarian thinking, and about the implications which they might have for the lives and welfare of women. In particular, one of the central concerns in this debate is the need to rediscover, or to redescribe, the sources of transformation by which social changes can be encouraged, and around which moral arguments can focus. The extent to which feminism is caught up in Enlightenment humanism, with its emphasis on individual obedience to universal rational principles as the source of transformative power in society, is now problematic, as feminists themselves search for other ways in which to describe the potential for social renewal. Here again, the impact of postmodern ways of thinking is to suggest new alternatives for political change, which do not rely upon individual reflection and action, and which may offer a more helpful framework for feminist revisions. That these proposals may also be costly to feminism is one of the major questions addressed in contemporary writing. A particular response to these matters is formulated by Christian feminists in a theology of relationship, which centres on the theme of redemption.

Individualism is singled out by feminists as a major feature of modernism. The Enlightenment opened up possibilities both for the expression of personal freedom, and for the guarantee of a society of minimal interference in this exercise of autonomy. To be free, in thinking and in making choices, was believed to embody the full potential and dignity of human nature, and at the same time to lie at the centre of what the moral project was understood to be. Liberal humanism affirmed the individual, as the one who can know and be obedient to rational principles, and placed great significance upon the development of self in accordance with these. To become authentic was the personal task of ordering one's life around the demands of freedom, of acknowledging this centre of freedom as the inner self essential to being a person, of taking responsibility for one's own decisions and actions. Life together with other free and rational individuals needed only to be bounded by laws to prevent interference and harm, and to allow individuals to use, wherever possible, their capacity for making decisions in accordance with right principles. Liberal feminists, as we have seen, realise clearly the inclusive potential of such individualism, since gender has no place to reside in this self-understanding, and many have engaged in this way of approaching the moral and political project.

However, it has also been the case that feminists have resisted this individualistic approach to morality and to social life, and have not been entirely happy to draw women into a way of thinking and acting which they believe is seriously flawed. Individualism, so the challenges go, not only distorts the embodied and the social character of the human person, but also becomes the ideological face of institutions that manifestly do not ensure, or even make provision for, the extension of the requirements of liberty and autonomy to all persons. Much that lies at the heart of the social constructionist and naturalistic paradigms of feminist ethics suggests alternatives to this emphasis on the separated self and its extraneous social interactions. Yet, within these paradigms too, there is a concern for the freedom of persons, and for the development of a life which is authentic to those concerned. Thus the very meaning of the central terms of feminism – liberation and self-determination, now takes on greater complexity, as their historical connections with individual choice and fulfilment alone, are challenged.[1]

Herein lies another of the dilemmas of contemporary feminism. For its historical roots in Enlightenment moral and political thinking offer to women the possibility of discovering transcendent rational principles on the basis of which social practices may be judged, and in reference to which personal lives may be measured and altered. Women who engage in this project resist any institution that obstructs their own exercise of reasonable self-determination, and believe that in personal relationships too, a basic respect for their equal right to autonomy is essential to healthy human interactions. Taking this individualism seriously, there seems no limit to the extension of this way of reasoning throughout the whole of life. Consistency in conforming to right principles becomes a source of social critique and of transformation.

At the same time, however, women are aware of the potential for being drawn away from precisely those relationships and practices which they believe are meaningful in human life, in which they are able to exercise other skills than that of impartial reasoning, and which they also claim to be essential to social well-being. The research of Gilligan brought out just these features. Women continually reported their difficulty with abstract considerations of justice, not because they could not understand them, but because to engage in what has now been labelled 'an ethic of justice', was to make them unrecognisable to themselves as persons, and to detach themselves from the relationships in which their lives held meaning. The 'ethic of care', which more closely approximated what women were saying about morality, has emphasised new issues about what kinds of persons we are, or are becoming, and about the quality of the relationships in which we are engaged. These place the stress in the moral life upon immanence rather than transcendence, upon discovering within situations and interactions what needs to be done, rather than appealing for guidance as if from outside these relationships. In this respect, the concerns of women seem to place them firmly on the side of intimacy, of emotional involvement between persons, of close ties with those most immediately sharing one's life, of small social units in which persons may be most fully nurtured, and lastly, of service to others which puts their needs before one's own.

In these emphases, and in their challenges to the individualism of western society and its traditions, the concerns of feminists overlap with those of other critics of liberalism. As Marilyn Friedman has noted, 'Some of these anti-individualist developments emerging from feminist thought are strikingly similar to other theoretical developments that are not specifically feminist.'[2] Thus, the renewed interest in a communitarian approach to morality takes precisely the features sketched above to be the outline of a new sort for society, as well as a more accurate rendering of the nature of moral reasoning. This similarity of issues to be found within feminist and communitarian challenges has led at least one feminist to argue that their causes should now be entirely common. For Elizabeth Fox-Genovese, feminism has, for too long, crippled itself with demands for autonomy and equal rights, while, at the same time, both believing in and enjoying the values that intimate relationships and life in the midst of close community entails. 'To the extent that feminism ... has espoused those individualistic principles, it has condemned itself to the dead-end toward which individualism is now plunging.'[3] This duplicity, or 'uneasy coexistence of communitarian and individualistic commitments', is writ large within feminism, according to Fox-Genovese, and suggests that only a *Feminism without Illusions* of liberal individualism can be appropriate in the midst of present needs for the reconstruction of communities.[4]

There is much in feminism that lends credibility to this analysis, and it may be helpful to examine just which features among the varieties of feminism support this new communitarianism, and in what ways that support presents critical issues for further developments in feminism and in Christian ethics. Clearly there is a strong emphasis in feminist moral thinking on the formation of the individual self in the midst of relationships. We are not first of all unattached beings, to whom interactions with others are then added, but primarily related beings who develop a sense of self-identity in different kinds of contexts. Those feminists, for example, who offer an object-relations analysis of human life, take as fundamental the qualities and characteristics of the earliest mother-child relationship. The foundations of the person are believed to lie here, in the differing ways in which responses are formed to separation and attachment, to anxiety and comfort, to deprivation and satisfaction. These begin to shape individual self-understanding, and form the essential matrix out of which persons emerge as distinctive and unique selves.[5] It is in the midst of this interactive setting that individual decisions are made which can confirm and strengthen these relations, or can deny and weaken them through lack of attention. The fundamental moral choice of the individual lies here, in giving priority to attachments among persons, and to the capacities for trust, acceptance, and loyalty which are essential within them. A strong feminist claim is made that authentic individuality recognises and enhances the relational character of the self.

Not only is this psychological theory important to new feminist reflections on individuality, but also epistemological considerations support this relational understanding. Feminists have questioned for some time the dependence of so-called objective knowledge upon the detachment of the knower. Central to modern epistemology has been the primary concern with describing the conditions for the legitimation of knowledge, so that rational persons, prepared to adopt the appropriate methodology for arriving at truth-claims, could be confident in the results of their inquiry. Such methods are open to any, provided that subjective considerations and particular aspects of the knower's life do not intrude upon them. Thus, knowledge which is reliable, which either corresponds most closely to reality, or is most internally coherent within a total framework of ideas, is derived by means of individual detachment from emotion, from relationships, and from historical circumstance.

This dichotomy between objectivity in knowledge and subjectivity in personal life is challenged by feminists as a thoroughly gendered account, and one which excludes those important ways of knowing in which women are quite specifically and specially involved.[6] Thus, as Lorraine Code has argued, 'the scope of epistemological inquiry has been too narrowly defined', and can be opened up to a whole range of new considerations through a recognition of the standpoint of the knower.[7] This standpoint is the position of the one who knows, as a situated being amidst a unique set of persons, structures, and circumstances that together make up a human life. Such standpoints are not merely interesting as background to the knower's life, nor are they to be dismissed as a bias that must be eradicated for true knowledge to be acquired. Rather, the recognition and conscious affirmation of standpoints clears the space for a feminist epistemology, built around women's experiences of exclusion and oppression.[8] In such a new approach, the knowledge which is important 'takes different perspectives into account', and at the same time, rests on the demonstration of 'the reality of social injustices and practices', which are experientially known by those involved.[9] This Code describes as a form of 'mitigated relativism'. To accept that individuals have distinctive standpoints from which they know and decide, gives moral priority to forms of co-operation whereby these positions may be upheld. Thus a feminist epistemology, that understands truth to be diverse and multifaceted, can be re-creative of communities, in ways that empower human beings to be co-operative, both with one another and with the natural world.[10]

The requirement of objectivity in knowledge is to be found in accounts of moral reasoning, since the kind of detachment required of the knower, has been been presumed essential to moral knowledge too, as we noted in Welch's critique of abstraction. To take account of the real differences between individuals can give rise to another moral outlook. Benhabib argues that in meetings with the 'concrete', rather than the 'generalized', other, we encounter 'all that belongs to them as embodied, affective, suffering creatures, their memory and history, their ties and relations to others'.[11] Such encounters themselves provide the grounds for interpersonal obligations, since, from them, arise moral norms of '*equity* and *complementary reciprocity*'.[12] The notion of emergent norms, Benhabib calls 'interactive universalism', since the necessary guides for behaviour are not imposed upon relationships, but are the conditions for the fruitful continuation of them. Welch extends this notion further by reference to the transformation which occurs, as those who engage in relationships are affected in, and transformed by, them. 'When mutual transformation occurs, there is the power of empathy and compassion, of delight in otherness, and strength in the solidarity of listening to others, bearing together stories of pain and resistance.'[13] While Benhabib speaks of the enlargement of the imagination that occurs through encounters like this, Welch describes the enlargement of the self. 'Genuine conversation occurs as one finds joy in listening to others and, even as previous and present worlds of meaning are challenged, experiences delight in the complexity of what emerges.'[14] These arguments for a communicative ethics suggest both the reality of continuous dialogue with others, whereby the participation of all in the common life is made possible, and the opportunities which such dialogue presents for that communal life also to be endlessly creative.

The above criticisms of 'the unencumbered self' of modern epistemology and moral philosophy bring with them assumptions about the human person as an interactive self, as a connected being, held together in the fabric of a common life, and shaped through continual intersubjective relations with others. That the individual is basically a communal being, and that attention must be given to the nurturing of persons in community, has been a central theme of the feminist ethic of care. The description of this ethic, given in works like that of Noddings, relies upon the special knowledge and feelings characteristic of women's embodiment, and thus encourages the uniquely important contribution of women to the sustenance of communal life. Women are believed to be in a privileged position, sensitive to precisely those concerns that are most necessary for the flourishing of human life, and bearing distinctive responsibilities for ensuring these conditions obtain.

Other feminists, however, argue for the wider acceptance of this ethic, both for men, and as a political framework for the restructuring of social life. Sara Ruddick argues that maternal thinking is itself a form of reasoning, concerned with the vigilance of preservative love, the realism of fostering growth, and the attention necessary for respectful training.[15] Each aspect of this reasoning is indicative of a cognitive capacity for thinking a certain way, and of a willingness to become a certain kind of person in relation to other persons. Men may engage in this reasoning too, for it emerges in the midst of the practical work of mothering, only part of which is giving birth. Indeed its relevance to a politics of peace for our world depends upon the belief that all persons can overcome the weighty tradition of dualistic thinking, which has separated rational from nurturing practice, and can reassess the meaning of individuality as engagement with others. The political dimensions of this ethic of care are closely explored by Joan Tronto, who questions the boundaries that have been drawn around the moral life in modern political thinking. These boundaries, which divide politics from morality, or which privilege the disinterested over the interested point of view, or which segregate public and private spheres of activity, have all been cultural creations, that a feminist emphasis on care can overthrow. 'In order to be created and sustained ... an ethic of care relies upon a political commitment to value care and to reshape institutions to reflect that changed value.'[16] This wider implication of caring work significantly challenges the belief that care is merely 'a parochial concern of women', by insisting that it is central to all human life. Thus, Tronto claims, 'It is time that we began to change our political and social institutions to reflect this truth.'[17]

In all of these ways, feminism traces a path alongside the new communitarianism, and, at several points, the concerns of both overlap and are interwoven. Feminist writings have been affirmative of communal life, as the place of personal and moral formation, and in that sense, have some sympathy with the Hegelian critique of Kant. To be able to formulate moral issues at all presumes a shared context, or *Sittlichkeit*, from which a common language of discourse and a set of values emerges, and thus morality is historically shaped and created. Feminist writings have contributed to this awareness by arguing that the moral agent is a situated, rather than a disembedded, self, and have given specific attention to the moral and political importance of ensuring the healthy quality of relationships essential to social well-being. Likewise, feminists have reaffirmed the importance of emotion in moral decision, in a way that is suggestive of the Humean suspicion of dispassionate reason. Feelings are affirmed, not as the private sensations of individuals that one must rise above in decisions of principle, but as important signs of our common humanity, from which may grow empathy and altruism.[18] Feminist writings have encouraged the training of these feelings in a relational ethic that more closely approximates the fullness of personhood. Lastly, feminists have recognised the moral centrality of the practices in which one engages, making the connection between *praxis* and reflection in a way that revives the Aristotelian notion of practical reason. To assert that one's standpoint is the position from which truth may be known and spoken, is to claim that the moral point of view is not from nowhere, but from precisely here, from the contingent circumstances of one's life. Feminists' descriptions of the rational activity of care, and their emphasis upon the formation of character in the midst of this work, are important affirmations of these renewed concerns in moral thinking.

Yet, some notes of caution need also to be sounded in this close overlapping of feminist and communitarian descriptions of morality, for there are important ways in which feminists need to be saying something quite distinctive and explicit about the possible implications of these descriptions for women. One of their concerns has to do with the proper place of detachment in personal life, with what Benhabib calls 'reflexive role-distance'.[19] In their enthusiasm for affirming interpersonal commitments and responsiveness to human need, there can be a danger that feminists will not give proper attention to the necessary space for some personal separation, and for reasoned reflection upon the relationships in which one is caught up. Grimshaw's hesitation about an ethic of care centred on the question of what the boundaries around the expectations of care would be, and how women would be able to resist their exploitation as carers in a generally uncaring society.[20] Precisely how one stands back to reflect in these situations is not only a matter of some delicacy between persons, but is also a problem of the nature of moral reasoning. Because there has been, in modern moral thinking, an opposition set up between individual freedom for self-determination, on the one hand, and being responsive to the requirements of relationship, on the other, decisions that may be needed between competing relational demands, or about doing something only for oneself, or about whether to enter into a new relationship, can appear to be affirming the first mode of individualistic moral thinking which feminists have so thoughtfully resisted. To provide a description of moral reflection that is true to a relational view of the self, is the challenge to feminism.

A second note of caution concerns the circularity of moral argument which is suggested in these feminist reconsiderations. Having clarified so helpfully women's ways of knowing and interacting with others, there needs also to be some consideration of the grounds upon which women might debate whether these forms of behaviour are good for them. There is a conservative tendency in some feminist writing, which seems to reaffirm the typical roles and responsibilities women have in society, now to be sanctioned by their agreement that these things are, after all, most natural to them. There may still be, however, an underlying moral question about whether the ways in which women have been socially formed thus far, are a good development or not. Benhabib suggests that 'Communitarians often seem to conflate the philosophical thesis concerning the significance of constitutive communities for the formation of one's identity with a socially conventionalist and morally conformist attitude.'[21] Thus there can be hidden assumptions in an emphasis on community, regarding the place and the function of women that do not receive due attention, and that sustain only the moral requirement to carry out one's role as fully as possible. When these assumptions are disclosed, feminists are much less sanguine about a renewed emphasis on communities, without retaining the 'specifically *modern* achievement of being able to criticize, challenge and question the content of these constitutive identities and the "prima facie" duties and obligations they impose upon us'.[22] To remove the culturally transcendent principles on the basis of which these practices could be prised open, is problematic for women, and reopens the question of whether there is something over the horizon of social constructions.

This brings us specifically to the issue of transformation, an area in which, again, the common interest of feminists and communitarians is problematic. For feminism shares with communitarianism a critique of modernism, which can result in a sense of wistfulness about some former period of social cohesiveness that has now been lost. The suggestion that before the emergence of modern individualism, before the birth of liberal democracies, and before the rise of feminism, there once were small social units, in which a common value scheme was shared and people knew what was expected of them, is evidence of a romantic streak in communitarian thinking, which seeks to recover from within history the sources of transformation of the present. Some feminist writings exhibit this tendency to urge the recovery of a lost past, which may be believed to predate the patriarchal rule of the father, or to dwell in the submerged memories of the oppressed, or to exist in places unaffected by the western tradition of controlling reason, or to have emerged within the early church, or even to precede the Fall. These sources of challenge to existing society are sought as an alternative to the abstractions of transcendent moral principles. However, many feminists are questioning whether this is in fact the only alternative, the only source of transformation, since, in particular, there is no clear way of judging between the radically different pictures of the lost utopias which may be desired. Without some means of making an intelligent choice here, women may abandon their emphasis on individual liberty, only to find themselves unable to discern or to effect positive changes in their lives.

It is now perhaps more obvious how forms of postmodern feminism offer what appear to be quite attractive ways through this dilemma of feminism, in which women seem to have to choose between a form of autonomous but abstract individualism, or a form of cohesive but potentially exploitative community. Iris Marion Young argues that, like most dichotomies, 'individualism and community have a common logic underlying their polarity, which makes it possible for them to define each other negatively'.[23] Looking more closely at these alternatives, it is possible to discover two shared assumptions in these different approaches, which, by exposing, may help us to see other ways through the debate. Both of these alternatives, Young claims, rely upon a denial of difference, by retaining the underlying logic of identity which has been characteristic of western rationality. Feminist writers have been concerned about this denial within individualism, finding that its assumption of the fundamental sameness of persons actually deprives the individual of a distinctive voice and point of view. What is unique cannot be taken into account in moral reasoning, and thus differences constitute a problem to be overcome, rather than an opportunity for new awareness and interaction. This suggests the second shared assumption, which is 'a desire to bring multiplicity and heterogeneity into unity'.[24] Again, feminists have questioned this desire within liberal thinking, since women have found themselves required to become like men in order to participate in political and moral debate. A critique of these two assumptions has helped feminists to challenge the place of individualism in modern moral philosophy.

However, Young herself finds that these same assumptions are characteristic of the emphasis on community as well, and therefore that having to choose between these alternatives is actually no helpful choice for women at all. Communitarians, in their emphasis upon the social construction of the self, express the same 'urge to unity', looking for forms of communal life which will result in 'harmony among persons . . . consensus and mutual understanding'.[25] Thus, those feminists who emphasise the relational character of the self, and the nurture which is required for the maintenance of good relations, presume that relationships will bring intersubjective harmony and will encourage respectful cooperation. Postmodern feminists are not only critical of these 'longings', which are dreams of another place that is not here, and which can therefore become controlling visions of what ought to be made to come true. They are also, as Young expresses so clearly, sceptical of the notion of subjectivity which underpins these hopes. At the centre of communitarian visions is an 'ideal of social relations as the copresence of subjects', an ideal which presupposes that subjects can be transparent to one another, that 'each understands the others and recognizes the others in the same way that they understand themselves, and all recognize that the others understand them as they understand themselves'.[26] Young accepts the Derridean critique of intersubjectivity, as an attempt 'to collapse the temporal difference inherent in language and experience into a totality that can be comprehended in one view'.[27] Her belief in the 'ontological difference within and between subjects' makes the alternative of community, in which 'persons cease to be other, opaque, not understood', also not a positive choice for feminism.

Postmodern feminism offers different affirmations of the fluid and decentred nature of the self, and of the diversely interactive nature of society. Without a centre of subjectivity that is either the seat of individual free will, or a source of feeling for other selves, this dilemma of modernism can be avoided. Particularly, there need no longer be the choice between the ideal of impartiality with its hierarchical consequences, sustained by individualism, and the ideal of smaller cohesive units with their exclusionary consequences, built upon fellow feeling. The decentred self is a web of interactions, that overlaps at various points and in various ways with other selves, and is thus, in an important way, elusive, mysterious, and unreachable in itself. Its fluidity means that there are practically unlimited possibilities for interactions, indeed for friendships, as Friedman argues, which are more supportive of human diversity and idiosyncracy, than other close personal relationships could be.[28]

A society of such fluctuating interactions is urban, and Young presents the outlines of the 'normative ideal of city life', claiming that we must look within our given experiences of cities 'for the virtues of this form of social relations'.[29] City life is characterised by interactions between strangers, within which there are smaller clusters of people who associate both voluntarily and nonvoluntarily, and beyond which there are wider networks of communication and provision. This kind of society can ensure justice through a continuous process of empowerment, which enables agents to participate in decision-making through an effective voice and vote, and thus liberates real human differences.[30] These new ways of thinking reveal important postmodern themes of heterogeneity and fluidity, and it is in the midst of these realities that social change occurs. Since human interactions are continually changing, there is always potential for disruption, as conventional boundaries are crossed, or as individual interests change. A society, which can accommodate these fluctuations, needs to be open to hear the different voices, and to be flexible in adapting to the participation of the many in collective life. Thus a postmodern alternative.

There is now within feminism considerable debate about what is the most helpful way to explain the nature and the logic of the moral life, in particular as it may provide the framework for personal and social transformation. Contemporary feminists are discovering the narrowness of the path between their rejection of Enlightenment individualism, in its ultimately abstract inwardness, and their potential submergence in the narrowness of communities. One description of this path is given by Benhabib in her form of interactive universalism, which avoids the generalised other, but none the less relies upon the emergence of norms for respecting differences that challenge social practices and structures. Another description of this path is provided by those ethicists of care, who recover a tradition submerged within the Enlightenment, and seek to place the capacities for nurture and for empathy at the centre of our human nature. This also provides a ground upon which social and political critique may be built. In these and in other ways, feminists are seeking to describe the possibility of an 'immanent critique' in ethics, given the problems identified with an individual knowledge of principles that transcends cultural contingencies. The postmodern emphasis on polyvocality does provide some vision for this, but at the cost of personal subjectivity, interpersonal encounter, and some rational considerations of social justice.

Lovibond provides a philosophical alternative in her analysis of *Realism and Imagination in Ethics*. With the rejection of Enlightenment notions of a rational 'view from nowhere' outside a common form of life, the position of the dissenter is more vulnerable. The question becomes how alternative insight is possible, of what it may be constructed, and how such insights may come to be recognised by, and later integrated into, the common life. Lovibond suggests that 'contradictions' emerge 'because of the incompleteness of intellectual authority within the moral language-game', and that these fragments of freedom become the sources of critique.[31] Individuals seek to 'find their way about' the world, through the personal exercise of imagination, as new ways of acting and being are considered, and, in the process, new language is introduced into the community.[32] This is an argument for empowerment, so that different voices are heard, but it is also an argument for rational discourse amongst those who share a common life, about the best responses to the human situation.

What is therefore important, recognising that social constructions of reality tend towards 'monopolistic value-systems', is for critics to remain within the community of discourse, to insist upon continued participation in the rational consideration of value, and to be living reminders to a community that its vision is fragmentary and incomplete. Our moral imagination, within the limits proposed, suggests that this conversation will lead, not to 'a conception of reality from which all traces of human perspective would be excluded', but rather to an immanent hope for a reality in which 'the individual or local perspectives of all human beings would be able to find harmonious expression'.[33] Such would be a form of non-foundational realism, that both recognises something of a shared humanity, and can allow critical spaces for the distinctive insights of feminist imagination. These contribute, through continued involvement in political and moral debate, to the fuller realisation of the common life.

Welch provides a theological version of an immanent critique in her feminist 'ethic of risk', for what happens in the occasions of interpersonal encounters is transformative of social life as well. This is so, not because of the exercise of imagination, but because of the discovery of solidarity in oppression. In dialogue with other standpoints, moments of transformation occur, as one 'feels the pain of the people who are oppressed', and, in this fellow-feeling, is able to acknowledge one's own pain.[34] Such shared memories of oppression become 'dangerous', in that they open up the space for questions about the necessity for such conditions of life. In these spaces, the work of liberation can occur, as attention is given to 'the cultural and the political matrix of our thought as well as our particular location within a tradition'.[35] Thus a critical distance is introduced in which it becomes possible to examine, together, our human experiences, and to create new ways of living.

Welch shares with postmodernism the recognition that our common life is a 'chaos of interdependence', and thus she does not urge a romantic return to some simpler or more unified form of community.[36] The point of moral debate is not to discover this perfect form of society which can then be imposed by the righteous. Rather, there is hope both for increasing diversity, as each new encounter brings with it new complexities, and for increasing harmony, as our compassion for others deepens, and as we struggle together to become the beloved community of God, in which 'the life-giving love constitutive of solidarity with the oppressed and love of oneself' is able to grow and be manifest.[37] It is clear that Welch understands this to be a continuous, active process of 'partial victories over injustice', which can 'lay the groundwork for further acts of criticism and courageous defiance'.[38] This, she proposes, is a more 'appropriate symbol for the process of celebrating life, enduring limits, and resisting injustice', than that symbol of final and complete victory – the kingdom of God.

In yet another form of immanent critique, Christian feminists are seeking, through the development of a theology of relationship, to bring the theme of redemption into this debate. For, as both Carter Heyward and Mary Grey have so carefully described, it is this theme which is at the heart of the Christian moral life. Redemption reveals the creative purposes of God in making all things to exist in relation, and the providential work of God in bringing the whole of creation into right and harmonious relationship. Redemption is, therefore, about integrity and wholeness, in the context of every aspect of the cosmos. Thus, as Grey writes, 'Redemption suggests the goal, the process and the method of reaching that desired wholeness.'[39] In her work, she seeks a model of redemption, which will show the integral relationship of self-affirmation, belonging to the natural world, and the forming of just social structures. An emphasis on any one of these, to the exclusion or to the detriment of the others, cannot provide the appropriate means for arriving at the goal, and it is so often into the gaps between these that women have fallen. Redemption which brings integrity to women's lives, and indeed which women consider to be essential to the fulfilment of all things, must hold these three – the self, relations with others, and connectedness with nature – in balance and in mutual tension. For each element brings a measure of transcendence to the others, in which the divine presence can be discovered at work. It is with reference to this theme that Christian feminism claims a source of critical distance, of power, and of envisioning a new future, which may lead towards a redemptive community.

With this concern for right relation, feminists are reclaiming a doctrine that has become too closely associated with 'overtones which ring of suffering, sacrifice, guilt and self-negation, the negativity of the cross of Jesus Christ and the severity of the atonement doctrines which try to explain it'.[40] As Ann Loades has argued, in her description of 'Why certain forms of holiness are bad for you', such overtones cluster within the tradition of the imitation of Christ, demanding that one replicate Christ's sufferings in personal life. Her insistence that this behaviour and belief is not only a form of disguised egotism, but is also seriously distorted when removed from 'the context of love', provides a powerful argument that this 'may be the last kind of Christianity that women are likely to need'.[41] To re-present this theme into feminist awareness is to challenge the cultural assumptions surrounding theories of the atonement, as well as understandings of Christ that are saturated with images of masculinity.[42] Indeed, since Ruether first raised the question of whether a male saviour could save women, this issue has not left the Christian feminist agenda.[43] Echoing Saiving's doubts about the description of the human situation in Protestant theology, Harrison too describes the irreconcilable oppositions, between self-assertion and self-denial, between eros and agape, between human choice and divine control, oppositions which are central to modern individualism and to neo-orthodoxy.[44] Women can participate in this scheme of theological ethics by agreeing to abandon the lesser-valued term, in a way that allows them to become just like their brothers in faith, but at the cost of colluding in the devaluation of those things that matter to them as persons. To the extent that the understanding of redemption, and the explanation of the work of Christ, have relied upon such presuppositions, they may hinder the very process which they seek to define. And redemption must include goal, process, and method.

There are three steps to this recovery of the theme of redemption for feminism. The first is to affirm that the relationships which form the matrix of our lives are not only natural given facts of existence, in which all things are bound together, but are purposive, in that we are meant for one another and for the earth. Women are sources of God-given and God-directed wisdom about the reality of this relational matrix, for, as Grey says, 'women are actually revealing a world that is relational at its very core'.[45] This has been an important contribution of green feminism, which, as Catherina Halkes has written, has developed a new ecological spirituality, in which 'there is amazement and admiration for the unity and the solidarity of all life'.[46] To affirm the connectedness of all things is, at the same time, to speak of the loving presence which upholds this creation. Thus our belonging to the created web of life, to the parameters of our embodiment, to our contingent circumstances, are the sites of the presence of God. Such teleological affirmations about the relational nature of all creation are also recognitions of the brokenness of our world in all its dimensions. Our spiritual awareness does not end in self-satisfied knowledge of these facts about our lives, but rather brings with it the sense, also, of creation as 'an enslaved reality in need of redemption'.[47] To believe that relationships are central to the divine creative will, is to become more sensitive to all forms of living and acting and interacting which deny relationship, or which pretend separation. Thus, affirmation of the relational nature of creation is also to long for integrity and wholeness in those relationships, and to believe that this longing is evidence of divine intention.

The second step in the recovery of this theme is to affirm that the end for which all things have been made is right relationship, in which integrity, wholeness, and harmony may be realised. The point of relationships is that they be right ones. In specifying these more closely, Grey suggests that redemptive relations include the necessity for resistance and protest on the basis of solidarity in suffering, but also surpass these, in their 'profounder dynamic'.[48] For, the 'level of broken mutuality refuses to be healed by political freedom struggles alone'.[49] Right relationships are also more than the entangled interactions of decentred selves, which happen to overlap in various and changing ways. For, right relation includes the journey of discovery of oneself as subject and agent, in which the integrity of the person may be known, and this, most especially, in the lives of women. Likewise, right relationship includes the process of self-affirmation as a distinctive person, a process which again is essential for the wholeness of women as persons in their own right. But it also strains forward both to the discovery of mutuality in interpersonal relationships, and to the transformation of structures in which such wholeness is blocked or denied. The end for which human life has been made, and in which it finds its most complete fulfilment, is mutuality-in-relation, an end which has broken through history in the passionate love of Christ, 'making possible in history endless possibilities of exchanged love'.[50] Thus Grey insists upon the uniqueness of incarnation and resurrection, as revelations of the 'divine passionate energy for justice', from which we claim 'resurrection energy' for the continuous renewal and transformation of the world.[51]

The third step in the recovery of the redemptive theme is to recognise that Christian feminism is hereby reclaiming the transcendence of the divine. While it is true that the dimension of God's immanence is highlighted, as for example in Harrison's claim that 'Our knowledge of God *is* in and through each other. Our knowledge of each other *is* in and through God', it is also the case that the divine is understood as 'the ground of relation', in a way that surpasses all actual relationships, and provides for them a continuing source of power for the work of justice.[52] In her definition of God, Carter Heyward writes:

that God is our power in relation to each other, all humanity, and creation itself. God is creative power, that which effects justice – right relation – in history ... God is not only our immediate power in relation, but is also our immediate re-source of power: that from which we draw power to realize actively who we are in relation.[53]

To make these claims about God is to suggest that God is constantly at work to do and to bring about and to support the forming of right relationships at all levels and types of inter-actions. It is on this basis that Christian feminists envision a new future, remembering 'the empowering actions of Jesus', which point us 'both to the estranged relational scene of the present, and to the creative envisioning of a transformed future'.[54] Grey claims that, 'The only hope-filled solution in the final analysis must lie in faith in a transcendental dimen-sion, in the sense which transcends finitude, embracing God and world, which will lead us from our limited human abilities for meaning-making.'[55]

The present question is whether, and how, such hopes for a redemptive community may live in a postmodern context, which, as Heller and Feher describe, 'is tremendously ill at ease with Utopianism'.[56] Indeed, they claim that 'Redemptive poli-tics of any kind are incompatible with the postmodern political condition', and thus there is very great difficulty in expressing what lies beyond the present, and encouraging moral action in accordance with such vision. Heller and Feher understand redemptive politics to be

one in which a single final gesture is seen as the carrier of ultimate redemption both for society and each and every person dwelling within it. The more de-centred a social system becomes, the more simple-minded redemptive politics appears ... It is this loss of relevance suffered by the redemptive paradigm that has led so many to despair.[57]

This realisation is an uneasy one for feminism, as feminists may be colluding in the very emphasis on immanence that makes their own hopes for redeeming the dream less plausible. The attempt of Christian feminists to sketch the theme of redemption, as 'the living out of increasing depth of redemptive relatedness', may be of some help in pointing the way to a renewing transcendence. In answering this question, feminism and Christian ethics are, once again, integrally related.

CHAPTER 10

Towards a new humanism

The search for an appropriate universalism within the writings of feminism suggests both an unwillingness to abandon the possibility of ethics altogether, and a desire to discover and to work towards the liberation of women and the greater fulfilment of human life. Their unwillingness is evidence of a profound awareness of fundamental questions about life in all of its dimensions, questions which press upon our consciousness, and which require the whole range of skills available to us to pursue and to understand, and of a belief that such awareness is a basic feature of being human. There is much that may still be developed within feminist thinking from what is basically a moral sense. It ensures, on the one hand, a most critical attitude towards, and assessment of, existing modes of reasoning in moral matters. Thus the dismantling of the notion of a disembodied thinking self, whose thoughts and actions need to be guided by transcendent rational principles, has been an exercise in developing a more adequate understanding of human life and the place of the moral within it. On the other hand, it is from this moral sense that women may recognise and speak of the different possibilities of morality, which may yet serve human life in new ways. Christian feminists have suggested that emphasis on the creation themes of finitude and of interdependence provides the setting for such new considerations, by placing morality firmly within an affirmation of creaturely life. To speak of these new conceptions of human life is to engage in an ethical inquiry, for which it is necessary to propose means of judgement and appropriate methodologies. Feminist attempts to formulate another understanding of the human person in community have been evidence of such a project.

Hopes for liberation and fulfilment are central to the feminist search for this redemptive community. Having been born in the midst of individualistic conceptions of liberation, feminism is left with an uncertain legacy. It has been significant in the feminist appropriation of liberal notions of freedom and self-legislation, that their call for the realisation of these was believed to be a way of affirming human unity, by allegiance to a shared set of principles, and further, of attending to injustices, in which the self-contradictory nature of treating persons as mere means to an end, becomes a powerful stimulus to social change. That these hopes are believed to have degenerated into privileges for the powerful, and to have failed to capture what is distinctive about women, has made continued reliance upon them fraught with difficulty for feminism.

Feminists' own challenges to these hopes stem from another conception of the human community, in which the notion of discrete, atomistic individuals is no longer plausible, and, instead, the interactive, relational nature of human life is affirmed. This requires a new description of the sources of transformation, which both keep alive the fundamental questions that are basic to our humanness, and at the same time offer helpful guidance towards greater and richer fulfilment. While many postmodern feminists have abandoned this search as unnecessary, given the multiplicity of fluctuating interactions between decentred selves, in which changes simply occur, other feminists have looked for these sources in various ways: – through the shared memories and experiences of oppression characteristic of the feminist standpoint, through the emergent norms of personal interactions, through the continuous exercise of imagination in finding one's way about the world. In all of these, new ways of expressing the desire for, and the means to, human fulfilment are suggested.

Christian feminists have interpreted these inquiries as a sign of the human longing for the redemptive recovery of what has been broken, and of a commitment to the discovery of resources for redemption, that may hold together, in one accord, the affirmation of the person, the possibility of interpersonal communion, and our embeddedness within the natural world. Both the vision of such redemption which is provided in individualistic religion, and that which is offered in new communitarian emphases, hold their dangers for women. The first may fail to provide a positive resource for human interactions, and for sensitive involvement in creation, in its overemphasis on the intercourse of the individual soul with the divine. The second may fail to offer a vision of transcendent wholeness, by comparison with which the efforts of particular communities may be known to be both partial and fragile achievements. For feminists to address this redemptive theme has had something of an apologetic function, in helping to contribute in a distinctive way to contemporary debates, but, equally, has been challenging to the Christian tradition itself, as this theme in its turn is held up for closer scrutiny. This new situation of critique and of opportunity holds the concerns of feminism and Christian theological ethics closely together.

There is, however, another matter to be tackled before completing the task of demonstrating the interactions, and the intrinsic relationship, of feminism and Christian ethics. This concerns the need to specify, in some way, what would constitute the fulfilment of human beings, and how that general conception of humanness relates particularly to the being, or the nature, of women. While the theme of redemption draws us on to consider the importance of right relationship, and places in the very centre of the divine intention for all creation the empowering of mutuality-in-relation, there is a question still to be addressed about how this purpose is manifest in the particular nature of human beings. To reaffirm the purposiveness of human life, and to believe that some intention is written throughout the fabric of creation, is to reopen the cluster of issues which surround an account of our essential humanness. This therefore is the third thread to be picked up from within the different paradigms of moral reasoning. Each of them has made assumptions about human nature, about the normative significance of female and male manifestations of that nature, and about those moral choices which would confirm the appropriate meaning of our being human, within the whole context of life. It will be useful to pull out this thread, as another way of comparing and contrasting the various moral approaches, and as a means of engaging with this highly contentious area of feminist and Christian ethical thinking. By bringing the major questions involved into the light of common concern, it is hoped that we may step forward together in understanding, towards a new humanism.

To claim that this is an issue at all is problematic in the context of contemporary feminism, and it may be useful to begin this discussion with a consideration of why that is so. There lie within feminist writings deep-seated suspicions about descriptions of human nature, of the meaning of the human body, and of the fulfilment for which humanity is intended. These descriptions, often called essentialist, speak about the common structure and content of human nature, and introduce another form of universalism into ethical discourse. This time, the ethical thinker reaches out to connect with the core of our humanity, rather than with abstract principles, drawing our attention thereby to those features of the human condition that are shared across contingent circumstances, and through historical changes. While the difficulty with Enlightenment universalism was its reliance upon transcendent reason, which must leave the body to one side during its inquiry, the difficulty here is precisely the opposite. Essentialism recalls us to bodily reality, to the materiality of existence, to the parameters of our embodied life, and asks that we find there the roots and the purpose of the moral project, already present. After all this effort, feminists are concerned that we not simply reproduce forms of sexual complementarity in which inequalities breed, or reaffirm that biology, after all, determines destiny.

In her analysis of theological anthropology within the Christian tradition, Ruether traces some of the dis-ease in feminist considerations of human nature. The tradition, she claims, has separated the question of existence, that is, how human beings actually live and interact in history, from the question of essence, that is, the authentic humanity intended for unity with God, expressed in the notion of being made in God's image. Basic to this separation is the assumption that the essence of the human person, as made by God, is good, and that this essence constitutes an original potential for full development into communion with the divine, which is the Creator's intention. On the other hand, the actual existence of humanity is marred by sin. The 'Fall' is understood to be the distortion of what God has made, which now obscures the *imago dei*, leaving human beings divided against themselves, their authentic essential being against their lived existential being. What Ruether is concerned to demonstrate is the way in which this kind of theological anthropology has become entangled in assumptions about man and woman, so that there is now 'an ambiguity in the way the *imago dei* / sin has been correlated with maleness and femaleness'.[1] This ambiguity is the tension between a belief that there is an 'equivalence of maleness and femaleness in the image of God', on the one hand, and a 'tendency to correlate femaleness with the lower part of human nature', in a way that links being female to sinful existential nature, on the other.[2] Such ambiguity is problematic and unresolved throughout Christian thinking, and continues to hamper our discussions of human nature today.

Ruether's analysis of 'patriarchal anthropology' shows just how pervasive are negative assumptions about female nature, that have now been described and documented by many other feminists. What is interesting in her discussion, is the way in which, consistently, in Roman Catholic and Protestant theologies, the *imago dei* is presented differentially for men and for women. Thus, Augustine wrote that 'the woman, together with her own husband, is the image of God', while the man is in God's image both alone and with his wife. For woman to be in touch with her own authentic being required marriage, since it was through her relation to man as 'helpmeet' that Augustine believed she shared in 'the whole substance' which could be 'one image'.[3] Aquinas accepted a biological hierarchy, within which woman was believed to be inferior to man in mind, body, and will, a created inequality intended by God for procreative purposes. Thus woman's 'imperfection' was placed into the context of the overall 'perfection' of nature, the original intention of which would be completed through her contribution in child-bearing. In the Protestant theologies of Luther and Calvin, there is a willingness to recognise the equality of man and woman in the original *imago dei*, so that there is something of an equivalence as far as the essential nature of each is concerned. However, the effect of sin means that, in their actual existence, this original equality is impossible to attain, and the impact of this fallen state is differently experienced by men and women in daily life. For Luther, woman's subjugation to man in the social world is justified as punishment for her sin; for Calvin, structures of subordination are ordered by God as the appropriate social order for a fallen world.

The accumulated weight of this theological tradition does not present a very positive prospect for consideration of the nature of women today, and makes it problematic for the Christian feminist to speak of the ways in which the purposes of the Creator may be known in and through women's lives. For the tradition presents only limited possibilities for a woman to know and to affirm her essential being. She can recover something of the fullness of this original nature in the expression of love between herself and her husband, although this loving relation has an impact upon her being, in the sense that it removes the offensive aspects of her being a woman at all, which it does not have upon her husband. She can fulfil this original nature by obedience to biological imperatives, which are, in Thomist thinking, valued more positively as the intention of the Creator, but which assume her inferiority to the male being. Or she can accept the Reformers' assumption that the entrance to this recovery of her essential nature is barred throughout human existence, and that the norms for her life are to be found in obedience to the divine will, in accepting her just punishment, or in conformity to the divine orders of creation. It is perhaps clearer in the Roman Catholic tradition that the notion of what constitutes essential humanness is male-centred, in that the man is, in himself, made in the image of God. He is the normative human being. However, while in Protestant thinking this essential humanness is understood to characterise man and woman equally, the norms for human existence in the sin-ridden historical and social world are set, not by the *imago dei*, but by God's commands, and these require the subordination of woman.

It may be said that the Enlightenment sought to develop this latter Protestant line of thinking, and, in particular, through feminist appropriations of its assumptions, to open up ways in which this original equality could actually be made available to existing human beings, and could be rendered socially and politically relevant, through envisioning a new society shaped on its premises. Liberal thinking is sustained by the belief that, in our essential humanness, there is a fundamental equality, which Wollstonecraft and others considered to be set in human nature at the creation. To believe that the way to the realisation of this essential humanness is not in fact barred by sin, is evidence of the secularisation of these theological assumptions, which gives into human hands the will and the reason with which to correct the impact of sin, as injustice, upon human existence. However, as we have seen, this in itself constitutes a mixed blessing for women, for their equality with men is ensured by a 'minimalist' understanding of this essential humanness, and by a devaluation of existential life as embodied and finite beings.[4] Thus, liberalism also reinforces, albeit unintentionally, the association of femaleness with a realm which must be transcended in moral reasoning and decision-making. The return to some discussion of an inclusive understanding of our essential being, and one that does not devalue actual embodied existence in history, is for many feminists an important matter on the theological and philosophical agenda.

Resistance to this conclusion has, however, been renewed and strengthened through postmodern considerations, and it is in these terms that the major discussions are taking place today. Contemporary suspicion of essentialism is indicative of an underlying mistrust of teleological explanations, of the impact of such explanations upon political and moral life, and, indeed, of metaphysics in general, for these are believed to require a return to pre-Enlightenment ways of thinking that are restrictive, impoverishing, and devaluing of women. This suspicion is centred, in feminist arguments, on the problem of identity, and is fuelled by the genealogical critique, adapted from Nietzsche and Foucault, which 'investigates the political stakes in designating as an *origin* and cause those identity categories that are in fact the *effects* of institutions, practices, discourses'.[5] This turns essentialist arguments on their head. Instead of looking for anything like 'a genuine or authentic sexual identity', the impact of this kind of argument is that questions of identity, and especially that of women, are rendered radically unstable and open to change.[6] Thus, it becomes the explicit task of feminism to subvert the notion of identity altogether, to 'denaturalize and resignify bodily categories'.[7] Feminism, according to this understanding, is a continuously radical deconstructive inquiry.

In various ways, this line of argument can be found running through the social constructionist paradigm. In her critique of the discourse of sexuality, Coward refers to the tendency of a discourse to seek some unity, within which its terms may cohere, and which will bring into the foreground those features of human embodiment that unite cultures and historical periods. In this search for unity, sexual identities are created by dominant ideological principles, a creation which is promptly disguised by the assertion that these identities are pre-existing. Coward accepts the ubiquitous nature of discourses, which set the terms of understanding, in which 'woman' and 'man' become established as concepts at all. Reality becomes a fabrication of discourse, a political project, built up of blocks of categories, and human life is set within its construction. Accordingly, the category of gender does not refer to any independent physical or material reality. Rather, as Butler writes, gender is 'the discursive/cultural means by which "sexed nature" or "a natural sex" is produced and established as "prediscursive", prior to culture, a politically neutral surface *on which* culture acts'.[8] The notion of sexual identity is thus believed to be a 'fictive construction', for there is nothing outside of its terms against which actions may be measured as authentic, or fulfilling of its requirements.[9] To understand gender as a cultural category is to reverse common-sense notions about the meaning of our language, an important step, as Weedon has argued, in finding new freedoms, and in illuminating features of the human situation that are hidden within gendered discourse.

The focus of this critique has been dualism, for the engendering of human life has consistently taken the form of dualistic separations of one kind of human being from another, and the positing of desire for one another. Thus, as we have noted, Coward speaks of the presumption that there is a constant heterosexual reproductive instinct, which always and everywhere accompanies human life, a presumption that conveniently empowers men and subordinates women, as it likewise renders homosexuality deviant. Frye too exclaims at the parading of sexual differences between men and women, and her wording is significant here, 'as if' their lives depended upon it. Biological facts disappear, becoming instead the projections of cultural preoccupations with patriarchal lineage. Indeed, this reproductive discourse 'marks and carves up the female body into artificial "parts"', so that the woman's body becomes a site of domination by man's desire.[10] Flax recognises the tremendous potential of this feminist deconstruction of the category of gender, and of the meaning of 'woman', since we may now begin to release the polymorphous perversity of our desires. This finds theological expression in Ruether's suggestion that the *imago dei* does not refer to God's creation of two gendered beings, but to the creation of complex human beings, who can relate to one another in a great variety of ways, once they are freed from adherence to dualistic categories that have been elevated to a 'supernatural apriority'. In this way also, the notion of the complementarity of man and woman, which relies upon an inequality that it attempts to deny, can be exposed and superceded.[11]

Running through these arguments is a concern about power. Language becomes the medium of social control, whereby the imaginations and desires of persons are structured in particular ways, and the choices available to them are limited by its categories. Thus, 'the construction of the category of women as a coherent and stable subject' becomes 'an unwitting regulation and reification of gender relations' that disciplines and controls the human body.[12] Language regulates our beliefs about the meaning of our bodies, shaping what is socially acceptable sexual behaviour, and giving to us an identity, by obedience to which we may conform to the ruling values of society. Accordingly, Butler claims:

There is no ontology of gender on which we might construct a politics, for gender ontologies always operate within established political contexts as normative injunctions, determining what qualifies as intelligible sex, invoking and consolidating the reproductive constraints on sexuality, setting the prescriptive requirements whereby sexed or gendered bodies come into cultural intelligibility. Ontology is, thus, not a foundation, but a normative injunction that operates insidiously by installing itself into political discourse as its necessary ground.[13]

Postmodern feminist politics requires the recognition of this process of 'naturalization', so that time is no longer wasted on discovering 'a normative sexuality that is "before", "outside", or "beyond" power', but instead is spent on 'rethinking subversive possibilities for sexuality and identity within the terms of power itself'.[14]

Two difficulties with this resistance to essentialism present themselves for feminist ethics. The first is that this deconstruction of the notion of identity suggests that the *raison d'être* of feminism itself is now more difficult to comprehend, and perhaps impossible to formulate at all, since the notion of 'woman' is broken down into limitless fragmentary expressions. Feminist writers identify with greater and greater precision who they are, what their standpoint is, and by what categories they may be distinguished, so that readers will understand 'where they are coming from', and be especially alert to any attempts to make universal what is particularly true only of the writer. The sense in which feminism may take seriously women's practical concerns, or may analyse and criticise women's living conditions, or may offer hope for more fulfilling possibilities, becomes an entirely local affair, in order to avoid the tendency of discourse to find some unity where there is none. To come to terms with a deconstructive politics of reality reduces the debate about what it means to be a woman to an internal dispute amongst those who subscribe to a particular set of categories, the result of which inquiry has no rational hold upon, or appeal to, those outside the discourse. At this point, proper respect for differences is urged, so that the potential damages of hegemony are limited, and the diversity of humanity is honoured. However, the logic of the argument turns against itself, and we are effectively left without a context in which these requirements make any sense, and without any means by which the most profound questions thrown up by human existence may be acknowledged and shared in rational debate and moral discourse.

This highlights the second problem, which is a nagging suspicion that this kind of critique is a further devaluation of embodiment, based upon a pervasive sense of the failure of language to speak the body, without repressive consequences. In many ways, this deconstruction of identity compares with the Protestant assertion that we are permanently cut off from our original creation, and that all attempts to reach this, to describe or to analyse its parameters, and indeed even to believe that such a basic humanness exists at all, are illegitimate extensions of particular points of view, that reinforce the privilege of the speaker. To locate the roots of resistance to identity in some elemental desires or interests, may succeed in overthrowing the authority of cultural hegemony, and avoiding the false 'valorization' of the body, but, at the same time, reveals the remnants of a curious idealism within feminism, with reference to which all of our feeble efforts at insight and dialogue are unravelled as hopelessly inadequate and flawed. The moral requirements which are given in such a context – to disturb, to rethink subversive possibilities, to expose, to challenge – seem to be derived from our mistakes, from our unwillingness to listen and our loss of faith that we have something to say to one another. From this quite influential kind of thinking amongst feminists, the meaning of broader considerations regarding woman's nature, and of some essential features of humanness, seems impossible to formulate at one level, and suspiciously power-hungry at another. That there could be found some divine purposes within such nature, or that the body might be of some physical and metaphysical significance, is equally inaccessible here.

To enter this debate about human nature is to recognise the huge intellectual scepticism about metaphysics in which contemporary feminism is caught up. The subject around which this controversy revolves for feminists is that of difference. For we have inherited a metaphysics of difference, which is based upon the normative male human being, in the context of which the female will, of necessity, be devalued and constituted by what she lacks. This is true not only of the particular assumptions regarding the *imago dei*, in which the essential nature of man is understood to be complete in itself, but is further reinforced by the identification of the female with the realm of existence, in which the fallenness of our human nature from this essence is experienced and known. It has been the great contribution of Ruether to demonstrate the way in which women are doubly disadvantaged by this kind of argument, firstly, by having no handle of their own on the *imago dei*, by which women's relation with the divine might be known in their own essential humanness, and secondly, by the accusation that all of the information from, and appeal to their experiences of the dimensions of humanness, are illegitimate attempts to build upon the fallen world what belongs to perfection. It is understandable that Enlightenment belief in the basic sameness of our essential humanity, as men and women, had some considerable attraction. It is understandable also, given this context, that naturalistic feminism finds such a receptive audience, for it very powerfully affirms precisely what the tradition seems reluctant to admit, namely that women are in some sense good in themselves.

An argument for a renewed consideration of our basic human nature requires a careful weaving through this scepticism, in which metaphysics is rejected altogether, as necessarily entailing a logic of difference that controls the engendering and the embodiment of women. For feminists to return to this subject in contemporary debate is a risky venture, for it is precisely here that the most powerful arguments against equality are constructed. Yet many feminists are reluctant to abandon this space to men, since that would deprive women of a way of reflecting upon their own knowledge of, and relation to, the divine. Likewise, there is a recognition that naturalistic feminism is incomplete in itself. It is weakened both by a tendency to confirm the status quo, with claims about the nature of women, as this is now experienced and formed in the midst of inequalities, and by what can degenerate into a rather facile assumption that everything women do is good, without reference to any other moral criteria. Neither the rejection of metaphysical inquiry, as a hindrance to the spontaneity of the feminist spirit, nor the circular arguments of naturalism, are adequate to the development of a suitable feminist humanism in which women may recognise themselves, affirm their godliness, and engage as partners with their brothers in the building of justice and peace. Contemporary feminist reconstructions of the dimensions of our humanness centre on precisely the two matters highlighted by Ruether as weaknesses in the tradition. There is, firstly, an attempt to recover the *imago dei* for women, a project in which the writing of Luce Irigiray is most valued. There is, secondly, a renewed interest in the natural law tradition, as a way of avoiding the dualism of existence and essence in which women have been trapped.

The writings of Irigiray, along with other new French feminists, are accused of being essentialist, by those feminists who believe that her strategy of 'entering further into womanhood', colludes with and reinforces existing definitions of 'woman'.[15] Her belief, that from the substance of woman's own deepest self-awareness, existing categories can be challenged from outside their terms, and an imaginative contribution can be made to the formulation of a new metaphysics of morals, strikes postmodern feminists as yet another form of 'epistemological imperialism', speaking a variation on the themes of 'global phallogocentrism'.[16] Irigiray agrees that the categories in which the nature of woman has been conceived are centred on the embodied experience and imagination of man, thus bearing 'the shape of the male body and the rhythms of male sexuality', and therefore that woman does not, and cannot appear as herself within them.[17] Woman is effectively sealed up in philosophical constructions, which reveal only the outline of her absence.[18] What Irigiray urges is that women discover how they may break into this symbolic order, with claims about their experience and lived reality, their sexuality and spirituality, which may unsettle assumptions regarding their 'difference' from men. And they do this by reaffirming the feminine from the site of their own bodies.

One step in this process is for woman to rediscover, as a woman, her relation to the divine. Man has defined himself as a distinctive gender, by reference to a God, who serves as the horizon of his identity, to 'orient his finiteness', and to guarantee his free and autonomous subjectivity.[19] Women have no such divine, and thus are alienated; 'deprived of God, they are forced to comply with models that do not match them, that exile, double, mask them, cut them off from themselves and from one another, stripping away their ability to move forward into love, art, thought, toward their ideal and divine fulfilment'.[20] The role which women are given within man's religion is a 'vocation for collaborating in the redemption of the world through suffering and chastity', and this, Irigiray believes, 'should not constitute the only means or path to our fulfillment as women'.[21] In her several references to Antigone, she questions the role of women, made into 'the guardians of death' by men, who '*incorporate* the feminine rather than recognizing women'.[22] What is missed in this process is the full coming into being of women, as they are in themselves, with reference to a divine horizon, that may also reflect their gender back to them for fulfilment.

In speaking of God, Irigiray understands 'not a transcendent entity that exists outside becoming',[23] but rather 'a *sensible transcendental* that comes into being through us'.[24] This coming is made possible in genuine love of self and other. 'Love of God has nothing moral in and of itself. It merely shows the way. It is the incentive for a more perfect becoming ... God forces us to do nothing except *become*. The only task, the only obligation laid upon us is: to become divine men and women, to become perfectly, to refuse to allow parts of ourselves to shrivel and die that have the potential for growth and fulfilment'.[25] Irigaray thus rejects the sense in which a metaphysical approach to morals must, necessarily, presume a conception of the human person already formed in the mind of God, to which actual persons must conform, and speaks instead of what we are to become through love. The entire way in which women imagine this divine, who appears 'with face unveiled' and who touches 'the sleeping understanding' of women,[26] and their encounter with the divine presence as a grace in which their own sanctification may occur, speaks a theological language that is alive within the Christian tradition, although deeply submerged by modernism.[27] Her hope is that women, through exploring its dimensions, will recover the divine in their own essential subjectivity, and know themselves, in their nakedness and vulnerability and utter uniqueness, to be enfolded in love.

Through the recovery of the transcendent for women, there is the possibility of a genuine otherness to emerge and be recognised between women and men. Since the symbolic order has been framed around the absence of woman, it actually 'covers over sexual difference', through the erection of hierarchical oppositions that presume a fundamental sameness, on the basis of which comparison of two terms can be made.[28] Here love takes place 'in the *One*. Two merely formed a one.'[29] In recovering the "other", and in claiming that 'it takes at least two to love', Irigaray seeks to restore the irreducible qualitative difference of the feminine, a difference which cannot be conceived within the terms of the 'Old Dream of Symmetry', and thus cannot effectively be discovered by the agreement of women to occupy the oppositional space laid out for them. Thus, she argues, 'If we keep on speaking sameness, if we speak to each other as men have been doing for centuries, as we have been taught to speak, we'll miss each other, fail ourselves'.[30] It is for this reason that Irigaray finds language of equality unhelpful,[31] and likewise looks beyond 'the circularity of discourse', which 'still defends its untouchable status', for the possibility of a new coming of the transcendent.[32]

In her ethics of sexual difference, Irigiray affirms the importance of woman's 'detachment from what is', of her 'love for the child that she once was', and of her 'openness . . . which allows access to difference'.[33] It is crucial for woman to form this intimacy with herself through the re-establishment of the mother–daughter relationship, which 'is one of the most difficult gestures for our culture'.[34] The importance of this relation is that, 'woman must be born into desire. She must be longed for, loved, valued as a daughter. An other morning, a new parousia that necessarily accompanies the coming of an ethical God.'[35] In speaking of love of other, Irigiray looks for the 'sense of the other that is not projective or selfish', and which recognises mutuality.[36] This happens, for example, in theological terms, as women consider the importance of their discovery and announcement of the resurrection, accepting their unique spiritual responsibility to witness to life.[37] Man may then respect 'the difference between him and her, in cosmic and aesthetic generation and creation. Sharing the heaven and the earth in all their elements, potencies, acts'.[38] Such would be genuine otherness-in-love, in which difference finds it true expression. This way of responding to the weaknesses in traditional descriptions of essential human nature highlights the importance of the recovery both of sexual difference, and of the divine as the *telos* of human existence toward which we may grow into the fullness of ourselves. In her speaking of the ways in which women may know themselves to be made in God's image, Irigiray offers an affirmation of women's goodness, which then becomes a strength in human relationships.

A second response to the discussion of human nature comes from those Christian feminists who find the most useful ethical context for these considerations within the natural law tradition, and they have set about recovering both Roman Catholic and Anglican forms of this ethic, in ways that are sensitive to contemporary concerns of women, and inclusive of women as full human persons. The Anglican theologian, Helen Oppenheimer, affirms the natural law approach as 'a methodology . . .

a way of looking at the world in a hopeful expectation that some sense can be made of it. It is not so much informative as encouraging.'[39] This approach presumes that all creation has been made for completion in happiness, and that human persons, who are intended for this fullness of life, may find their way forward through the exercise of conscience, which is the voice of their true nature.[40] It is crucial for the appropriation of this tradition for women, that our common humanity be recognised, and that the sense in which women and men are made in the image of God be both explained and proclaimed. The Thomist scholar, Jean Porter, has affirmed that, for Aquinas, 'women and men are equal with respect to what is essential to the nature of the species of humanity, namely, the possession of an intellectual nature ... enabling the individual to know and to love God'.[41] This normative equality, she claims, can help us to distinguish some of the mistaken assumptions in his anthropology, for example, about 'the relative mental inferiority of women', and likewise can serve as the basis for a more thorough critique of social institutions than Aquinas himself was prepared to undertake.[42]

This approach opens up a most fruitful area in which feminism and Christian ethics may be working together for mutual benefit. In her book, *Virtuous Woman*, Denise Lardner Carmody considers the central importance of the question of what constitutes the good life for women. In keeping with Thomist thinking, she accepts that a conception of what constitutes 'the good' for human beings is fundamental to our ability to decide and to act as rational agents, and thus to attain the fullness of our human life. She recognises the feminist criticism that, in descriptions of the good life in the western tradition, women have been 'objects rather than subjects', and thus that the ways in which women themselves might answer this question may differ quite a bit from what has been said of, or about them.[43] What she does not accept in contemporary feminist rhetoric, is that somehow this question is irrelevant to women, or that it is illegitimate to consider it. Noting the ways in which feminism is caught up in 'the reigning mentality in academic philosophy, which is agnostic about creation and destiny, if not uninterested', she suggests that for feminists to share in this scepticism will not be helpful to women's lives.[44] As we have explored in this chapter, much feminist resistance to these considerations is built upon a belief that the identity of woman has been pre-established by patriarchal ideology, or that there exists a perfect model somewhere of the good woman to which we particular women are to conform. Such assumptions are, however, not integral to this approach, which is centred much more on the affirmation of a person as an active agent, 'securing and enjoying her well-being through her own deliberate choices'.[45]

It is in this same sense that Oppenheimer speaks of the formation of personal identity around what matters to us, and that to define a person 'as an irreplaceable centre of minding', is both to affirm the sacredness of persons in the sight of the divine, and to set a task for human life in sorting out what we really do care about.[46] Such arguments are based on the assumption, with which this chapter began, that the asking of fundamental questions about our existence is a basic feature of being human, and that such inquiry is indicative of the human search for understanding which is given by God. It is thus of primary importance that women ask themselves and each other, what is the highest good which 'ought to illumine their moral activity, help them live in the light rather than darkness, in the truth rather than foolishness'.[47] Women wonder about what their lives are for, and are concerned to act in ways that enhance their humanity, rather than dull it, and that strengthen their own sense of self-worth and dignity, and in this wondering a freedom to question and to grow becomes possible. Not only is this search for making sense of things a natural human desire, it is also the place in which we may encounter the divine, as both the answer to, and the mystery of, our existence. Carmody argues that the 'most significant datum about women, as about men, is that we do not furnish our own reason to be', and she urges women to continue to ponder the meaning of this mysterious 'elementary reality', without reference to which their lives become 'ultimately uninteresting ephemera'.[48] Her choice of words here, while not directly referring to postmodern feminist arguments, suggests the importance of the discovery of a centre for personal consciousness, within which the 'deepest capacities' of our human souls may be affirmed, and allowed to develop in the presence of a loving and purposive deity.

Such an affirmation of the full humanness of women comes also as a challenge to the continuing formation of the Christian tradition and to the church. For it carries the recognition that 'God has left witnesses to the divine wisdom and love everywhere', and therefore that the kinds of things which women are saying, and all of the reasonable and passionate arguments of feminists, are expressions of a search for truth and goodness which we may not ignore.[49] As we noted earlier, Cahill had affirmed that the natural law tradition is 'hospitable' to insights derived from experience, and thus that women's account of their own life experiences is a legitimate contribution to normative ethics.[50] Accordingly, in her response to *Veritatis Splendor*, she argues that the attempt to discuss 'the moral meaning of the human body', a most important and controversial issue in contemporary debate, will be hampered, so long as the final appeal is the reassertion of 'sexual norms which had their origin in the primacy of procreation and in women's subordination to men through their procreative role', rather than the continued, difficult rational debate and analysis 'from both a natural law and a feminist perspective' of the meaning, and the balance of importance, of the basic terms of the debate.[51] On the basis of a normative equality, Christian feminists have much to contribute to wider feminist considerations in our world, their enthusiasm for which task is dampened only by their anxiety that they will be shot from behind with appeals to the authority of normative masculinity.

Lastly, it is within this tradition that a positive understanding of our common life and culture may be found, for it is clear that Aquinas finally equates 'the true good of the individual and the common good in such a way that the highest natural good of the individual consists in participation in a just community'.[52] This may offer to feminism a positive way in which to hold together the importance of 'truly loving oneself', with a

commitment to 'the common good of her community'.[53] Esther
Reed has explored the ways in which this conception might be
useful in the present debate about pornography, which 'seems
to have reached a curious deadlock'.[54] Her exploration suggests a way for Christian feminists to do justice to their political
responsibilities, not abandoning society as a series of endless
struggles between universalising discourses and battles for the
signified, but becoming involved in the making of laws, by
which the universal values of 'human dignity, respect and
honour due to the body', may become woven into the fabric of
our common life.[55] The postmodern alternative, of living
without generalisations at all, and of continuously celebrating
the diverse possibilities of living, is indicative of the need, so
deeply felt and clearly expressed by women, for some recognition of the fullness of the human person, which exceeds the
bounds of our categories, and for the shaping of a society which
is not based upon 'false universals which hide differences of sex,
gender, race or class'.[56] Thomistic thinking may provide a
framework for such decisions about 'the common good which
depends on the political, economic, personal and cultural
choices of each person', and upon the uniqueness of each
person's life as a rational being.[57]

There is a curious sound, as Reed acknowledges, to the
notion of a 'Thomistic feminist approach', since 'Vast tracts of
Aquinas' writings ... are texts of horror which perpetuated
misogynism'.[58] Yet it is a sign of the continuing appeal of
Aquinas' theory of goodness, with its specification of what
would be the human good, and a sign of the important sense in
which his theory is not bound to the particular account of the
natural world as he then believed it to be,[59] that feminists may
find it a useful framework for moral reasoning. 'Happiness,
felicitas is, of course, from *feo*, to produce, whence also *fecundus*
and *femina*. It may or may not be coincidental that the fulfilment of common good is characterised within Christian tradition by fecundity and the feminine.'[60] That feminists are speaking from this happiness which is not yet, and are calling the
world into the more full realisation of its possibilities, is

evidence of feminism as a 'transforming grace' in which a 'genuinely new Christian consciousness' is emerging.[61] Through the recovery of a new humanism in which woman and man are both known to be made in the image of God, and intended for communion with one another and with God in the context of their creaturely life, Christian feminism may both transcend itself, and press 'the tradition to transcend itself, to become the hope, the future that is promised'.[62]

Notes

1 ON DIVERSITY

1 There is now extensive literature in the USA and Canada which documents this diversity. See the bibliography in Beverly Wildung Harrison's book *Our Right to Choose, Toward A New Ethic of Abortion* (Boston, Beacon Press, 1983). Now also material describing the debates in Poland and in the newly unified Germany reveals similar diversity, see the *Bulletin of Medical Ethics*, numbers 75, 78, and 82, 1992–3.

2 See Harrison, *Our Right*, for the initial emergence of this kind of understanding of the issue.

3 This view is expressed in a recorded interview of Ginette Paris, a psychologist, by James Hillman, entitled 'The Sacrament of Abortion', available from Spring Publications, Dallas, Texas, USA.

4 Here one thinks not only of work within the Roman Catholic tradition, but also of Oliver O'Donovan: *Begotten or Made?* (Oxford, Clarendon Press, 1984).

5 Thus the debate within the Polish Chamber of Physicians in December 1991 regarding the adoption of a new code of medical ethics was described in the *Bulletin of Medical Ethics* as follows: 'Discussions between these two factions turned into scandal when the "fundamentalists" began to scream and shout in opposition to the reading of an "open letter" . . . written by a physician who favours "democracy",' (no. 78, May 1992, p. 17, report written by Witold Jacorzynski and Marek Wichrowski of the Department of Philosophy and Medical Ethics at the Academy of Medicine, Warsaw). The chairman refused to allow the letter to be read, and forty people left the room in protest at the undemocratic procedures before the vote was even taken (no. 75, Jan/Feb. 1992, pp. 23–4).

6 It is interesting that many feminist thinkers are political philosophers by training and profession, for their historical investigation into alternative theories of the state has led them into revisioning contemporary political analysis in ways which are, on the whole, uncommon in this more conservative discipline.

7 For the most thorough description, analysis, and critique of the differing forms of feminism, see Alison Jagger, *Feminist Politics and Human Nature* (Sussex, Harvester Press, 1983).

8 The latest work of Alasdair MacIntyre explicitly refers to rivalry and suggests that there are 'very different and mutually antagonistic conceptions of moral enquiry'. *Three Rival Versions of Moral Enquiry* (London, Duckworth, 1990), p. 2.

9 See for example William Oddie: *What Will Happen to God?* (London, SPCK, 1984).

10 See for example Mary Daly: *Gyn/Ecology: The Metaethics of Radical Feminism* (London, The Women's Press, 1979) and *Pure Lust: Elemental Feminist Philosophy* (London, The Women's Press, 1984).

11 Initial explorations in this area were made in my 'Feminism and the Logic of Morality: A Consideration of Alternatives', in E. Frazer, J. Hornsby, and S. Lovibond: *Ethics: A Feminist Reader* (Oxford, Blackwell, 1992).

2 THE LIBERAL PARADIGM

1 Susan Dowell and Linda Hurcombe first drew attention to the existence of this 'Declaration', in *The Dispossessed Daughters of Eve: Faith and Feminism* (London, SCM Press, 1981). It has now been found and translated into English by Terry Garley, the Ecumenical Officer for Nottinghamshire and Derbyshire.

2 Mary Wollstonecraft: *A Vindication of the Rights of Woman*, reprinted in Alice S. Rossi, ed.: *The Feminist Papers* (New York, Bantam Books, 1973), p. 64.

3 Wollstonecraft: *Vindication*, p. 64.

4 Wollstonecraft: *Vindication*, p. 72. The central part of the *Vindication* was written as an attack on the educational ideas of Jean-Jacques Rousseau. See his *Emile*, translated by Barbara Foxley (London, Dent, 1911), originally published in 1762.

5 Wollstonecraft: *Vindication*, p. 49.

6 Wollstonecraft: *Vindication*, p. 63.

7 *Ibid.*

8 Wollstonecraft: *Vindication*, p. 59.

9 Wollstonecraft: *Vindication*, p. 49.

10 Wollstonecraft: *Vindication*, p. 81.
11 Wollstonecraft: *Vindication*, p. 66.
12 Wollstonecraft: *Vindication*, p. 79.
13 Judith Sargent Murray: *On the Equality of the Sexes*, reprinted in Rossi: *Feminist Papers*, p. 20.
14 Murray: *Equality*, p. 19. Murray here outlines the four types of intelligence as imagination, reason, memory, and judgement.
15 Murray: *Equality*, p. 21.
16 *Ibid.*
17 Murray: *Equality*, p. 23.
18 Simone de Beauvoir: *The Second Sex*, translated and edited by H. M. Parshley (New York, Bantam Books, 1961), p. 575.
19 De Beauvoir: *Second Sex*, p. 33. Cf. also 'This accounts for our lengthy study of the biological facts; they are one of the keys to the understanding of woman. But I deny that they establish for her a fixed and inevitable destiny' p. 29.
20 De Beauvoir: *Second Sex*, p. 33.
21 De Beauvoir: *Second Sex*, p. 685.
22 De Beauvoir: *Second Sex*, p. 686.
23 De Beauvoir: *Second Sex*, p. 580.
24 De Beauvoir: *Second Sex*, p. 674.
25 De Beauvoir: *Second Sex*, p. 585. Cf. also de Beauvoir's criticisms of the church: 'Religion sanctions woman's self-love; it gives her the guide, father, lover, divine guardian she longs for nostalgically; it feeds her daydreams; it fills her empty hours. But, above all, it confirms the social order, it justifies her resignation, by giving her the hope of a better future in a sexless heaven. This is why women today are still a powerful trump in the hand of the Church; it is why the Church is notably hostile to all measures likely to help in woman's emancipation' pp. 587–8.
26 De Beauvoir: *Second Sex*, p. 591.
27 Jean Paul Sartre: *Existentialism and Human Emotions* translated by Bernard Frechtman (New York, The Philosophical Library, 1957). 'Of course, freedom as the definition of man does not depend on others, but as soon as there is involvement, I am obliged to want others to have freedom at the same time that I want my own freedom' p. 46.
28 De Beauvoir: *Second Sex*, p. 671.
29 De Beauvoir: *Second Sex*, p. 249
30 Janet Radcliffe Richards: *The Sceptical Feminist* (Harmondsworth, Penguin Books, 1982).
31 John Stuart Mill: *The Subjection of Women*, first published in England in 1869, reprinted in Rossi, ed.: *Feminist Papers*,

pp. 196–238, a work considered by most feminists to be jointly written with Harriet Taylor.

32 Radcliffe Richards: *Sceptical Feminist*, p. 65.

33 Radcliffe Richards: *Sceptical Feminist*, pp. 65–7 *passim*.

34 Radcliffe Richards: *Sceptical Feminist*, p. 69.

35 Radcliffe Richards: *Sceptical Feminist*, p. 90, author's emphasis.

36 Radcliffe Richards: *Sceptical Feminist*, p. 99.

37 Radcliffe Richards: *Sceptical Feminist*, p. 120, author's emphasis.

38 Radcliffe Richards: *Sceptical Feminist*, p. 121, author's emphasis.

39 Radcliffe Richards: *Sceptical Feminist*, p. 73.

40 Rosemary Radford Ruether: *Liberation Theology* (New York, Paulist Press, 1972), p. 32.

41 Ruether: *Liberation Theology*, p. 4.

42 Ruether: *New Woman / New Earth* (New York, Seabury Press, 1975), p. 83.

43 Ruether: *New Woman*, p. 66.

44 Ruether: *New Woman*, p. 73.

45 Ruether: 'A Method of Correlation', in Letty Russell, ed.: *Feminist Interpretation of the Bible* (Oxford, Blackwell, 1985), p. 115.

46 Ruether: 'Method', p. 118.

47 Ruether: 'Method', p. 117.

48 Ruether: *New Woman*, p. xi.

49 Letty M. Russell: *Human Liberation in a Feminist Perspective* (Philadelphia, Westminster Press, 1974), p. 39.

50 Russell: *Human Liberation*, p. 52. Russell is here quoting from Gustavo Gutiérrez: *A Theology of Liberation*, translated and edited by Caridad Inda and John Eagleson (Maryknoll New York, Orbis Books, 1972), p. 145.

51 Russell: *Human Liberation*, p. 103.

52 Russell: *Human Liberation*, p. 138.

53 See her essay, 'Authority and the Challenge' in Russell, ed.: *Feminist Interpretation of the Bible*. 'In the light of this understanding of authority as partnership, it is no longer necessary to accept the dilemma of choice between faithfulness to the teaching of scripture or to our own integrity as human beings' p. 146.

54 Russell: *Human Liberation*, p. 19.

55 Russell: 'Authority', p. 139.

56 Beverly Wildung Harrison: 'Keeping Faith in a Sexist Church: Not for Women Only' in *Making the Connections: Essays in Feminist Social Ethics*, edited by Carol S. Robb (Boston, Beacon Press, 1985), pp. 221–2.

3 CRITIQUE OF LIBERALISM

1 Charlotte Perkins Gilman: *The Yellow Wallpaper* (London, Virago, 1987).
2 Charlotte Perkins Gilman: *The Living of Charlotte Perkins Gilman. An Autobiography* (New York, D. Appleton-Century Co., 1935), p. 119.
3 Gilman: *Autobiography*, p. 120.
4 Carl Degler, ed.: *Women and Economics* (reprint edn., New York, Harper & Row, 1966), p. xiii.
5 Gilman: *Yellow Wallpaper*: p. 10.
6 Gilman: *Yellow Wallpaper*: p. 15, p. 10.
7 Gilman: *Yellow Wallpaper*: p. 13.
8 Gilman: *Yellow Wallpaper*: p. 20.
9 Gilman: *Yellow Wallpaper*: p. 13.
10 Gilman: *Yellow Wallpaper*: p. 24.
11 Brian Easlea: *Science and Sexual Oppression: Patriarchy's Confrontation with Woman and Nature* (London, Weidenfeld & Nicolson, 1981), pp. 144–5. This book provides an alternative version of the history of the modern period to the one suggested by Enlightenment optimism.
12 Gilman: *Yellow Wallpaper*: p. 21–2, p. 14.
13 See especially Margery Collins and Christine Pierce: 'Holes and Slime: Sexism in Sartre's Psychoanalysis' in Carol C. Gould and Marx W. Wartofsky: *Women and Philosophy: Toward a Theory of Liberation* (New York, G. P. Putnam's Sons, 1976), pp. 112–127.
14 De Beauvoir: *Second Sex*, p. 60.
15 Michèle Le Doeuff: *Hipparchia's Choice: An Essay Concerning Women, Philosophy, etc.*, translated by Trista Selous (Oxford, Blackwell, 1991), pp. 62–74, 84–9, for her insightful analysis of women in Sartre's *Being and Nothingness*, translated by Hazel E. Barnes (New York, The Citadel Press, 1965).
16 De Beauvoir: *Second Sex*, p. 681.
17 Le Doeuff: *Hipparchia's Choice*, p. 116.
18 De Beauvoir: *Second Sex*, p. 678.
19 De Beauvoir: *Second Sex*, p. 679.
20 De Beauvoir: *Second Sex*, p. 681.
21 De Beauvoir: *Second Sex*, p. 682.
22 Valerie Saiving Goldstein: 'The Human Situation: A Feminine View', in *The Journal of Religion*, 40, April 1960, 100–12. Since the publication of this article, the author has changed her name to Ms. Saiving.

23 Saiving: 'Human Situation', p. 107.
24 Saiving: 'Human Situation', p. 102.
25 Saiving: 'Human Situation', p. 105.
26 *Ibid.*
27 *Ibid.*
28 Saiving: 'Human Situation', p. 109.
29 Rosemary Radford Ruether: *Sexism and God-Talk: Towards a Feminist Theology* (London, SCM Press, 1983) pp. 102–3.
30 Carol Gilligan: *In a Different Voice: Psychological Theory and Women's Development* (Cambridge, Massachusetts, Harvard University Press, 1982), p. 35.
31 Gilligan: *Different Voice*, p. 31. The notion of moral maturity is traced by Genevieve Lloyd in *The Man of Reason: 'Male' and 'Female' in Western Philosophy* (London, Methuen, 1984). She locates its origin in Kant, and in the general belief that through the use of reason, mankind was progressing from primitive belief into Enlightened rationality. Kant's description of the process of self- improvement through the development of moral consciousness appears to be an assertion of what is common to all persons. However, as Lloyd notes, 'Ironically, the Kantian picture of morality, with its emphasis on what is supposedly universal about the mind, has been a major strand in more recent ideas of the lesser moral development of women. There are, for example, echoes of Kant's contrast between mere inclinations and the impersonality of duty in Freud's notorious claim that the moral development of women falls short of the full moral consciousness of men' p. 69.
32 Gilligan: *Different Voice*, p. 132.
33 Gilligan: *Different Voice*, p. 142.
34 Gilligan: *Different Voice*, p. 166.
35 See Jean Bethke Elshtain: *Public Man, Private Woman: Women in Social and Political Thought* (Oxford, Martin Robertson, 1981), pp. 228–255. See also Andrea Nye: *Feminist Theory and the Philosophies of Man* (London, Routledge, 1989), chapter 2.
36 Ruether: *Sexism*.
37 Ruether: *Sexism*, pp. 97–9 in which she considers the patriarchal anthropology of the Reformation.
38 Ruether: *Sexism*, p. 23.
39 Ruether: *Sexism*, p. 18.
40 *Ibid.*
41 Ruether: *Sexism*, p. 24, author's emphasis.
42 Ruether: *Sexism*, p. 27.
43 Ruether: *Sexism*, p. 41.

44 Ruether: *Sexism*, p. 44.
45 Ruether: *Sexism*, p. 218.
46 Ruether: *Sexism*, p. 221.
47 Ruether: *Sexism*, p. 30.
48 Ruether: *Sexism*, p. 32
49 Judith Plaskow: *Sex, Sin and Grace: Women's Experience and the Theologies of Reinhold Niebuhr and Paul Tillich* (Washington DC, University Press of America, 1980).
50 Plaskow: *Sex, Sin and Grace*, p. 76.
51 Plaskow: *Sex, Sin and Grace*, p. 129.
52 *Ibid.*
53 Plaskow: *Sex, Sin and Grace*, p. 132.
54 Linda Woodhead: 'Love and Justice' in *Studies in Christian Ethics*, 5:1, 1992, 46.
55 Woodhead: 'Love and Justice', p. 55.
56 *Ibid.*
57 Woodhead: 'Love and Justice', p. 56.
58 Le Doeuff: *Hipparchia's Choice*, p. 337, fn 41.

4 THE SOCIAL CONSTRUCTIONIST PARADIGM

1 De Beauvoir: *Second Sex*, p. 249.
2 Harriet Martineau: *Society in America*, edited by Seymour Martin Lipset (Garden City, New York, Anchor Doubleday and Co., 1962). The section on 'Women' has been reprinted in Rossi: *Feminist Papers*, from which these references are drawn.
3 Rossi: *Feminist Papers*, p. 125.
4 Rossi: *Feminist Papers*, p. 127.
5 Rossi: *Feminist Papers*, p. 125.
6 *Ibid.*
7 *Ibid.*
8 Rossi: *Feminist Papers*, p. 128.
9 Rossi: *Feminist Papers*, p. 126.
10 Rossi: *Feminist Papers*, p. 127.
11 Rossi: *Feminist Papers*, p. 133.
12 Rossi: *Feminist Papers*, p. 134.
13 Rossi: *Feminist Papers*, p. 141.
14 *Ibid.*
15 Rossi: *Feminist Papers*, p. 142.
16 Rossi: *Feminist Papers*, pp. 125–6.
17 Rossi: *Feminist Papers*, p. 134.
18 Rossi: *Feminist Papers*, pp. 142–3.

19 Cicely Hamilton: *Marriage as a Trade* (London, The Women's Press, 1981). Important extracts from this work are reprinted in Frazer, et. al.: *Ethics* from which these references are drawn.
20 Frazer, et. al.: *Ethics*, pp. 47–8.
21 Frazer, et. al.: *Ethics*, p. 36.
22 Frazer, et. al.: *Ethics*, p. 36.
23 Frazer, et. al.: *Ethics*, pp. 39–40.
24 Frazer, et. al.: *Ethics*, p. 40.
25 *Ibid.*
26 Betty Friedan: *The Feminine Mystique* (New York, Dell Publishing Co., 1963), p. 7.
27 Friedan: *Feminine Mystique*, p. 7.
28 Friedan: *Feminine Mystique*, p. 15.
29 Friedan: *Feminine Mystique*, p. 27.
30 Friedan: *Feminine Mystique*, p. 26.
31 Gerda Lerner: *The Creation of Patriarchy* (Oxford University Press, 1986), p. 239.
32 Juliet Mitchell: *Woman's Estate* (New York, Random House, Inc. – Vintage Books Edition, 1973), p. 40.
33 Mitchell: *Woman's Estate*, p. 150.
34 Mitchell: *Woman's Estate*, p. 120.
35 Mitchell: *Woman's Estate*, p. 122.
36 Mitchell: *Woman's Estate*, p. 140.
37 Mitchell: *Woman's Estate*, pp. 94–5, on which a chart of comparisons between 'Radical Feminists' and 'Abstract Socialists' is provided.
38 Mitchell: *Woman's Estate*, p. 66.
39 Rosalind Coward: *Patriarchal Precedents: Sexuality and Social Relations* (London, Routledge & Kegan Paul, 1983). See also her collection of essays: *Female Desire: Women's Sexuality Today* (London, Collins – Paladin Grafton Books, 1984).
40 Coward: *Patriarchal Precedents*, p. 16.
41 Coward: *Patriarchal Precedents*, pp. 188 and 255.
42 Coward: *Patriarchal Precedents*, p. 259.
43 Coward: *Patriarchal Precedents*, p. 261.
44 Coward: *Patriarchal Precedents*, p. 272.
45 Coward: *Patriarchal Precedents*, p. 265.
46 Coward: *Patriarchal Precedents*, p. 280.
47 See the cultural study of the creation of 'otherness' in Edward W. Said: *Orientalism: Western Conceptions of the Orient* (London, Penguin Books, 1991).
48 bell hooks: *Yearning: race, gender, and cultural politics* (London, Turnaround, 1991), p. 8.

49 hooks: *Yearning*, p. 3.
50 hooks: *Yearning*, p. 29.
51 hooks: *Yearning*, p. 54.
52 *Ibid.*
53 hooks: *Yearning*, p. 55.
54 hooks: *Yearning*, p. 27.
55 *Ibid.*
56 hooks: *Yearning*, p. 22.
57 hooks: *Yearning*, p. 77.
58 Dorothee Sölle: *Thinking About God: An Introduction to Theology* (London, SCM Press, 1990), p. 3.
59 Sölle: *The Strength of the Weak: Toward a Christian Feminist Identity*, translated by Robert and Rita Kimber (Philadelphia, Westminster Press, 1984), see especially chapter 9 'Paternalistic Religion as Experienced by Woman', pages 106–17.
60 Sölle: *Thinking About God*, p. 38.
61 Sölle: *Thinking About God*, p. 71. The quote is taken from Elisabeth Schüssler Fiorenza's essay 'For the Sake of our Salvation', in *Bread Not Stone: The Challenge of Feminist Biblical Interpretation* (Boston, Beacon Press, 1984), p. 41. The approach of Schüssler Fiorenza to biblical hermeneutics is also an example of the social constructionist paradigm at work.
62 Sölle: *Thinking About God*, p. 72.
63 Sölle: *Thinking About God*, pp. 74–5.
64 Ruether: *New Woman*, and 'Dualism and the Nature of Evil in Feminist Theology', in *Studies in Christian Ethics*, 5:1, 1992.
65 Ruether: *New Woman*, p. 194.
66 Ruether: *New Woman*, p. 195.
67 Ruether: 'Dualism', p. 38.
68 *Ibid.*
69 Ruether: 'Dualism', p. 39.
70 Ruether: *New Woman*, p. 69.
71 Ruether: 'Dualism', p. 33.
72 Ruether: 'Dualism', p. 34.
73 Ruether: *New Woman*, p. 211.
74 Rebecca Chopp: *The Power to Speak: Feminism, Language, God* (New York, Crossroad, 1989), p. 12.
75 Chopp: *Power to Speak*, p. 1.
76 Chopp: *Power to Speak*, p. 2.
77 Chopp: *Power to Speak*, p. 103.
78 Chopp: *Power to Speak*, p. 14.
79 Chopp: *Power to Speak*, p. 116.
80 Chopp: *Power to Speak*, p. 14.

81 Chopp: *Power to Speak*, p. 125.
82 Chopp: *Power to Speak*, p. 122.
83 Chopp: *Power to Speak*, p. 128.
84 Sölle: *The Strength of the Weak*, p. 90.

5 CRITIQUE OF SOCIAL CONSTRUCTIONISM

1 L. Frank Baum's novel, *The Wizard of Oz* (London, Fontana, 1969), originally published in 1900, was made into a film in 1939, with a number of changes to the text. Here, reference is made both to the book and to the screenplay of the film, and it is in the latter that this sentence appears. According to Salman Rushdie, 'The truth is that this great movie, in which the quarrels, sackings and near-bungles of all concerned produced what seems like pure, effortless and somehow inevitable felicity, is as near as dammit to that will-o'-the-wisp of modern critical theory: the authorless text.' See his *The Wizard of Oz* in British Film Classics (London, British Film Institute, 1992), p. 16. It seems appropriate that this composite story of a young woman, as told by many others, reflects the themes of this chapter.
2 Naomi Scheman: *Engenderings: Constructions of Knowledge, Authority, and Privilege* (London, Routledge, 1993), p. xii.
3 Scheman: *Engenderings*, p. xiii.
4 Scheman: *Engenderings*, pp. 196–7.
5 Rushdie, *Wizard*, p. 56.
6 Chris Weedon: *Feminist Practice and Poststructuralist Theory* (Oxford, Blackwell, 1992), p. 32, author's emphasis.
7 Weedon: *Feminist Practice*, p. 33.
8 *Ibid.*
9 *Ibid.*
10 Weedon: *Feminist Practice*, p. 83.
11 Weedon: *Feminist Practice*, p. 77.
12 Weedon: *Feminist Practice*, p. 84.
13 Weedon: *Feminist Practice*, p. 98.
14 Weedon: *Feminist Practice*, pp. 112–13.
15 Weedon: *Feminist Practice*, p. 125.
16 Weedon: *Feminist Practice*, p. 167.
17 Susan Hekman, *Gender and Knowledge: Elements of a Postmodern Feminism* (Oxford, Blackwell, 1992), p. 62.
18 Hekman: *Gender and Knowledge*, p. 79.
19 Hekman: *Gender and Knowledge*, p. 81.
20 Hekman: *Gender and Knowledge*, p. 103.

21 Hekman: *Gender and Knowledge*, p. 93.
22 Hekman: *Gender and Knowledge*, p. 175. She makes use here of Derrida's description of the 'supplement' in his work *Positions*, translated by Alan Bass (University of Chicago Press, 1981).
23 Hekman: *Gender and Knowledge*, p. 179.
24 Hekman: *Gender and Knowledge*, p. 185.
25 Hekman: *Gender and Knowledge*, p. 187.
26 Hekman: *Gender and Knowledge*, p. 189.
27 Hekman: *Gender and Knowledge*, p. 188.
28 Kate Soper, *Humanism and Anti-Humanism* (London, Hutchinson, 1986), p. 11.
29 Soper: *Humanism*, p. 133.
30 Soper: *Humanism*, p. 12.
31 Soper: *Humanism*, p. 141.
32 Soper: *Humanism*, p. 133.
33 Soper: *Humanism*, p. 97.
34 Soper: *Humanism*, p. 128. She refers here explicitly to the rejection of humanism in the writings of Jacques Lacan.
35 Soper: *Humanism*, p. 128.
36 Soper: *Humanism*, p. 131.
37 Soper: *Humanism*, p. 152.
38 Soper: *Humanism*, p. 138.
39 Soper: *Humanism*, p. 139.
40 Soper: *Humanism*, p. 153.
41 Marilyn Frye: *The Politics of Reality* (Trumansburg, New York, The Crossing Press, 1983), p. 153.
42 Frye: *Politics of Reality*, p. 2.
43 Frye: *Politics of Reality*, p. 19.
44 Frye: *Politics of Reality*, p. 29.
45 Frye: *Politics of Reality*, p. 37, author's emphasis.
46 Frye: *Politics of Reality*, p. 173.
47 Ann Foreman: *Femininity as Alienation: Women and the Family in Marxism and Psychoanalysis* (London, Pluto Press, 1977), p. 156.
48 Foreman: *Femininity*, p. 157.
49 Foreman: *Femininity*, p. 155.
50 Michèle Barrett: *Women's Oppression Today: Problems in Marxist Feminist Analysis* (London, Verso, 1986), p. 35.
51 Barrett: *Women's Oppression*, p. 35.
52 *Ibid.*
53 Barrett: *Women's Oppression*, pp. 35–6.
54 Barrett: *Women's Oppression*, p. 93.
55 Barrett: *Women's Oppression*, p. 96.

56 *Ibid.*
57 Jane Flax: *Thinking Fragments: Psychoanalysis, Feminism, and Postmodernism in the Contemporary West* (Berkeley, University of California Press, 1990), pp. 25–6.
58 Flax: *Thinking Fragments*, p. 27.
59 Flax: *Thinking Fragments*, pp. 27–8.
60 Flax: *Thinking Fragments*, p. 28.
61 *Ibid.*
62 Flax: *Thinking Fragments*, p. 177.
63 *Ibid.*
64 Flax: *Thinking Fragments*, p. 183.
65 Flax: *Thinking Fragments*, p. 178.
66 Flax: *Thinking Fragments*, p. 183.
67 Flax: *Thinking Fragments*, p. 233.
68 Flax: *Thinking Fragments*, p. 236.
69 Frye: *Politics of Reality*, p. 4.
70 Rosi Braidotti: *Patterns of Dissonance: A Study of Women in Contemporary Philosophy*, translated by Elizabeth Guild (Cambridge, Polity Press, 1991), p. 278.
71 Braidotti: *Patterns of Dissonance*, p. 278.
72 Braidotti: *Patterns of Dissonance*, p. 279.
73 Braidotti: *Patterns of Dissonance*, p. 277.
74 Braidotti: *Patterns of Dissonance*, p. 278.
75 Braidotti: *Patterns of Dissonance*, p. 280.
76 *Ibid.*
77 *Ibid.*
78 Braidotti: *Patterns of Dissonance*, p. 281.
79 Braidotti: *Patterns of Dissonance*, p. 282.
80 Braidotti: *Patterns of Dissonance*, p. 283.
81 Braidotti: *Patterns of Dissonance*, p. 284. Braidotti here draws upon Italo Calvino's *Lezioni Americane: sei proposte per il prossimo millenio* (Milan, Garzanti, 1988). Braidotti is particularly interested in Calvino's interpretation of a painting by Boccaccio, in which the Italian Renaissance poet-philosopher, Cavalcanti, deep in meditation on the ruins of past civilisation, makes his escape from the threat of attack by a gang on horseback, by jumping 'ever so lightly over to the other side of the fence, disappearing ever so lightly around the corner, leaving his interlocutors aghast'. Braidotti is 'deeply struck by the mixture of elegance and basic strategy with which the thinker confronts the challenges and difficulties of his times' pp. 283–4.
82 Braidotti: *Patterns of Dissonance*, p. 15.

83 Sabina Lovibond: 'Feminism and Postmodernism', in *New Left Review*, 178, 1989, 15.
84 Lovibond: 'Feminism and Postmodernism', 19, author's emphasis.
85 Lovibond: 'Feminism and Postmodernism', 26, author's emphasis.
86 Lovibond: 'Feminism and Postmodernism', 28.

6 THE NATURALIST PARADIGM

1 Margaret Fuller: 'The Great Lawsuit: Man versus Men. Woman versus Women', in Rossi: *Feminist Papers*, p. 182.
2 Fuller: 'Great Lawsuit', p. 169.
3 Fuller: 'Great Lawsuit', p. 166.
4 Fuller: 'Great Lawsuit', p. 164.
5 Fuller: 'Great Lawsuit', p. 167.
6 Fuller: 'Great Lawsuit', p. 169.
7 Fuller: 'Great Lawsuit', p. 180.
8 Fuller: 'Great Lawsuit', p. 167.
9 Fuller: 'Great Lawsuit', p. 181.
10 Emma Goldman: 'The Tragedy of Woman's Emancipation', in Rossi: *Feminist Papers*, p. 509.
11 Goldman: 'Tragedy', p. 511.
12 *Ibid.*
13 Goldman: 'Tragedy', p. 515.
14 Emma Goldman: 'Jealousy: Causes and a Possible Cure', in Frazer, et. al.: *Ethics*, p. 325.
15 Goldman: 'Jealousy', p. 320.
16 Goldman: 'Jealousy', p. 326.
17 Virginia Woolf: *A Room of One's Own* (London, Penguin Books, 1945), p. 37.
18 Woolf: *Room*, p. 67.
19 Virginia Woolf: *Three Guineas*, New Edition (London, Hogarth Press, 1943), p. 147.
20 Woolf: *Three Guineas*, p. 179.
21 Woolf: *Three Guineas*, p. 324.
22 Woolf: *Three Guineas*, p. 303.
23 Woolf: *Room*, p. 53.
24 Woolf: *Room*, p. 13.
25 Daly: *Gyn/Ecology*, p. 2.
26 Daly: *Gyn/Ecology*, p. 353.
27 Daly: *Gyn/Ecology*, p. 386.
28 Daly: *Gyn/Ecology*, p. 7.
29 *Ibid.*

30 See especially *Websters' First New Intergalactic Wickedary of the English Language* (London, The Women's Press, 1988), a book which is 'Conjured by Mary Daly in cahoots with Jane Caputi'.
31 Daly: *Gyn/Ecology*, p. 12.
32 Daly: *Gyn/Ecology*, p. 13.
33 Daly: *Gyn/Ecology*, p. 11.
34 *Ibid.*
35 Daly: *Gyn/Ecology*, p. 34.
36 Carol McMillan: *Women, Reason and Nature* (Oxford, Blackwell, 1982), pp. 55–6.
37 McMillan: *Women, Reason and Nature*, p. 59.
38 McMillan: *Women, Reason and Nature*, p. 128.
39 McMillan: *Women, Reason and Nature*, pp. 135–6, in which McMillan describes the takeover by obstetricians of women's role in birthing.
40 McMillan: *Women, Reason and Nature*, p. 92.
41 McMillan: *Women, Reason and Nature*, p. 58.
42 McMillan: *Women, Reason and Nature*, p. 94.
43 McMillan: *Women, Reason and Nature*, p. 85.
44 McMillan acknowledges her indebtedness to Hannah Arendt: *The Human Condition* (University of Chicago Press, 1974)
45 McMillan: *Women, Reason and Nature*, p. 88.
46 McMillan: *Women, Reason and Nature*, p. 151.
47 Nel Noddings: *Caring: A Feminine Approach to Ethics and Moral Education* (Los Angeles, University of California Press, 1984), pp. 1–2.
48 Noddings: *Caring*, p. 1.
49 Noddings: *Caring*, p. 2.
50 Noddings: *Caring*, p. 3.
51 Noddings: *Caring*, p. 27.
52 Noddings: *Caring*, p. 128. Noddings here stresses that mothering is a relationship, not a social role, and therefore that 'Biology has the final word in that task.' The possibility of men 'reproducing' this role is thus not admitted.
53 Noddings: *Caring*, p. 130.
54 Noddings: *Caring*, pp. 40–4, in which she compares the Greek figure of Ceres as a model of feminine sensibility with that of the biblical figure of Abraham, whose 'relative' duty to his son was displaced by his 'absolute' duty to his God.
55 Noddings: *Caring*, p. 14.
56 Noddings: *Caring*, p. 56.
57 Noddings: *Caring*, p. 79.
58 Noddings: *Caring*, p. 49.

59 Noddings: *Caring*, p. 82.
60 Noddings: *Caring*, p. 107.
61 Noddings: *Caring*, p. 86.
62 Noddings: *Caring*, p. 115.
63 Lisa Sowle Cahill: *Women and Sexuality* (New York, Paulist Press, 1992), p. 45.
64 Cahill: *Women and Sexuality*, p. 46.
65 Cahill: *Women and Sexuality*, p. 7.
66 Cahill: *Between the Sexes: Foundations for a Christian Ethics of Sexuality* (Philadelphia, Fortress Press, 1985), p. 84.
67 Cahill: *Women and Sexuality*, pp. 45–6. The importance of Ruether is here acknowledged by Cahill, who considers that Ruether 'is never more Catholic than when she insists on "the full humanity of women" as the final court of appeal'. This reference to Ruether's *Sexism and God-Talk* is further evidence of the richness of her writing.
68 Cahill: *Between the Sexes*, p. 150.
69 Cahill: *Between the Sexes*, p. 89.
70 Cahill: *Between the Sexes*, p. 10.
71 Cahill: *Between the Sexes*, pp. 87–8.
72 Cahill: *Between the Sexes*, p. 88.
73 Cahill: *Between the Sexes*, p. 89. The important work of Mary Midgley is here recognised.
74 Cahill: *Between the Sexes*, p. 150.
75 Cahill: *Women and Sexuality*, p. 78.
76 Cahill: *Women and Sexuality*, pp. 66–7.
77 Cahill: *Women and Sexuality*, p. 47.
78 Cahill: *Women and Sexuality*, p. 69.
79 Carter Heyward: *Our Passion for Justice: Images of Power, Sexuality, and Liberation* (Cleveland, Ohio, The Pilgrim Press, 1984), pp. 228–9.
80 See especially her essays, 'Lesbianism and the Church', 'Coming Out: Journey without Maps', and 'Sexuality, Love, and Justice' in the above. To this may be added the concerns of green Christian feminists that the creative relation to the earth has also been too narrowly conceived as a form of domination or control. See Anne Primavesi: *From Apocalypse to Genesis* (Tunbridge Wells, Burns and Oates, 1991) and Catherina J. M. Halkes: *New Creation: Christian Feminism and the Renewal of the Earth* (London, SPCK, 1991).
81 Heyward: *Our Passion*, p. 89.
82 Heyward: *Our Passion*, p. 245.
83 Heyward: *Our Passion*, p. 140.

84 Heyward: *Our Passion*, p. 198, author's emphasis.
85 Heyward: *Our Passion*, p. 184.

7 CRITIQUE OF NATURALISM

 1 Margaret Atwood: *The Handmaid's Tale* (London, Virago Press, 1987).
 2 Atwood: *Handmaid's Tale*, p. 279.
 3 Atwood: *Handmaid's Tale*, p. 29.
 4 Atwood: *Handmaid's Tale*, p. 35.
 5 Atwood: *Handmaid's Tale*, pp. 176–7.
 6 Atwood: *Handmaid's Tale*, pp. 70–1.
 7 Atwood: *Handmaid's Tale*, p. 146.
 8 Atwood: *Handmaid's Tale*, p. 156.
 9 Atwood: *Handmaid's Tale*, p. 242.
10 Atwood: *Handmaid's Tale*, p. 247.
11 Atwood: *Handmaid's Tale*, p. 83.
12 Atwood: *Handmaid's Tale*, p. 84.
13 Atwood: *Handmaid's Tale*, p. 303.
14 Londa Schiebinger: *The Mind has no Sex? Women in the Origins of Modern Science* (Cambridge, Massachusetts, Harvard University Press, 1989), p. 1.
15 Schiebinger: *Mind*, p. 180.
16 Schiebinger: *Mind*, p. 181.
17 Schiebinger: *Mind*, pp. 182–3. The illustrations on these pages are from Vesalius' *Epitome* (Basel, 1543). They show the different shapes and reproductive organs of the female and male bodies, but reveal the same skeleton, common to both.
18 Schiebinger: *Mind*, p. 190.
19 Schiebinger: *Mind*, pp. 203–6. In an exercise of comparative anatomy in 1829, John Barclay drew the skeleton of the ideal male body beside that of an animal 'which would highlight the distinctive features of the male skeleton', namely, a horse, 'remarkable for its strength and agility'. The skeleton of the female body, on the other hand, was compared to an animal 'noted for its large pelvis and long, willowy neck – the ostrich' which, as a womb on legs with a very small brain well illustrated the important differences of female anatomy.
20 Sabina Lovibond: *Realism and Imagination in Ethics* (Oxford, Blackwell, 1983), p. 133.
21 Lovibond: *Realism*, p. 116.
22 Lovibond: *Realism*, p. 177.

23 McMillan: *Women, Reason and Nature*, see especially her 'Concluding Remarks'.

24 Lovibond: *Realism*, p. 183. The phrase is from the title of an essay by E. P. Thompson, reprinted in Thompson:*Writing by Candlelight* (London, Merlin Press, 1980).

25 Lovibond: *Realism*, pp. 186–7.

26 Jean Grimshaw: *Feminist Philosophers: Women's Perspectives on Philosophical Traditions* (Brighton, Wheatsheaf Books, 1986), pp. 89–90.

27 Grimshaw: *Feminist Philosophers*, p. 211.

28 Grimshaw: *Feminist Philosophers*, pp. 216–17.

29 In conversation, Atwood has indicated that the novel is also intended as a critique of a certain kind of feminism, whose 'positions and slogans run the risk of being taken over by a dominant power group, only to be exploited as a new instrument of female oppression (even with female collaborators)'. Coral Ann Howells: YORK NOTES on *The Handmaid's Tale* (Essex, Longman York Press, 1993), p. 9. The reference is to Earl G. Ingersoll (editor): *Margaret Atwood: Conversations* (London, Virago Press, 1992).

30 Grimshaw: *Feminist Philosophers*, p. 259.

31 Grimshaw: *Feminist Philosophers*, p. 261.

32 Susan Brooks Thistlethwaite: *Sex, Race, and God: Christian Feminism in Black and White* (London, Geoffrey Chapman, 1990), p. 59. See also pp. 12–15, on the 'conceptual instability of white feminism'.

33 Thistlethwaite: *Sex, Race, and God*, pp. 60–1.

34 Thistlethwaite: *Sex, Race, and God*, p. 86. Cf. her critique of Daly, p. 58.

35 Thistlethwaite: *Sex, Race, and God*, pp. 12–13.

36 Thistlethwaite: *Sex, Race, and God*, pp. 71–4.

37 Elaine Marks and Isabelle de Courtivron (editors): *New French Feminisms: An Anthology* (Brighton, Harvester Press, 1986), pp. 7–8.

38 De Beauvoir: *Second Sex*, p. xvii.

39 De Beauvoir: *Second Sex*, p. xix.

40 De Beauvoir: *Second Sex*, p. xxviii.

41 Moira Gatens: *Feminism and Philosophy: Perspectives on Difference and Equality* (Oxford, Polity Press, 1991), pp. 114–15. Her chapter on 'Psychoanalysis and French Feminisms' is a most helpful analysis.

42 Susan F. Parsons: 'Feminist Reflections on Embodiment and Sexuality' in *Studies in Christian Ethics*, 4:2, 26.

43 Helene Cixous: 'The Laugh of the Medusa', translated by Keith Cohen and Paula Cohen, in Marks and de Courtivron: *New French Feminisms*, p. 253.

44 Cixous: 'Laugh', p. 263.
45 Cixous: 'Laugh', p. 259.
46 *Ibid.*
47 Cixous: 'Laugh', p. 253.
48 Cixous: 'Laugh', p. 261.
49 Cixous: 'Laugh', p. 259.
50 Cixous: 'Laugh', p. 257.
51 Cixous: 'Laugh', p. 245.
52 Cixous: 'Laugh', p. 248.
53 Cixous: 'Laugh', p. 264.
54 Cixous: 'Laugh', p. 262.
55 Cixous: 'Laugh', p. 246.
56 Cixous: 'Laugh', p. 260.
57 Cixous: 'Laugh', p. 251.
58 Cixous: 'Laugh', p. 252.
59 Cixous: 'Laugh', p. 264.
60 *Ibid.*
61 Phyllis Trible: *Texts of Terror: Literary-Feminist Readings of Biblical Narratives* (Philadelphia, Fortress Press, 1984), p. 3.
62 Jeremiah 31: 15–22.
63 Phyllis Trible: *God and the Rhetoric of Sexuality* (Philadelphia, Fortress Press, 1978), p. 40.
64 'Is Ephraim my dear son? my darling child?
For the more I speak of him,
  the more I do remember him.
Therefore, my womb trembles for him;
I will truly show motherly-compassion upon him.
  Oracle of Yahweh.'   Jeremiah 31: 20. Trible's translation,
                        Rhetoric, p. 45.
65 Trible: *Rhetoric*, p. 44.
66 Jeremiah 31: 22b.
67 Trible: *Rhetoric*, p. 48.
68 Trible: *Rhetoric*, p. 173.
69 Trible: *Rhetoric*, p. 191.
70 Trible: *Rhetoric*, p. 196.

8 TOWARDS AN APPROPRIATE UNIVERSALISM

1 Margaret A. Farley: 'Feminism and Universal Morality', in Gene Outka and John P. Reeder, Jr. eds.: *Prospects for a Common Morality* (Princeton University Press, 1993), p. 170.
2 See the excellent study by Susan Bordo: *The Flight to Objectivity: Essays on Cartesianism and Culture* (Albany, State University of New York Press, 1987).

3 Susan Moller Okin: *Justice, Gender and the Family* (New York, Basic Books, 1989), p. 23.
4 Okin: *Justice*, p. 105.
5 Okin: *Justice*, p. 5, author's emphasis.
6 Okin: *Justice*, p. 171.
7 Grace Jantzen: 'Connection or Competition: Identity and Personhood in Feminist Ethics', in *Studies in Christian Ethics*, 5:1, 1992, 4–5.
8 See the study of Hobbes, Marx, and Mill by Christine Di Stefano: *Configurations of Masculinity: A Feminist Perspective on Modern Political Theory* (Ithaca, New York, Cornell University Press, 1991).
9 Sara Ruddick: *Maternal Thinking: Towards a Politics of Peace* (London, The Women's Press, 1989), pp. 17–23. See also discussion of the notion of demands from Iris Murdoch's moral philosophy, as background to 'maternal thinking', in Grimshaw, *Feminist Philosophers*, chapter 8.
10 Iris Young: *Justice and the Politics of Difference* (Princeton University Press, 1990), p. 4.
11 Sharon D. Welch: *A Feminist Ethic of Risk* (Minneapolis, Fortress Press, 1990), p. 127.
12 Welch: *Ethic of Risk*, p. 127, author's emphasis.
13 Seyla Benhabib: *Situating the Self: Gender, Community and Postmodernism in Contemporary Feminism* (Oxford, Polity Press, 1992), p. 13.
14 *Ibid.*
15 Young: *Politics of Difference*, p. 115.
16 Young: *Politics of Difference*, p. 98. See chapter 5 above for discussion of Frye's work.
17 Judith Butler: *Gender Trouble: Feminism and the Subversion of Identity* (London, Routledge, 1990)
18 Young: *Politics of Difference*, p. 116.
19 *Ibid.*
20 See especially her earlier work: *Communities of Resistance and Solidarity: A Feminist Theology of Liberation* (New York, Orbis Books, 1985). See chapter 5 above for discussion of Trible's work.
21 Lois McNay: *Foucault and Feminism: Power, Gender and the Self* (Oxford, Polity Press, 1992), p. 7.
22 *Ibid.*
23 Catherine Wilson: 'How did the Dinosaurs die out? How did the Poets survive?' a reply to Richard Rorty, in *Radical Philosophy*, 62, Autumn 1992, 24.
24 Wilson: 'Dinosaurs', p. 20.
25 Lovibond: 'Feminism', p. 19.
26 *Ibid.*

27 Susan Bordo: 'Feminism, Postmodernism and Gender-Scepticism', in Linda J. Nicholson, ed.: *Feminism/Postmodernism* (London, Routledge, 1990), p. 144.
28 *Ibid.*
29 Kate Soper: 'Feminism as Critique', in *New Left Review*, 176, 1989, 108.
30 Bordo: 'Feminism', p. 149.
31 McNay: *Foucault*, p. 197.
32 Benhabib: *Situating*, p. 16.
33 *Ibid.*
34 Benhabib: *Situating*, p. 230.
35 Welch: *Ethic of Risk*, p. 33.
36 Welch: *Ethic of Risk*, p. 23.
37 Welch: *Ethic of Risk*, p. 111.

9 TOWARDS A REDEMPTIVE COMMUNITY

1 Agnes Heller and Ferenc Feher: *The Postmodern Political Condition* (Cambridge, Polity Press, 1991), pp. 35–6.
2 Marilyn Friedman: 'Feminism and Modern Friendship: Dislocating the Community' in Eve Browning Cole and Susan Coultrap-McQuin, eds.: *Explorations in Feminist Ethics* (Bloomington, Indiana University Press, 1992), p. 89.
3 Elizabeth Fox-Genovese: *Feminism without Illusions: A Critique of Individualism* (Chapel Hill, University of North Carolina Press, 1991), p. 241.
4 Fox-Genovese: *Feminism without Illusions*, p. 41.
5 See the work of feminist object-relations theorists, who note the social and political implications of the mother/child relationship, especially: Nancy Chodorow: *The Reproduction of Mothering: Psychoanalysis and the Sociology of Gender* (Berkeley, University of California Press, 1978) and Dorothy Dinnerstein: *The Mermaid and the Minotaur: Sexual Arrangements and Human Malaise* (New York, Harper and Row, 1976).
6 See Mary Field Belenky, Blythe McVicker Clinchy, Nancy Rule Goldberger, and Jill Mattuck Tarule: *Women's Ways of Knowing: The Development of Self, Voice, and Mind* (New York, Basic Books, 1986).
7 Lorraine Code: *What Can She Know? Feminist Theory and the Construction of Knowledge* (Ithaca, New York, Cornell University Press, 1991), p. 7.
8 See the original work on feminist standpoint epistemology by Nancy Hartsock: 'The Feminist Standpoint: Developing the

Ground for a Specifically Feminist Historical Materialism', in Sandra Harding and Merrill Hintikka, eds.: *Discovering Reality: Feminist Perspectives on Epistemology, Methodology, and the Philosophy of Science* (Dordrecht, Reidel, 1983); and Sandra Harding: *The Science Question in Feminism* (Ithaca, New York, Cornell University Press, 1986).

9 Code: *What Can She Know?*, p. 320.
10 Code: *What Can She Know?*, p. 324.
11 Benhabib: *Situating*, p. 161, author's emphasis.
12 Benhabib: *Situating*, p. 159.
13 Welch: *Ethic of Risk*, p. 135.
14 *Ibid.*
15 Sara Ruddick: *Maternal Thinking: Towards a Politics of Peace* (London, The Women's Press, 1989). See especially Part II.
16 Joan C. Tronto: *Moral Boundaries: A Political Argument for an Ethic of Care* (London, Routledge, 1993), p. 178.
17 Tronto: *Moral Boundaries*, p. 180. See also the earlier work by the feminist political scientist, Jean Bethke Elshtain: *Public Man, Private Woman*, chapters 5 and 6.
18 See Annette Baier: *Postures of the Mind: Essays on Mind and Morals* (Minneapolis, University of Minnesota Press, 1985), chapters 11–15; and her 'Hume, The Women's Moral Theorist?' in Eva Kittay and Diane Meyers, eds.: *Women and Moral Theory* (Maryland, Rowman and Littlefield, 1987). See also Tronto, *Moral Boundaries* in which she recovers the main figures of the Scottish Enlightenment to develop a politics of care.
19 Benhabib: *Situating*, p. 74.
20 Grimshaw: *Feminist Philosophers*, chapter 7.
21 Benhabib: *Situating*, p. 74.
22 *Ibid.*
23 Young: *Politics of Difference*, pp. 228–9.
24 Young: *Politics of Difference*, p. 229.
25 *Ibid.*
26 Young: *Politics of Difference*, p. 231.
27 *Ibid.*
28 Friedman: 'Feminism and Modern Friendship', p. 94.
29 Young: *Politics of Difference*, p. 238.
30 Young: *Politics of Difference*, p. 251.
31 Lovibond: *Realism*, p. 179.
32 Lovibond: *Realism*, p. 181.
33 Lovibond: *Realism*, p. 218.
34 Welch: *Ethic of Risk*, p. 135.
35 Welch: *Ethic of Risk*, p. 156.

36 Welch: *Ethic of Risk*, p. 35.
37 Welch: *Ethic of Risk*, pp. 160–1.
38 Welch: *Ethic of Risk*, p. 161.
39 Mary Grey: *Redeeming the Dream: Feminism, Redemption and Christian Tradition* (London, SPCK, 1989), p. 4.
40 Grey: *Redeeming*, p. 1. Cf. Isabel Carter Heyward's analysis of redemption in *The Redemption of God: A Theology of Mutual Relation* (Lanham, Maryland: University Press of America, 1982), chapter 4.
41 Ann Loades: *Searching for Lost Coins: Explorations in Christianity and Feminism* (London, SPCK, 1987), p. 57. This section includes a close analysis of the life and death of Simone Weil. See also her reference to Iris Murdoch's novel, *Henry and Cato*, p. 39.
42 See Grace Jantzen: 'Ascension and the Road to Hell', in *Theology*, 94:759, May/June 1991. In what was to be her last editorial, Jantzen wrote: 'Women are well used to men of power rushing off to do high-profile things, leaving us to get on with the everyday tasks that make their work possible, and returning to judge us by the results' p. 163.
43 Ruether: *Sexism*, chapter 5.
44 Beverly Wildung Harrison: 'Sexism and the Language of Christian Ethics' in Harrison and Robb: *Making the Connections*, p. 28.
45 Grey: *Redeeming*, p. 31.
46 Halkes: *New Creation*, p. 124.
47 Halkes: *New Creation*, p. 127.
48 Grey: *Redeeming*, p. 8.
49 Grey: *Redeeming*, p. 10.
50 Grey: *Redeeming*, p. 106.
51 Grey: *Redeeming*, pp. 107–8. In her Christology, Grey seeks a path between the work of Carter Heyward, who claims that emphasis on the uniqueness of Christ 'would *weaken* relational power in history', and that of Ruether, who argues that 'Christ needs to be set over-against the oppressive structures of society', see pages 107 and 199.
52 Harrison: 'Sexism', p. 41, author's emphasis.
53 Heyward: *The Redemption of God*, p. 6.
54 Grey: *Redeeming*, p. 152.
55 Grey: *Redeeming*, p. 155.
56 Heller and Feher: *Postmodern Political Condition*, p. 4.
57 Heller and Feher: *Postmodern Political Condition*, p. 32.

10 TOWARDS A NEW HUMANISM

1 Ruether: *Sexism*, p. 93.
2 Ruether: *Sexism*, p. 93.
3 Ruether: *Sexism*, p. 95. The quotation is from Augustine's *De Trinitate* 7. 7. 10.
4 Ruether: *Sexism*, p. 102 ff. in which she analyses liberal feminism.
5 Butler: *Gender Trouble*, p. xi.
6 Butler: *Gender Trouble*, p. x.
7 Butler: *Gender Trouble*, p. xii.
8 Butler: *Gender Trouble*, p. 7, author's emphasis.
9 Butler: *Gender Trouble*, p. xi.
10 Butler: *Gender Trouble*, p. 157, note 54.
11 Ruether: *New Woman*, p. 194. See also Ruether: 'Dualism and the Nature of Evil in Feminist Theology' for the more recent influence of postmodernism on her theological thinking.
12 Butler: *Gender Trouble*, p. 5.
13 Butler: *Gender Trouble*, p. 148.
14 Butler: *Gender Trouble*, p. 30.
15 Luce Irigaray: *Speculum of the Other Woman*, translated by Gillian C. Gill (Ithaca, New York, Cornell University Press, 1974), p. 60.
16 Butler: *Gender Trouble*, p. 13.
17 Margaret Whitford: *Luce Irigaray: Philosophy in the Feminine* (London, Routledge, 1991), p. 150.
18 Irigaray: *Speculum*. The entire book is a demonstration of this thesis throughout the history of western thought.
19 Irigaray: *Sexes and Genealogies*, translated by Gillian C. Gill (New York, Columbia University Press, 1987), pp. 61–2.
20 Irigaray: *Sexes and Genealogies*, p. 64.
21 Irigaray: *Sexes and Genealogies*, p. 66. Cf. Whitford: *Luce Irigaray*, pp. 145–6.
22 Whitford: *Luce Irigaray*, p. 142. Cf. Irigaray: *An Ethics of Sexual Difference*, translated by Carolyn Burke and Gillian C. Gill (London, The Athlone Press, 1984), pp. 107–8, author's emphasis.
23 Irigaray: *Sexes and Genealogies*, p. 63.
24 Irigaray: *Ethics*, p. 129, author's emphasis.
25 Irigaray: *Sexes and Genealogies*, pp. 68–9.
26 Irigaray: *Speculum*, p. 197 and 200.
27 See Whitford: *Luce Irigaray*, p. 141ff, for references to the influence of Feuerbach on Irigaray's thinking, particularly as he notes 'the anomaly that in Protestantism the Holy Family excludes the mother.'

28 Irigiray: *This Sex which is not One*, translated by Catherine Porter (Ithaca, New York, Cornell University Press, 1977), p. 159.

29 Irigiray: *Ethics*, p. 66.

30 Irigiray: *This Sex*, p. 205.

31 Irigiray: 'Equal to Whom?', p. 74. In this piece, which is partly a review of Elisabeth Schüssler Fiorenza's *In Memory of Her*, Irigiray exclaims that 'sociology quickly bores me when I'm expecting the divine'. I am grateful to Ann Claire Mulder for her very helpful seminar on this article.

32 Irigiray: *Ethics*, pp. 129 and 112.

33 Irigiray: *Ethics*, p. 69.

34 *Ibid.* It is in this context that the quotation from Irigiray used in the preface is to be understood. See also the important work by Jessica Benjamin: *The Bonds of Love: Psychoanalysis, Feminism, and the Problem of Domination* (London, Virago Press, 1993) in which she also argues for the recovery of desire for women in chapters 3 and 5.

35 Irigiray: *Ethics*, p. 150.

36 Irigiray: *Ethics*, p. 111.

37 Irigiray: *Ethics*, p. 141.

38 Irigiray: *Ethics*, p. 150.

39 Helen Oppenheimer: *The Hope of Happiness: A Sketch for a Christian Humanism* (London, SCM Press, 1983), p. 19.

40 Oppenheimer: *Hope of Happiness*, p. 15.

41 Jean Porter: *The Recovery of Virtue: The Relevance of Aquinas for Christian Ethics* (Louisville, Kentucky, Westminster/John Knox Press, 1990), p. 138.

42 Porter: *Recovery of Virtue*, p. 140.

43 Denise Lardner Carmody: *Virtuous Woman: Reflections on Christian Feminist Ethics* (Maryknoll, New York, Orbis Books, 1992), p. 8.

44 Carmody: *Virtuous Woman*, p. 8.

45 Porter: *Recovery of Virtue*, p. 70.

46 Oppenheimer: *Hope of Happiness*, pp. 92–3.

47 Carmody: *Virtuous Woman*, p. 8.

48 Carmody: *Virtuous Woman*, p. 9.

49 Carmody: *Virtuous Woman*, p. 10.

50 Cahill: *Women and Sexuality*, p. 45.

51 Cahill: 'Accent on the Masculine', *Veritatis Splendor* in focus: 9, in *The Tablet*, 11 December 1993, p. 1619.

52 Porter: *Recovery of Virtue*, p. 51.

53 Porter: *Recovery of Virtue*, p. 50.

54 Esther D. Reed: 'Pornography and the End of Morality?' in *Studies in Christian Ethics*, 7:2, 79.

55 Reed: 'Pornography', p. 81.
56 Reed: 'Pornography', p. 87.
57 Reed: 'Pornography', p. 89.
58 Reed: 'Pornography', p. 86.
59 See Porter: *Recovery of Virtue*, pp. 52–8, for her extended treatment of this issue in light of contemporary philosophical considerations.
60 Reed: 'Pornography', p. 90.
61 Anne E. Carr: *Transforming Grace: Christian Tradition and Women's Experience* (San Francisco, Harper & Row, 1990), p. 113.
62 *Ibid.*

Select bibliography

Alcoff, Linda and Potter, Elizabeth, eds.: *Feminist Epistemologies*, London: Routledge, 1993.

Andolsen, Barbara Hilkert, Gudorf, Christine E., and Pellauer, Mary D. eds.: *Women's Consciousness, Women's Conscience: A Reader in Feminist Ethics*, New York: Seabury, 1985.

Arendt, Hannah: *The Human Condition*, University of Chicago Press, 1974.

Assiter, Alison: *Althusser and Feminism*, London: Pluto Press, 1990.

Atwood, Margaret: *The Handmaid's Tale*, London: Virago Press, 1987.

Bacchi, Carol Lee: *Same Difference: Feminism and Sexual Difference*, Australia: Allen and Unwin, 1990.

Baier, Annette: 'Hume, The Women's Moral Theorist?' in Eva Kittay and Diane Meyers, eds.: *Women and Moral Theory*.

Postures of the Mind: Essays on Mind and Morals, Minneapolis: University of Minnesota Press, 1985.

Barrett, Michèle: *Women's Oppression Today: Problems in Marxist Feminist Analysis*, London: Verso, 1986.

Bartky, Sandra Lee: *Femininity and Domination: Studies in the Phenomenology of Oppression*, London: Routledge, 1990.

Baum, L. Frank: *The Wizard of Oz*, London: Fontana, 1969.

Belenky, Mary Field, Clinchy, Blythe McVicker, Goldberger, Nancy Rule, and Tarule, Jill Mattuck: *Women's Ways of Knowing: The Development of Self, Voice, and Mind*, New York: Basic Books, 1986.

Benhabib, Seyla and Cornell, Drucilla, eds.: *Feminism as Critique: Essays on the Politics of Gender in Late-Capitalist Societies*, Oxford: Polity Press, 1987.

Benhabib, Seyla: *Situating the Self: Gender, Community and Postmodernism in Contemporary Feminism*, Oxford: Polity Press, 1992.

Benjamin, Jessica: *The Bonds of Love: Psychoanalysis, Feminism, and the Problem of Domination*, London: Virago Press, 1993.

Bordo, Susan: 'Feminism, Postmodernism and Gender-Scepticism', in Linda J. Nicholson, ed.: *Feminism/Postmodernism*.

The Flight to Objectivity: Essays on Cartesianism and Culture, Albany: State University of New York Press, 1987.

Braidotti, Rosi: *Patterns of Dissonance: A Study of Women in Contemporary Philosophy*, translated by Elizabeth Guild, Cambridge: Polity Press, 1991.

Butler, Judith: *Gender Trouble: Feminism and the Subversion of Identity*, London: Routledge, 1990.

Cahill, Lisa Sowle: 'Accent on the Masculine', *Veritatis Splendor* in focus: 9, in *The Tablet*, 11 December 1993.

Between the Sexes: Foundations for a Christian Ethics of Sexuality, Philadelphia: Fortress Press, 1985.

Women and Sexuality, New York: Paulist Press, 1992.

Carmody, Denise Lardner: *Virtuous Woman: Reflections on Christian Feminist Ethics*, Maryknoll, New York: Orbis Books, 1992.

Carr, Anne E.: *Transforming Grace: Christian Tradition and Women's Experience*, San Francisco: Harper & Row, 1990.

Chodorow, Nancy: *The Reproduction of Mothering: Psychoanalysis and the Sociology of Gender*, Berkeley: University of California Press, 1978.

Chopp, Rebecca: *The Power to Speak: Feminism, Language and God*, New York: Crossroad, 1989.

Cixous, Helene: 'The Laugh of the Medusa', translated by Keith Cohen and Paula Cohen, in E. Marks and I. de Courtivron, eds.: *New French Feminisms*.

Cixous, Helene and Clement, Catherine: *The Newly Born Woman*, translated by Betty Wing, University of Manchester, 1986.

Clark, Lorenne M. G. and Lange, Lynda, eds.: *The Sexism of Social and Political Theory*, University of Toronto Press, 1979.

Cocks, Joan: *The Oppositional Imagination: Feminism, Critique and Political Theory*, New York: Routledge, 1989.

Code, Lorraine: *What Can She Know? Feminist Theory and the Construction of Knowledge*, Ithaca, New York: Cornell University Press, 1991.

Code, Lorraine, Mullett, Sheila, and Overall, Christine, eds.: *Feminist Perspectives: Philosophical Essays on Method and Morals*, University of Toronto Press, 1988.

Cole, Eve Browning and Coultrap-McQuin, Susan, eds.: *Explorations in Feminist Ethics*, Bloomington: Indiana University Press, 1992.

Collins, Margery and Pierce, Christine: 'Holes and Slime: Sexism in Sartre's Psychoanalysis', in Carol Gould and Marx Wartofsky eds.: *Women and Philosophy: Toward a Theory of Liberation*.

Coward, Rosalind: *Patriarchal Precedents: Sexuality and Social Relations*, London: Routledge & Kegan Paul, 1983.

Female Desire: Women's Sexuality Today, London: Collins, Paladin Grafton Books, 1984.

Daly, Mary: *Beyond God the Father: Toward a Philosophy of Women's Liberation*, Boston: Beacon Press, 1974.

Gyn/Ecology: The Metaethics of Radical Feminism, London: The Women's Press, 1979.

Pure Lust: Elemental Feminist Philosophy, London: The Women's Press, 1984.

Daly, Mary and Caputi, Jane: *Websters' First New Intergalactic Wickedary of the English Language*, London: The Women's Press, 1988.

De Beauvoir, Simone: *The Second Sex*, translated by H. M. Parshley, New York: Bantam Books, 1961.

Degler, Carl, ed.: *Women and Economics*, New York: Harper & Row, 1966.

Dinnerstein, Dorothy: *The Mermaid and the Minotaur: Sexual Arrangements and Human Malaise*, New York: Harper & Row, 1976.

Di Stefano, Christine: *Configurations of Masculinity: A Feminist Perspective on Modern Political Theory*, Ithaca, New York: Cornell University Press, 1991.

Dowell, Susan and Hurcombe, Linda: *The Dispossessed Daughters of Eve: Faith and Feminism*, London: SCM Press, 1981.

Easlea, Brian: *Witchhunting, Magic and the New Philosophy: An Introduction to Debates of the Scientific Revolution 1450–1750*, Brighton: Harvester Press, 1980.

Science and Sexual Oppression: Patriarchy's Confrontation with Woman and Nature, London: Weidenfeld & Nicolson, 1981.

Elshtain, Jean Bethke: *Public Man, Private Woman: Women in Social and Political Thought*, Oxford: Martin Robertson, 1981.

Farley, Margaret A.: 'Feminism and Universal Morality', in Gene Outka and John P. Reeder, Jr. eds.: *Prospects for a Common Morality*.

Flax, Jane: *Thinking Fragments: Psychoanalysis, Feminism and Postmodernism in the Contemporary West*, Berkeley: University of California Press, 1990.

Foreman, Ann: *Femininity as Alienation: Women and the Family in Marxism and Psychoanalysis*, London: Pluto Press, 1977.

Fox-Genovese, Elizabeth: *Feminism without Illusions: A Critique of Individualism*, Chapel Hill: University of North Carolina Press, 1991.

Fraser, Nancy and Bartky, Sandra Lee, eds: *Revaluing French Feminism: Critical Essays on Difference, Agency and Culture*, Bloomington: Indiana University Press, 1992.

Frazer, Elizabeth, Hornsby, Jennifer, and Lovibond, Sabina, eds.: *Ethics: A Feminist Reader*, Oxford: Blackwell, 1992.

Friedan, Betty: *The Feminine Mystique*, New York: Dell Publishing Co., 1963.

Friedman, Marilyn: 'Feminism and Modern Friendship: Dislocating the Community', in Eve Browning Cole and Susan Coultrap-McQuin eds.: *Explorations in Feminist Ethics*.

Frye, Marilyn: *The Politics of Reality*, Trumansburg, New York: The Crossing Press, 1983.

Fuller, Margaret: 'The Great Lawsuit: Man versus Men, Woman versus Women', reprinted in Alice S. Rossi, ed.: *The Feminist Papers*.

Furlong, Monica: *A Dangerous Delight: Women and Power in the Church*, London: SPCK, 1991.

Gallop, Jane: *The Daughter's Seduction: Feminism and Psychoanalysis*, Ithaca, New York: Cornell University Press, 1982.

Gatens, Moira: *Feminism and Philosophy: Perspectives on Difference and Equality*, Oxford: Polity Press, 1991.

Gilligan, Carol: *In a Different Voice: Psychological Theory and Women's Development*, Cambridge, Massachusetts: Harvard University Press, 1982.

Gilligan, Carol, Ward, Janie Victoria, Taylor, Jill McLean and Bardige, Betty, eds.: *Mapping the Moral Domain*, Cambridge, Massachusetts: Harvard University Press, 1988.

Gilman, Charlotte Perkins: *The Yellow Wallpaper*, London: Virago, 1987.

The Living of Charlotte Perkins Gilman: An Autobiography, New York: D. Appleton-Century Co., 1935.

Goldman, Emma: 'Jealousy: Causes and a Possible Cure' in E. Frazer, J. Hornsby, and S. Lovibond eds.: *Ethics: A Feminist Reader*.

'The Tragedy of Women's Emancipation' reprinted in Alice S. Rossi, ed.: *The Feminist Papers*.

Gould, Carol C. ed.: *Beyond Domination: New Perspectives on Women and Philosophy*, New Jersey: Rowman & Allenheld, 1984.

Gould, Carol C. and Wartofsky, Marx W., eds.: *Women and Philosophy: Toward a Theory of Liberation*, New York: G. P. Putnam's Sons, 1976.

Grey, Mary: *Redeeming the Dream: Feminism, Redemption and Christian Tradition*, London: SPCK, 1989.

The Wisdom of Fools? Seeking Revelation for Today, London: SPCK, 1993.

Griffin, Susan: *Women and Nature: The Roaring Inside Her*, New York: Harper & Row, 1978.

Griffiths, Morwenna and Whitford, Margaret, eds.: *Feminist Perspectives in Philosophy*, London: Macmillan Press, 1988.

Grimshaw, Jean: *Feminist Philosophers: Women's Perspectives on Philosophical Traditions*, Brighton: Wheatsheaf Books, 1986.

Grosz, Elizabeth: *Jacques Lacan: A Feminist Introduction*, London: Routledge, 1990.

Gunew, Sneja, ed.: *Feminist Knowledge: Critique and Construct*, London: Routledge, 1990.

Halkes, Catherina J. M.: *New Creation: Christian Feminism and the Renewal of the Earth*, London: SPCK, 1991.

Hamilton, Cicely: *Marriage as a Trade*, London: The Women's Press, 1981.

Harding, Sandra: *The Science Question in Feminism*, Ithaca, New York: Cornell University Press, 1986.

Harding, Sandra and Hintikka, Merrill, eds.: *Discovering Reality: Feminist Perspectives on Epistemology, Methodology, and the Philosophy of Science*, Dordrecht: Reidel, 1983.

Harding, Sandra, ed.: *Feminism and Methodology*, Bloomington: Indiana University Press, 1987.

Harrison, Beverly Wildung: *Our Right to Choose: Toward A New Ethic of Abortion*, Boston: Beacon Press, 1983.

Harrison, Beverly Wildung: *Making the Connections: Essays in Feminist Social Ethics*, edited by Carol S. Robb, Boston: Beacon Press, 1985.

Hartsock, Nancy: 'The Feminist Standpoint: Developing the Ground for a Specifically Feminist Historical Materialism' in S. Harding and M. Hintikka, eds.: *Discovering Reality*.

Hekman, Susan: *Gender and Knowledge: Elements of a Postmodern Feminism*, Oxford: Blackwell, 1992.

Heller, Agnes and Feher, Ferenc: *The Postmodern Political Condition*, Cambridge: Polity Press, 1991.

Heyward, Isabel Carter: *The Redemption of God: A Theology of Mutual Relation*, Lanham, Maryland: University Press of America, 1982.

Our Passion for Justice: Images of Power, Sexuality, and Liberation, Cleveland, Ohio: The Pilgrim Press, 1984.

Touching Our Strength: The Erotic as Power and the Love of God, New York: HarperCollins, 1989.

hooks, bell: *Yearning: Race, Gender, and Cultural Politics*, London: Turnaround, 1991.

Howells, Coral Ann: YORK NOTES on *The Handmaid's Tale*, Essex: Longman York Press, 1993.

Hunt, Mary E.: *Fierce Tenderness: A Feminist Theology of Friendship*, New York: Crossroad, 1992.

Irigiray, Luce: *Speculum of the Other Woman*, translated by Gillian C. Gill, Ithaca, New York: Cornell University Press, 1974.
This Sex Which is Not One, translated by Catherine Porter, Ithaca, New York: Cornell University Press, 1977.
An Ethics of Sexual Difference, translated by Carolyn Burke and Gillian C. Gill, London: The Athlone Press, 1984.
Sexes and Genealogies, translated by Gillian C. Gill, New York: Columbia University Press, 1987.
'Equal to Whom?' in *differences*, a Journal of Feminist Cultural Studies, Volume 1, Number 2.
Jagger, Alison: *Feminist Politics and Human Nature*, Brighton: Harvester Press, 1983.
Jagger, Alison and Bordo, Susan, eds.: *Gender/Body/Knowledge: Feminist Reconstructions of Being and Knowing*, New Jersey: Rutgers University Press, 1989.
Jantzen, Grace: 'Ascension and the Road to Hell', in *Theology*, 94, May/June 1991.
'Connection or Competition: Identity and Personhood in Feminist Ethics', in *Studies in Christian Ethics*, 5:1, 1992.
Jardine, Alice: *Gynesis: Configurations of Women and Modernity*, Ithaca, New York: Cornell University Press, 1985.
Keller, Catherine: *From a Broken Web: Separation, Sexism and Self*, Boston: Beacon Press, 1986.
Keohane, Nannerl O., Rosaldo, Michelle Z., and Gelpi, Barbara C. eds.: *Feminist Theory: A Critique of Ideology*, Brighton: Harvester Press, 1982.
Kittay, Eva and Meyers, Diane, eds.: *Women and Moral Theory*, Maryland: Rowman and Littlefield, 1987.
Kristeva, Julia: *The Kristeva Reader*, edited by Toril Moi, Oxford: Blackwell, 1986.
Le Doeuff, Michèle: *Hipparchia's Choice: An Essay Concerning Woman, Philosophy, etc.*, translated by Trista Selous, Oxford: Blackwell, 1991.
Lerner, Gerda: *The Creation of Patriarchy*, Oxford University Press, 1986.
Lloyd, Genevieve: *The Man of Reason: 'Male' and 'Female' in Western Philosophy*, London: Methuen, 1984.
Loades, Ann: *Searching for Lost Coins: Explorations in Christianity and Feminism*, London: SPCK, 1987.
Loades, Ann, ed.: *Feminist Theology: A Reader*, London: SPCK, 1990.
Lovibond, Sabina: *Realism and Imagination in Ethics*, Oxford: Blackwell, 1983.
'Feminism and Postmodernism', in *New Left Review*, 178, 1989.

MacIntyre, Alasdair: *Three Rival Versions of Moral Enquiry*, London: Duckworth, 1990.

MacKinnon, Catharine A.: *Toward a Feminist Theory of the State*, Cambridge, Massachusetts: Harvard University Press, 1991.

Maitland, Sara: *A Map of the New Country: Women and Christianity*, London: Routledge & Kegan Paul, 1983.

Marks, Elaine and de Courtivron, Isabelle eds.: *New French Feminisms: An Anthology*, Brighton: Harvester Press, 1986.

Martin, Emily: *The Woman in the Body*, Milton Keynes: Open University Press, 1989.

Martineau, Harriet: *Society in America*, edited by Seymour M. Lipset, Garden City, New York: Anchor Doubleday & Co., 1962.

McFague, Sallie: *Models of God: Theology for an Ecological, Nuclear Age*, Philadelphia: Fortress Press, 1987.

McMillan, Carol: *Women, Reason and Nature*, Oxford: Blackwell, 1982.

McNay, Lois: *Foucault and Feminism: Power, Gender and the Self*, Oxford: Polity Press, 1992.

Midgley, Mary: *Beast and Man: The Roots of Human Nature*, Brighton: Harvester Press, 1979.

Mill, J. S. and Taylor, Harriet: 'On the Subjection of Women', reprinted in Alice S. Rossi, ed.: *The Feminist Papers*.

Mitchell, Juliet: *Women's Estate*, New York: Random House, Vintage Books, 1973.

Murdoch, Iris: *The Sovereignty of Good*, London: Routledge & Kegan Paul, 1970.

Murray, Judith Sargent: *On the Equality of the Sexes*, reprinted in Alice S. Rossi, ed.: *The Feminist Papers*.

Nicholson, Linda J. ed.: *Feminism/Postmodernism*, London: Routledge, 1990.

Noddings, Nel: *Caring: A Feminine Approach to Ethics and Moral Education*, Los Angeles: University of California Press, 1984.

Nussbaum, Martha: 'Human Functioning and Social Justice: In Defense of Aristotelian Essentialism', in *Political Theory*, 20:2, May 1992.

'Justice for Women!: Susan Moller Okin *Justice, Gender and the Family*', in *Women: A Cultural Review* 4:3, Winter 1993.

Nye, Andrea: *Feminist Theory and the Philosophies of Man*, London: Routledge, 1989.

Oddie, William: *What Will Happen to God?*, London: SPCK, 1984.

O'Donovan, Oliver: *Begotten or Made?*, Oxford: Clarendon Press, 1984.

O'Faolain, Julia and Martines, Lauro, eds.: *Not in God's Image: Women in History*, London: Virago, 1979.

Okin, Susan Moller: *Women in Western Political Thought*, Princeton University Press, 1979.
Justice, Gender and the Family, New York: Basic Books, 1989.
Oliver, Kelly, ed.: *Ethics, Politics and Difference in Julia Kristeva's Writing*, London: Routledge, 1993.
Oppenheimer, Helen: *The Hope of Happiness: A Sketch for a Christian Humanism*, London: SCM Press, 1983.
Outka, Gene and Reeder, John P. Jr. eds.: *Prospects for a Common Morality*, Princeton University Press, 1993.
Paris, Ginette: 'The Sacrament of Abortion', a recorded interview with James Hillman, available from Spring Publications, Dallas, Texas USA.
Parsons, Susan F.: 'Feminism and the Logic of Morality: A Consideration of Alternatives', in E. Frazer, J. Hornsby and S. Lovibond, eds.: *Ethics*.
'Feminism and Moral Reasoning', in *Australasian Journal of Philosophy*, Supplement 64 (June 1986)
'The Intersection of Feminism and Theological Ethics: A Philosophical Approach', in *Modern Theology*, 4 (April 1988)
'Feminist Reflections on Embodiment and Sexuality' in *Studies in Christian Ethics*, 4:2, 1991.
Plaskow, Judith: *Sex, Sin and Grace: Women's Experience and the Theologies of Reinhold Niebuhr and Paul Tillich*, Washington, DC: University Press of America, 1980.
Porter, Jean: *The Recovery of Virtue: The Relevance of Aquinas for Christian Ethics*, Louisville, Kentucky: Westminster/John Knox Press, 1990.
Primavesi, Anne: *From Apocalypse to Genesis*, Tunbridge Wells: Burns and Oates, 1991.
Radcliffe Richards, Janet: *The Sceptical Feminist*, Harmondsworth: Penguin Books, 1982.
Reed, Esther D.: 'Pornography and the End of Morality?' in *Studies in Christian Ethics*, 7:2, 1994.
Rhode, Deborah L. ed.: *Theoretical Perspectives on Sexual Difference*, New Haven: Yale University Press, 1990.
Rossi, Alice S., ed.: *The Feminist Papers*, New York: Bantam Books, 1973.
Ruddick, Sara: *Maternal Thinking: Towards a Politics of Peace*, London: The Women's Press, 1989.
Ruether, Rosemary Radford: *Liberation Theology*, New York: Paulist Press, 1972.
New Woman/New Earth, New York: Seabury Press, 1975.
Sexism and God-Talk: Towards a Feminist Theology, London: SCM Press, 1983.

Women-Church: Theology and Practice, New York: Harper & Row, 1985.

'A Method of Correlation' in Letty Russell, ed: *Feminist Interpretation of the Bible*.

'Dualism and the Nature of Evil in Feminist Theology' in *Studies in Christian Ethics*, 5:1, 1992.

Rushdie, Salmon: *The Wizard of Oz* in British Film Classics series, London: British Film Institute, 1992.

Russell, Letty M.: *Human Liberation in a Feminist Perspective*, Philadelphia: Westminster Press, 1974.

Russell, Letty M., ed.: *Feminist Interpretation of the Bible*, Oxford: Blackwell, 1985.

Said, Edward W.: *Orientalism: Western Conceptions of the Orient*, London: Penguin Books, 1991.

Saiving, Valerie: 'The Human Situation: A Feminine View' in *The Journal of Religion*, 40, April 1960.

Sartre, Jean Paul: *Existentialism and Human Emotions*, translated by B. Frechtman, New York: The Philosophical Library, 1957.

Being and Nothingness, translated by Hazel E. Barnes, New York: The Citadel Press, 1965.

Sawicki, Jana: *Disciplining Foucault: Feminism, Power and the Body*, London: Routledge, 1991.

Sayers, Janet: *Biological Politics*, London: Tavistock, 1982.

Sayers, Sean and Osborne, Peter, eds.: *Socialism, Feminism and Philosophy*, A *Radical Philosophy* Reader, London: Routledge, 1990.

Scheman, Naomi: *Engenderings: Constructions of Knowledge, Authority, and Privilege*, London: Routledge, 1993.

Schiebinger, Londa: *The Mind has no Sex? Women in the Origins of Modern Science*, Cambridge, Massachusetts: Harvard University Press, 1989.

Schüssler Fiorenza, Elisabeth: *In Memory of Her: A Feminist Theological Reconstruction of Christian Origins*, London: SCM Press, 1983.

Bread Not Stone: The Challenge of Feminist Biblical Interpretation, Boston: Beacon Press, 1984.

Sölle, Dorothee: *The Strength of the Weak: Toward a Christian Feminist Identity*, translated by Robert and Rita Kimber, Philadelphia: Westminster Press, 1984.

Thinking About God: An Introduction to Theology, London: SCM Press, 1990.

Soper, Kate: *Humanism and Anti-Humanism*, London: Hutchinson, 1986.

'Feminism as Critique', in *New Left Review*, 176, 1989.

Thistlethwaite, Susan Brooks: *Sex, Race and God: Christian Feminism in Black and White*, London: Geoffrey Chapman, 1990.

Tong, Rosemary: *Feminist Thought: A Comprehensive Introduction*, London: Unwin Hyman, 1989.

Trible, Phyllis: *God and the Rhetoric of Sexuality*, Philadelphia: Fortress Press, 1978.

Texts of Terror: Literary-Feminist Readings of Biblical Narratives, Philadelphia: Fortress Press, 1984.

Tronto, Joan C.: *Moral Boundaries: A Political Argument for an Ethic of Care*, London: Routledge, 1993.

Vetterling-Braggin, Mary, Elliston, Frederick A., English, Jane, eds.: *Feminism and Philosophy*, New Jersey: Littlefield, Adams & Co., 1977.

Weedon, Chris: *Feminist Practice and Poststructuralist Theory*, Oxford: Blackwell, 1992.

Welch, Sharon D.: *Communities of Resistance and Solidarity: A Feminist Theology of Liberation*, New York: Orbis Books, 1985.

A Feminist Ethic of Risk, Minneapolis: Fortress Press, 1990.

Whitford, Margaret: *Luce Irigiray: Philosophy in the Feminine*, London: Routledge, 1991.

Wilson, Catherine: 'How did the Dinosaurs die out? How did the Poets survive?' in *Radical Philosophy*, 62, Autumn 1992.

Wollstonecraft, Mary: *A Vindication of the Rights of Women*, reprinted in Alice S. Rossi, ed.: *The Feminist Papers*.

Woodhead, Linda: 'Love and Justice', in *Studies in Christian Ethics*, 5:1, 1992.

Woolf, Virginia: *Three Guineas*, New Edition, London: Hogarth Press, 1943.

A Room of One's Own, London: Penguin Books, 1945.

Young, Iris: *Justice and the Politics of Difference*, Princeton University Press, 1990.

Index

New Studies in Christian Ethics

Rights and Christian ethics by Kieran Cronon
Power and Christian ethics by James Mackey
Biblical interpretation and Christian ethics by Ian McDonald
Plurality and Christian ethics by Ian S. Markham
Sex, gender and Christian ethics by Lisa Sowle Cahill
Moral action and Christian ethics by Jean Porter
The environment and Christian ethics by Michael S. Northcott
Health and Christian ethics by Alastair V. Campbell
Feminism and Christian ethics by Susan F. Parsons
The market economy and Christian ethics by Peter Sedgwick
Responsibility and Christian ethics by William Schweiker
Justice and Christian ethics by E. Clinton Gardner
Moral philosophy and Christian ethics by David A. S. Fergusson
Biology and Christian ethics by Stephen R. L. Clark

Lightning Source UK Ltd.
Milton Keynes UK
UKOW030610050213

205837UK00001B/23/A